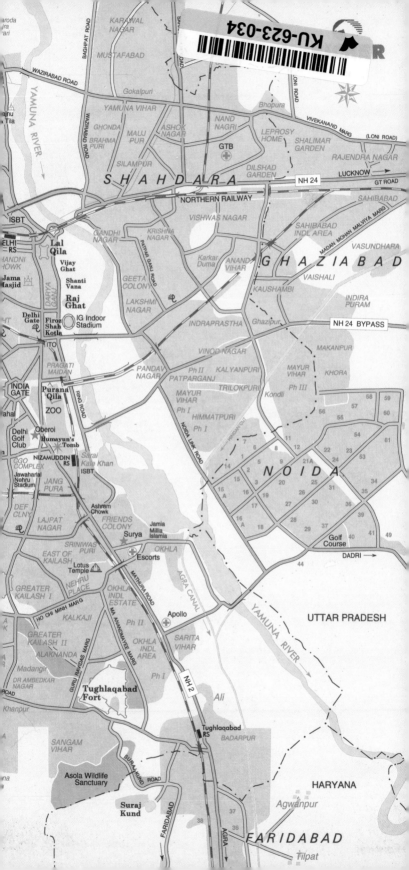

AN EICHER GOODEARTH PUBLICATION

Copyright © 1998 EICHER GOODEARTH LTD, NEW DELHI
ISBN 81-900601-2-0

Editor & Publisher : Swati Mitra
Design : Anando Dutta
Photography : Satish Sharma
Cartography : Lt Gen S M Chadha (Retd)
Academic Editor : Professor Narayani Gupta

CONTRIBUTORS
Delhi in History : Narayani Gupta
Introducing Delhi : Bhaskar Ghosh, Jasjit Mansingh, Amba Sanyal,
Subhadra Sengupta, Shyamala Shiveshwarkar, Emma Tarlo,
Rahul Varma, Gillian Wright
Delhi : Area by Area : Narayani Gupta, Monica Juneja,
Ripin Kalra, Ratish Nanda, Reena Nanda, Rosemary Sachdev
Arts and Entertainment : Bhaskar Ghosh, Partho Dutta, Bulbul Sharma
Nita Srinivasan, Vikrant Sood, Urmila Verma
Short Excursions : Bill Aitken
Travellers Needs : Shona Adhikari, Shyamala Shiveshwarkar
Architectural Drawings : Himanish Das
Miniature Paintings : M Firozuddin
Additional Photographs :
Ajay Sethi (pp 214-24); Deepak Hiranandani (pp 24 Above Right, 26 R, 32 A, 32 BR, 35 BL,
113 BR, 195 ML, 199ML); Lolita Dutta (pp 287 B, 288 A); Manish Swaroop (pp 75 M, 77 M,
91AR, 103 BL, 149-50, 156); Mimanshak (pp 207-10); Peter McManus (pp 48B, 49B, 51B,
52AR, 52B, 53A, 57M, 66B,193M, 265A, 266B, 280B, 283B, 286A, 286B)
Editorial Assistance :
Sulagna Chattopadhyay, Himanjali Mitra, C.K.Sathian

Great care has been taken in the compilation, updation and validation of
information, and every effort has been made to ensure that all information is
as up-to-date as possible at the time of going to press. Details like telephone
and fax numbers, opening hours, prices and travel information may change.
However, the Publishers are not responsible for errors, if any, and
their consequences.

The Publishers would be happy to receive suggestions and corrections for
inclusion in the next edition. Please write to Head of Publishing,
Eicher Goodearth Ltd, Eicher House, 12 Commercial Complex,
Greater Kailash II (Masjid Moth), New Delhi 110 048.

This publication has been supported by **Delhi Tourism and Transportation
Development Corporation Ltd** (A Government Undertaking)
18A DDA SCO Complex, Defence Colony, New Delhi 110024.

Printed by Ajanta Offset & Packagings Ltd, New Delhi
on behalf of Eicher Goodearth Ltd.

Price: Rs 345

Chandni Chowk, 1998. Impressions of a Mughal miniature artist, Firozuddin.

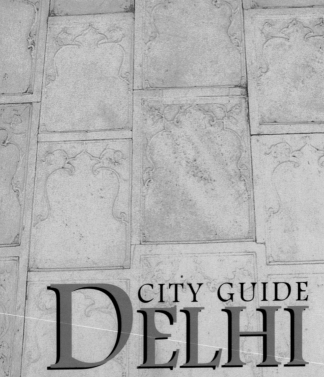

EICHER

CITY GUIDE
DELHI

CONTENTS

About this Guide VI

ABOUT THIS GUIDE

This is the first encyclopaedic guidebook of Delhi, blending the cultural with the practical, artistic excellence with scientific precision. The highly visual Eicher City Guide, with over 700 photographs, above 25 architectural drawings and 42 detailed maps, is the perfect companion not just for the intrepid tourist but also for every armchair traveller and even the curious Dilliwala.

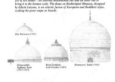

Delhi in History

The opening chapter places modern Delhi in its historical context. The authoritative text takes you through layers of Delhi's history and culture, inspiring you to love and understand this vast and vibrant city.

Introducing Delhi

This section is for those who wish to enter the soul of this city through the chapters on Environment, Clothes, Food, Bazaars, Festivals and Crafts. It ensures that the city remains with you long after you have left it.

Delhi: Area by Area

For the ease of the explorer the city has been divided into eight areas, each demarcated by colour-coded minarets on the upper right-hand corner of every page. Each area has its own road map – major sights indicated with reference numbers in the text as well as on the map. This makes it easy to relate the map with historical and architectural details given in the text. Every chapter is a tour, complete in itself. The text is organised in a manner that you can move from one place of interest to the next closest to it.

Arts and Entertainment

A critical description of museums and art galleries. Listing of auditoria, cinema halls, sports complexes, etc., with full details of opening hours and admission prices.

Gandhi National Museum

Across the road from Raj Ghat is Gandhi National Museum which has on display a few personal belongings of a man who hardly possessed anything. A stone bowl and a brass plate, the clothes Gandhiji wore on the day he was assassinated, a pair of wooden sandals, his bamboo walking stick, a few stud pens he carried himself and a diary in his own handwriting are the few interesting items on display. There is a library and an information centre in the same complex.

Gandhi Smriti

Birla House is the place where Mahatma Gandhi was assassinated on 30 January 1948, on his way for his customary evening prayers. The museum has a large collection of photographs on his life and a few of his personal belongings. Gandhi's life has been illustrated in an unusual way at this museum by using a series of small dolls' houses and terracotta dolls portraying the major events in his life. The spartan room where he lived during his periodic visits to Delhi is preserved as it was during his lifetime. Gandhiji's last footsteps from this room to the garden have been marked out.

NOIDA Golf Course: Sector 38, NOIDA ☎515293. Green fees are Rs 100 on weekdays and Rs 300 on weekends. Per foreign nationals green fees are US $30 on weekdays and US $40 for weekends.

Away from the city's noise and pollution, this lush green 18 hole course is also very popular with golfers from south Delhi and foreigners.

Aravali Golf Club HP, Faridabad ☎5214815. Green fees are Rs 50 on weekdays and Rs 100 on weekends and holidays. For foreigners green fees are US $10 for weekdays and US $25 for weekends and holidays.

This 9 hole golf course is laid out with a lot of greenery. This is the only course which has a motel run by Haryana Tourism.

Sterling Golf & Sports Complex Club D46, Sector 46, NOIDA ☎527980-3. Green fees are Rs 400 on weekdays and Rs 500 on weekends.

This is a new 18 hole golf course, designed by Greg Norman, 45 km from Connaught Place.

The Resort Country Club Pachgaon-Tauru Road, Gurgaon, Haryana ☎510380. City offices ☎3221388/4469900. Green fees are Rs 500 on weekdays and Rs 250 on weekends.

This is a 9 hole golf course on the Jaipur highway.

Meadows Golf and Country Club Faridpur Jharsa Village, Gurgaon Sohna Road, Haryana ☎5134 7/360. City office ☎3141148. Green fees for non-members are Rs 400 for weekdays and Rs 500 for weekends.

A pretty 18 hole course on the main Sohna Road, about 30 km from the Dhaula Kuan roundabout.

DDA Siri Fort Sports Complex ☎6497481/6496637. Casual membership for the Driving Range is Rs 25 per day and Rs 50 for a batch of 10 balls.

Agra

One of the world's most sought after tourist destinations (56 km from Mathura, 200 km from Delhi), it is vital for the visitor to approach Agra with eyes open to its treasures but firmly close to its less salubrious manifestations. Go by train, either the Shatabdi or Taj Express (both leave early morning), and can book a good hotel near Taj Mahal. The Taj is closed on Mondays. Entry fee is Rs 15 during the day but a glimpse of the Taj at sunrise (6 to 8 am) or sunset (5 to 7 pm) will cost Rs 100. Entry is free on Fridays.

If you have to go by road to Agra choose a Sunday when there are fewer trucks. Agra does not lack accommodation to suit every pocket.

Short Excursions

Over 25 destinations around Delhi are outlined for those seeking a weekend out of the city. A useful map at the beginning of the chapter helps you get your bearings.

Architectural Drawings

This is the first time that the architectural splendour of the city's many monuments have been captured by the unique architectural drawings which help the reader to visualise the monuments.

Where to Eat

Delhi could be very exciting for those interested in food. It offers good food from all over the world and all parts of India. So, you will not be homesick for your kind of food. If you are not an Indian and adventurous about food, it may be worth your while to sample Indian food, both the food typical of north India and other parts of the country. The restaurants in the city are varied – not only in their ambience, or the lack of it, but also in their rates.

In an earlier chapter, Food, we have written about the traditional cuisines of Delhi, especially about the many similar religions strewn across the city.

Booking – it is advisable to book a table in a restaurant, especially during the festive season to avoid a tedious wait or even disappointment.

Taxes – Certain additional taxes are levied now and above the listed price on the menu. It may be worthwhile to check at the restaurant.

Here we give you a list of the better-known restaurants in the city. The list has been made area-wise so as to make it convenient for you to find an eatery close to where you are staying or working. There is something to suit every pocket and palate. Also, each restaurant comes with a description of its speciality cuisine. A sumptuous meal for two could cost anything from Rs 200 to over Rs 2000 (and that's not including wine)! Read on and make your choices.

NAME, TYPE OF FOOD WITH LOCATION, ADDRESS, PHONE, FACILITIES, PRICE RANGE			
Connaught Place, Paharganj			
Amber Indian	N Block, Connaught Circus Opp. Scindia House ☎3312062		T •
Appetitte European	Vishal Hotel Main Bazaar Road Paharganj ☎527629-		T •
Balochi Indian	New Delhi Hilton Barakhamba Avenue ☎3320101		T •
Berco's Chinese	E Block, Connaught Place ☎3318134		
Blue Elephant Oriental (Thai)	New Delhi Hilton Barakhamba Avenue ☎3320101		T •

★ Price Range in Rupees (priced for two)			
Below 300•	300-600•	600-900•••	900+ •

Travellers Needs

A detailed list of restaurants has been made area-wise. There is something to suit every pocket and palate. The listing of hotels is according to preferred localities and price ranges. A shopping guide with reference to items, markets and prices is also provided.

Emergency
HOSPITALS

Delhi has several government as well as many privately run hospitals and nursing homes. All government hospitals have modern medical facilities, and due to the patient turnout, medical assistance is slow. Service at the privately run hospitals and nursing homes is more efficient and assistance quicker.

Practical Information

Sequentially arranged, this section gives you all the information that you would need from the time you decide to visit Delhi till you leave the city. Comprehensive and up-to-date details on visas, embassies, tourist information offices, banks, money changers and much else. A lucid Phrase Book and Glossary adds to the utility of this guide.

Maps

The maps are separately numbered from 1 to 42. They cover in minute detail an area of about 190 sq km of Delhi that would be of interest to the tourist. You can locate the place you want from the index as well as with the help of the Key given on the back end pages.

Once upon a time, the Aravalli Hills, matted with
keekar, tapered off into a wide and abundant
Yamuna. The river, also called Kalindi, was fed by
many streams that made gentle indentations in the
hills. The earth had hardened into stratified russet
sandstone or had been transmuted into grey
quartzite. Deep in the earth were glittering veins of
mica. From the 10th century these rocks were
chipped away to get slabs, rubble and gravel for
building. Delhi was quarried into a new landscape.
The hill slopes became shallower, and undulating
stretches were flattened into fields. And the hills hid
away their secrets – the secrets of the men and
women who centuries ago had kindled their fires
and hunted for their food, using the little stone
implements that came to light in 1991 in Anangpur,
near Surajkund.

DELHI IN History

And the forests that reached down to the Yamuna
grew thick and impenetrable. The Mahabharata
describes how this Khandava forest was given by
Duryodhana to the Pandavas, and how Arjuna,
helped by Krishna, set the forest on fire and levelled
the ground to lay out Indraprastha, the grandest of
the five townships established by the Pandavas.
The climate of India made it possible for towns to
be reclaimed swiftly by forests, and so it happened
with Delhi. An inscription on a slab of sandstone
from the reign of Emperor Ashoka tells us that
Delhi was on the great northern highway of the
Mauryas, linking their capital, Pataliputra (near
modern Patna in Bihar), with Takshashila (Taxila,
near modern Rawalpindi in Pakistan) which was
the route Buddhist monks took on their way to
central Asia.

Surajkund.

More than a millennium was to pass before Delhi made its presence felt again. For the princes of the fiefdoms in the deserts of Rajasthan, Delhi was a frontier area from where to essay expansion into the land of the five rivers, Punjab. For princes in Afghanistan, Delhi was a frontier town in India, holding the key to the interfleuve, the Doab.

Jogmaya Mandir near the Qutb complex.

The Tomar Rajputs built a fort on the southern Ridge, which their successful rivals, the Chauhans, enlarged (both Tomars and Chauhans can be found in a modern telephone directory for Delhi). The red fortress, Lalkot, was surrounded by the larger complex, Qila Rai Pithora, named for King Prithviraj Chauhan. Raja Jaichand, whose daughter had married Prithviraj against her father's wishes, enlisted the help of Mohammed of Ghur (in Afghanistan) and Prithviraj was killed in a battle north of Delhi. His *qila* was appropriated by Mohammed of Ghur, who returned to his own country after leaving Qutbuddin Aibak as his viceroy in Delhi. In 1206, when Mohammed died, Aibak crowned himself Sultan of Delhi.

Qutb in Arabic means axis or pillar. Within a few decades, the area around Lalkot knew three *qutbs*, Sultan Qutbuddin Aibak, Qutb Minar of which he built the first storey, and the Sufi saint, Qutbuddin Bakhtiyar Kaki, whose shrine is near the citadel. And Lalkot became, instead of a frontier town, the *qutb* of a kingdom that was later called the *Saltanat* (sultanate) of Delhi.

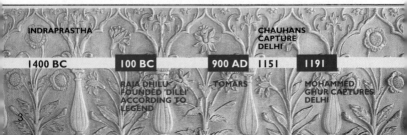

INDRAPRASTHA		CHAUHANS CAPTURE DELHI	
1400 BC	100 BC	900 AD 1151	1191
	RAJA DHILU FOUNDED 'DILLI' ACCORDING TO LEGEND	TOMARS	MOHAMMED GHUR CAPTURES DELHI

3

Qutb Minar.

Delhi remained a capital city almost throughout the
period between 1190 and 1526, of a state whose
boundaries kept shifting and which included
Afganisthan and the Dakshin (Deccan). The
Mamluks/Ilbaris were succeeded by Khaljis,
Tughlaqs, Sayyids and Lodis.

FIRST STOREY OF QUTB MINAR BUILT		TUGHLAQABAD BUILT		BEGUMPURI MASJID BUILT		TOMB OF SIKANDER LODI BUILT
1200	1305	1323	1354	1388	1489	1517
	HAUZ KHAS BUILT		FIROZABAD BUILT		MOTH KI MASJID BUILT	

4

Like the kingdom, the city of Delhi also varied in size. As in medieval Europe, the capital was where the ruler happened to be. Citadels were abandoned and new ones built, around which grew dense settlements usually surrounded by a wall. Sections of the walls and gateways of Lalkot, Siri and Jahanpanah still survive. The walled houses were surrounded by gardens, orchards or forests. From the 13th century a network of canals was laid out to irrigate the fields and orchards of Delhi. Hunting *kushks* (kiosks) on the Ridge and near the palace recall a time when the thick forests here afforded game for the sultan's *shikar*. When things seemed secure, suburbs grew around the city walls. Summer houses set in gardens were later used to house their owners' mortal remains. At its greatest extent, in the 14th century, urban Delhi stretched from Mehrauli to Daryaganj, from the hills to the river.

A ceiling in the Qutb complex.

DINPANAH (PURANA QILA)	CAPITAL SHIFTED TO SHAHJAHANABAD	BRITISH TAKE OVER DELHI	DURBAR IN DELHI
1538	1565	1648	1724	1803	1857	1877
	HUMAYUN'S TOMB BUILT	JANTAR MANTAR BUILT	SIEGE OF DELHI

Purana Qila.

A crossroads city, many of the Indian languages, and those of western and central Asia and even of Europe, could be heard in the bazaars of Delhi. Around the city lived Jat farmers and Gujjar herdsmen, both part of communities that were spread all over north India. Within the city lived nobles, soldiers, merchants and artisans who were Persian, Mongol, Turkish and Afghan. Languages met and mingled, central and west Asian with local Hindawi, particularly among the soldiers. Thus developed the lingua franca named for the army, Urdu, which between the 13th and the 18th century became a language in its own right, in Delhi and in faraway Hyderabad. Free of its rough-and-ready moorings, it became a language of poetry, with an Indian grammar and a highly Persianised vocabulary. Its writers wrote poems about their city, and it was this language that bridged Persian and Hindi, to which the scholar J.B. Gilchrist gave the name Hindustani, the language of Hindustan, north India.

The imposing gateway to Humayun's Tomb.

| 1911 | 1931 | 1947 | 1950 | 1962 | 1985 | 1992 |

NEW DELHI INAUGURATED

DELHI MADE THE CAPITAL OF THE REPUBLIC

NATIONAL CAPITAL REGION DEMARCATED

CORONATION DURBAR IN DELHI

INDIA BECOMES INDEPENDENT

MASTER PLAN FOR DELHI DRAWN UP

DELHI BECOMES A STATE

6

Dargah of Nizamuddin Auliya.

Not only was Delhi the site of royal power but, after the fall of Baghdad in 1358, when the *Khilafat* (Caliphate) shifted to Cairo, it became the capital of Islam in India. Along with Ajmer it was a major centre of Sufism, the popular Islam which came close to Hindu mysticism. Qutbuddin Bakhtiyar Kaki, Nizamuddin Auliya and Roshan Chiragh Dehlvi, became known far beyond Delhi, and their resting places continue to afford solace to thousands who throng to them every year. The strong thread of Sufi faith bound India together permanently, as did the Bhakti cults, more than the army of any ruler.

Domes

Domes have been an inseparable element of architecture down the ages. The dome on Alai Darwaza is shallow and represents very elementary knowledge of dome construction, using squinches. The dome on Ghiyasuddin's Tomb built over a decade latter shows more sophisticated knowledge. Over time the profile of the dome shifted from the single pointed 'Tartar' dome of Ghiyasuddin's Tomb to the bulbous one of Ghata Masjid. Humayun's Tomb and Rashtrapati Bhawan employ the use of two domes – an external monumental one and an inner one to bring it to the human scale. The dome on Rashtrapati Bhawan, designed by Edwin Lutyens, is an eclectic fusion of European and Buddhist styles, evoking the great stupa at Sanchi.

Alai Darwaza (1311)

Ghiyasuddin Tughlaq's Tomb (1321-1325)

Bara Gumbad, Lodi Garden (1484)

Humayun's Tomb (1565)

Dargah of Qutbuddin Bakhtiyar Kaki.

Atgah Khan's Tomb.

Delhi's architecture and opulence dazzled the eye. It was a magnet not only for the politically ambitious, the soldier of fortune, the merchant and the devout, but also for the marauder. Timur had the unique distinction of being a dreaded name both in Russia and in north India. In 1398, his soldiers, wild-eyed at the sight of so much wealth, ransacked Delhi just as the crusaders had pillaged Constantinople in 1204. He paid a compliment to the city when he took all its artisans back with him to build in Samarkand, a city as beautiful as Delhi.

The same predatory spirit that spurred on a Timur prompted Vasco da Gama to look for a new route to India. Nearly thirty years after Gama's ship reached Calicut, a small band led by Prince Babur of Samarkand, made its way through Kabul to north India. This descendant of Timur and Genghis Khan was invited to challenge Ibrahim Lodi by the Sultan's cousin, Daulat Khan Lodi, and the ruler of Mewar, Rana Sanga. The Lodis had moved their capital to Agra, and as Babur wandered through the shrines and ruins of Delhi, he made disparaging comments on the lack of a city-building tradition in India. Perhaps he might have decided to return to Kabul or Samarkand, but he died before he could do so.

The carkasse of old Dely, called the nine castles and fifty-two gates is now inhabited only by Googers. [Gujjars - shepherds]

William Finch, British traveller, 1611.

Ghata Masjid (1711)

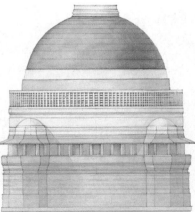

Rashtrapati Bhawan (1931)

8

Late Mughal period silver coins.

Diwan-e-Am, Lal Qila.

Dehli is one of the greatest cities of antiquity. It was first called Indrapat…. Humayun restored the citadel of Indrapat and named it Dinpanah.

Abul Fazl, minister at the court of Akbar, 1600.

Babur's book-loving son Humayun, and his rival, Sher Shah Suri, between them built the foundation of an empire in India. Their dynasty was named Mughal by the Europeans, a term never used by the rulers themselves. Its capital was a citadel in Delhi, on the Yamuna, Dinpanah, with an imposing mosque and gateways. Near it, some years later, Humayun's widow laid out a magnificent mausoleum for him, set in a formal garden which Babur would have approved. Not far from it was later built another majestic memorial, that of Abdur Rahim Khan-i-Khanan. He was a Renaissance man, a scholar-soldier in the court of Emperor Akbar who has been immortalised through his Hindi writings. Rahim's *dohe* (verses) are known to every Indian child.

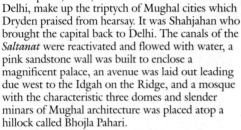

*Jama Masjid
by Thomas Daniell, 1795.*

Akbar and Jehangir preferred to treat Agra and Lahore as their capitals; these, with Delhi, make up the triptych of Mughal cities which Dryden praised from hearsay. It was Shahjahan who brought the capital back to Delhi. The canals of the *Saltanat* were reactivated and flowed with water, a pink sandstone wall was built to enclose a magnificent palace, an avenue was laid out leading due west to the Idgah on the Ridge, and a mosque with the characteristic three domes and slender minars of Mughal architecture was placed atop a hillock called Bhojla Pahari.

While Louis XIV in France was building his escape-city of Versailles, Shahjahan's city was being built and peopled. Traders built *katras and kuchas* (enclosed markets and lanes), the aristocrats their *havelis* and *karkhanas* (mansions and workshops), philanthropists *serais*, *shifakhanas* and *madarsas* (inns, hospitals and schools) and the pious built *masjids* (mosques). The central avenue was called Chandni Chowk, for the *chowk* (open space) where a pool reflected the *chandni* (moonlight). Kinship groups or guilds created *mohallas* (neighbourhoods). Beyond the city walls lay gardens (Shalimar Bagh, Karol Bagh), and extensive properties of friendly rajas and nawabs. The emperors went every year to Mehrauli after it was refreshed by monsoon showers, to Palam to hunt, to the shrine of Nizamuddin to pay homage.

Lal Qila from the Yamuna.

COURTESY : M.M. KAYE (EDITED), THE GOLDEN CALM, VIKING PRESS, NEW YORK, 1980.

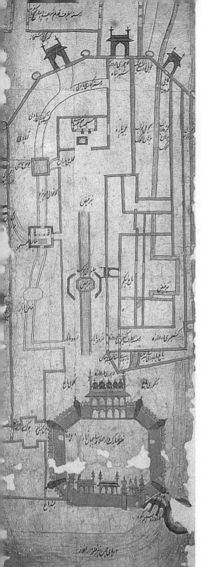

A map of Shahjahanabad, probably made around 1770-80.

COURTESY : SUSAN GOLE, INDIAN MAPS AND PLANS, MANOHAR PUBLICATIONS, DELHI, 1989.

The eighteenth century was a time of wars in Europe and in India. The decline of the Bourbons in France paralleled that of the Mughals in India. There was one difference, the Bourbons' weakness did not lead to the shrinking of their kingdom. The Mughal empire, built up in successive conquests like the Ottoman and the Romanov empires, found sections becoming independent until, as the popular jingle went,

> *The kingdom of Shah Alam*
> *Is only from Delhi to Palam.*

Mughal lifestyles and Mughal architecture were being zealously copied in Lucknow, Hyderabad and other towns. In Delhi, the combination of an opulent palace and a weak government attracted the locusts - the Persians under Nadir Shah, the Afghans led by Ahmed Shah Abdali, Marathas, Jat rebels and the British. The last came to stay.

Unlike Indians, they were meticulous in preparing maps and demarcating boundaries. The only disconcerting thing was that the boundary of British India kept moving outwards. For half a century, the Mughal emperors remained sovereign in the palace while the city was governed by the *kotwal* (city magistrate) and the British Resident, whose office was in a building which had been the library of the ill-fated Prince Dara Shikoh, now modified and anglicised with the addition of a classical facade.

Brackets
Brackets have traditionally been used for different purposes: span openings, support eaves, chhajjas, balconies and jharokhas. The examples drawn from diverse buildings in the long history of Delhi demonstrate the ingenuity of the Indian craftsman in transforming a functional item into an object of beauty.

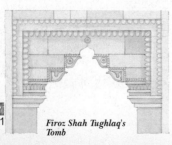

Firoz Shah Tughlaq's Tomb

Sikander Lodi's Tomb

Lahore Gate

11

Bahadur Shah Zafar (ascended the throne 1837, deposed 1857).

The Metcalfes were a parallel Delhi dynasty, Charles Metcalfe, his nephew Thomas and the latter's son, Thomas Theophilus. Thomas Metcalfe laid out a spacious house north of the city, and used Shalimar Garden and the Qutb area for weekend picnics. His enthusiasm for the older buildings of Delhi spurred on the young Sayyid Ahmad Khan to write the first detailed account of these in Urdu, *Asar us Sanadid* (Remains of the Past), which was the basis of the first English guide to Delhi by Carr Stephen.

Delhi's foremost *madarsa* outside Ajmere Gate, that had been named for Ghaziuddin, was called Anglo-Arabic School after the British teachers introduced books on science and mathematics to enthusiastic students who were happy to translate them into

Urdu. Ghalib, Zauq, Emperor Bahadur Shah under the pen name *Zafar* (sword), wrote verse, the distinguished hakims treated patients from all over north India, the merchants did brisk business....

Mirza Ghalib (1786-1869).

Delhi is a very suggestive and moralising place - such stupendous remains of power and wealth passed and passing away - and somehow I feel we horrid English have just 'gone and done it', merchandised it, revenued it and spoilt it all.

Emily Eden, English writer and artist, 1837.

Talaqi Gate, Purana Qila.

Digamber Jain Mandir, Chandni Chowk.

Wrought iron bracket in a haveli in Chandni Chowk.

The British army storming the Kashmere Gate on 14 September 1857.

Until the peace was broken on a hot May morning in 1857 by the sound of running feet over the bridge of boats across the river Yamuna. Delhi was the obvious homing-ground for the rebels seeking to force the British to the ground. For four months the city gates were closed, with thousands of rebel soldiers within, and the British and loyalist troops huddled on the northern Ridge. Theme of memorials, theses, novels and plays, the 'Mutiny', as far as the inhabitants of Delhi were concerned, meant the desecration of Shahjahan's city. The gentle, 82-year old Emperor Bahadur Shah, was cruelly shipped off to Yangaon, his palace, now called the Red Fort, was occupied by British soldiers and most of its buildings were demolished.

The flower that for long adorned a garden

Is now lying dead in dust and thorny bushes.

Wandering through the ruins I hear people exclaim

Only some time ago there were gardens and houses here.

Mir Dard, Delhi poet, 1719-85. (Translated from Urdu by Ishrat Haque).

The soldiers were everywhere, Daryaganj was made a cantonment, the Ridge remained an army preserve. The tradition of military occupation of large parts of the city continues till today. A distinctly British landscape was overlaid on the Mughal city, a spacious Town Hall, a clock tower and an elegant railway station, all at the cost of many neighbourhoods and gardens. Near the railway station grew the crowded Sadar Bazaar, a wholesale market, and in the north, the Sahibs lived in their exclusive Civil Lines, with its own hotels and club. There were exceptions, Mark Twain, the American writer visiting Delhi in 1896, described the house he stayed in – 'built by a rich Englishman who had become orientalised, so much so that he had a *zenana*… To please his harem he built a mosque; to please himself he built an English church. That kind of man will arrive, somewhere.' (Actually the 'Englishman' was the Anglo-Indian Colonel Skinner

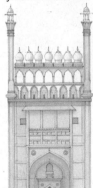

Lahore Gate is the entrance to Lal Qila from Chandni Chowk

Sher Shah's Gate, Lal Darwaza, was most likely the western gate of Shergarh

Talaqi Darwaza of Purana Qila

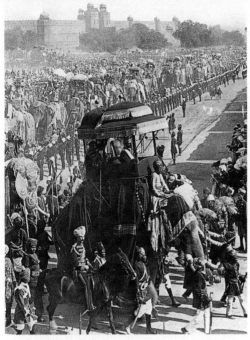

Viceregal party outside Red Fort proceeding to the Coronation Durbar, 1903.

who built St. James Church). In the south, the Archaeological Survey set to work to document and list Delhi's monuments, using Sayyid Ahmad's book as a base.

A political decision changed Delhi's fate. Bengal politics got so inflamed that it was decided to shift the capital from Calcutta to Delhi. These were the years of the high noon of empire, when architecturally arresting capitals were being built in Ottawa, Pretoria and Canberra. To design a grand capital at 'New' Delhi, Edwin Lutyens, builder of stately homes, a man with a quiet sense of fun and a wonderful concern for detail, teamed up with Herbert Baker, who had given Pretoria its secretariat buildings. Riding paths and wide avenues for carriages curved round spacious rondpoints while carefully chosen trees were planted, which, in some decades, made a dusty landscape one of the greenest capitals in the world.

India Gate was designed by Edwin Lutyens and built in 1931

Kashmere Gate was the northern entrance to Shahjahanabad

The three-storeyed Hathi Darwaza is the gateway to Zafar Mahal in Mehrauli, built by Bahadur Shah Zafar

Tree-lined Chandni Chowk, 1910.

The hill at Raisina decided the issue of the location. Some officials wondered whether the capital would not be best around the axis of the Coronation Pillar in north Delhi, which commemorated the Durbar of 1911-12, and some dared to suggest a city on the left of the river. Lutyens, viewing the ground from elephant back, noticed that Dinpanah, site of Indraprastha, was directly east from Raisina. There the Viceroy's palace would be built, linked by a procession way to the oldest Delhi.

In the years after the First World War, Chandni Chowk echoed to the speeches of nationalist leaders, and in the evening Jaisinghpura hummed with the soft sounds of hammer on stone, as Rajasthani workers built a capital to last 500 years! New Delhi was replete with a massive War Memorial, and statues of Viceroys, and behind the trees were elegant bungalows for the officials to live in from October to March. An act of the British parliament conferring a parliament on the Indians made new demands; the building for this was tucked into a vacant space.

1947 was a year of exhilaration and grief - the exhilaration seen when a cavalcade of Mountbatten, Jawaharlal Nehru and other leaders were mobbed by excited crowds at 'India Gate' and the tricolour of independent India fluttered above the palace of Shahjahan, the tragedy when thousands of Muslims from Delhi left their homes to build new lives in Pakistan. The return flow of Hindu and Sikh refugees from Pakistani Punjab converged instinctively on Delhi.

Archways

Quwwatul Islam Mosque (1192–98)

Ghiyasuddin Tughlaq's Tomb (1321-25)

Sikander Lodi's Tomb (1517)

From a Guidebook of Delhi published almost a hundred years ago.

A week, or at least five days, may well be devoted to Delhi, many of the sights of which deserve repeated visits. For those who can give three days to the place, the following plan of sight-seeing will perhaps be found the most convenient :

First Day

Morning : Drive through Kashmere Gate to the Fort and Palace, the Jama Masjid, and the Chandni Chowk.

Afternoon : Drive to the further end of Ridge, and from there along it to the south end. Then proceed along the route of the sites of the siege batteries and the breaches, finishing with the spot where General Nicholson was shot and the grave where he is buried.

Second Day

Morning : Drive to the Qutb by the direct route of the Ajmere Gate and Safdarjang's tomb. Spend the day there - one cannot see all that is worth seeing in less than four hours - and return in the evening by the same road, pausing to see the group of tombs at Khairpur, now Lodi Garden. (By starting at 7.30 am and having a second relay of horses, it is possible to include Tughlaqabad in the day's trip; this, however, involves a 35 mile drive and 6 hours of sight-seeing).

Third Day

Morning : Visit the Purana Qila, Humayun's Tomb, and Nizamuddin; if possible also the tomb of Isa Khan and of Khan-i-Khanan.

Afternoon : Visit the Delhi Palace again, the Kala Masjid, and the tomb and college of Ghaziyuddin at the Ajmere Gate.

Connaught Place in the early 1950s.
COURTESY : THE HINDUSTAN TIMES.

Afsarwala's Tomb (1566-67)

Secretariat Gate (1931)

India Habitat Centre (1994)

16

Rashtrapati Bhawan.

The municipal properties, mostly agricultural land around the city, were parcelled out and little homes were built in Malviya Nagar, Lajpat Nagar, Rajendra Nagar, all the townships which embodied a tough spirit of courage and hard work. Delhi was also expected to house many new departments of government and houses of officials, hospitals, schools, institutes of research....

All this called for a major planning exercise. The Delhi Development Authority, created in 1957, produced a Master Plan in 1962 (since modified into 'Delhi 2001') in which European and American planning practices were overlaid on Delhi. The qualities of the garden city were continued in the network of parks and forests, but the demand for housing continues unabated. Delhi now merges into the neighbouring states of Uttar Pradesh and Haryana, and forms part of a larger area demarcated as the National Capital Region.

Vikas Minar, headquarters of Delhi Development Authority.

The villages that surrounded the twin cities are now reduced to enclaved habitats, as the 'colonies' proliferate. The rulers of the country moved into the spacious houses built by the British, the Viceroy's palace is now Rashtrapati Bhawan, the Commander-in-Chief's house was in his lifetime the residence of Jawaharlal Nehru (later a museum in his memory). The ceremonial Kingsway became Rajpath, ideally suited for an annual procession to celebrate the formation of the Republic. The Temporary Secretariat in north Delhi houses the Delhi Assembly. There are other architectural statements, in the form of public buildings and places of worship, reflecting international architectural fashions. The various histories that make up Delhi make its tale one of many cities, an endless game of discovery.

In some years, the Mass Rapid Transport System will be a reality, and Delhi's commuter zone will extend further. Many of the shabbier areas will become elegant neighbourhoods, shopping precincts will become more glitzy. But children and their parents will still fly kites in the monsoon breeze, and the weaver birds will return every year to hang their nests from the branches of trees in Mehrauli.

Into the total blue

The domes of the mausolea

- Dark, shut round on their own thoughts -

Suddenly send forth Birds.

Octavio Paz, 'In the gardens of the Lodis'.

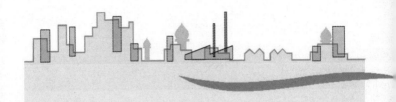

Introducing
DELHI

Connaught Place, 1998.
Impressions of a Mughal miniature artist, Firozuddin.

squeezed dry of rain,
a host of clouds
	palest silver like delicate sea-shells,
float free in places,
waved back and forth
	by brisk winds with the utmost ease;
the sky appears like a great king
fanned by a hundred fleecy cowries.

KALIDASA, *RITUSAMHARA*

Environment

A six pointed star, about 5 cm across, with Delhi at the heart of the hexagon, placed on a map of India of the scale 1 cm to 120 km, embraces the major regions of northern India. The north apex reaches the high Himalayas where lie Jammu, Kashmir and Ladakh, the cold desert with its magical moon landscape. The curve to the right to the next point of the star follows the sweep of the central Himalayas and the apex encompasses the holy Manasarovar Lake in Tibet. The second curve towards the right embraces the mountains of Nepal and its two lofty peaks - Everest and Kanchenjunga. The third point of the star almost reaches Allahabad, the heartland of the fertile and populous Indo-Gangetic plain and the confluence of the rivers Ganga and Yamuna. The holy city of Varanasi is 185 km downstream.

To the west of Delhi, lying between the two points of the star, is the Great Indian Desert, most of which is in the Indian state of Rajasthan. The southern point of the star reaches the forested highlands of central India beyond which is the Deccan peninsula, an ancient land mass of volcanic origin.

Seasons

The climate of Delhi is created by these geographic features. Hot winds blow from the desert in the summer months, and temperatures soar to 40° C, occasionally reaching a high of 46° C. Violent dust storms – locally called *loo* – are a feature of this hot, dry season in Delhi. The blessed relief of rain follows by end-June when the monsoon reaches Delhi, having hit Kerala around the first week of June, crossed the Deccan and the Bay of Bengal to be finally deflected along the sweep of the Himalayas from east to west. Temperatures for the next few months remain in the high 30s and the humidity makes for some discomfort. Winter is the pleasantest season in Delhi, sunny and cool but the minimum temperature drops sharply in late December and January. Every time there is heavy snowfall in the mountains, icy winds blow down.

The Gulmohur flower in shades of fire red and orange.

The royal dressage of the Queen's Flower.

There is a brief change of season between winter and the hot weather. Spring lasts only a few weeks in February and March, but it is sweet and sensuous. It is the season of new leaf – many of Delhi's indigenous forest trees are dressed in shades of vivid green. This is followed soon after by the procession of colour of the ornamental flowering trees. The Hindu festivals of Basant Panchami and Holi celebrate this season, known in Hindi as *Basant*.

The Laburnum, or Amaltas, festooned with cascades of gold.

In the Indian tradition, there are six seasons - *Grishma, Varsha, Sharad, Hemant, Sheet* and *Basant*. They correspond roughly to Summer, Rains, Post-rains, Early winter, Winter and Spring. The passing of seasons has been immortalised in Indian art and literature. The most famous literary work on this theme is the 5th century Sanskrit poet, Kalidasa's *Ritusamhara*, literally the gathering of seasons.

Natural Ecosystems

The natural vegetation of the region around Delhi can best be described as thorny scrub which can still be seen on the outskirts of the city. If one sees the city as a triangle, the western side is a natural divide, an extension of the ancient Aravalli hills which run through Rajasthan. The outcrops in Delhi are called the Ridge. The undulating terrain runs through the Cantonment area in west Delhi, and the section in the north includes Delhi University. From the highest point in the south at Bhatti, 318 metres above sea level, the fall is 100 metres to the river Yamuna which forms a natural boundary of the city on the east. The base of the triangle is rocky, broken country where small water bodies fill with monsoon run-off and where agricultural land around small villages is cultivated for vegetables and flowers for the urban market.

The Jacaranda flower, a delicate filigree of mauve and violet.

The magnificent remains of the older cities of Delhi, once fed by the Yamuna, invite exploration – Surajkund, Tughlaqabad, Mehrauli, Hauz Khas, Siri and Jahanpanah. Quarrying for stone at Bhatti, and in the neighbouring state of Haryana, has recently been curtailed through legislation as an environmental health measure.

The Ridge today is an important lung of metropolitan Delhi. Its evolution from thorny scrub began in the 19th century with the British, who started planting drought resistant indigenous trees, largely Neem (*Azadirachta indica*) and Babul (*Acacia nilotica*). Palas or Flame of the Forest (*Butea monosperma*), a small tree with a gnarled and crooked trunk, occurs naturally. It heralds spring with bright red flowers from which a dye is extracted. In 1878, the Ridge was declared a Reserved Forest. Lutyens, the architect of New Delhi, used the undulating land to great advantage while siting the Viceroy's House, now Rashtrapati Bhawan, the home of the President of India, on Raisina Hill.

Early blossoms of spring.

At the southern base of the triangle, the urban sprawl has made inroads with agricultural land being converted into luxurious estates for the elite. Architecturally, these 'farmhouses' are completely out of tune with the past or contemporary landscape of the area. In planning colonial Delhi, Lutyens and Baker laid out a geometric pattern of roads radiating from roundabouts while keeping the Mughal and pre-Mughal monuments as axis points. They thus achieved an architectural synthesis of history and, at the same time, extended the garden concept integral to the buildings of the Mughal period to the avenues of New Delhi.

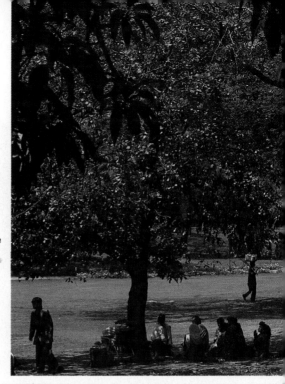

Pipal, the most common of the ficus species.

The credit for planting indigenous forest species, a brilliant and practical idea, is shared with Lutyens by William Robertson Mustoe, a gardener from London's Kew Gardens, who came to India in 1919. Together they created a garden city while not tampering with the old parks: Roshanara, the garden created by Shahjahan's daughter, Qudsia and Shalimar Gardens in north Delhi. The Ridge area in north Delhi, with Flagstaff Tower at the highest point, was a rambling wilderness until the idea of 'beautification' came up. This was the British cantonment during the 1857 war from where their attack was launched to recapture Delhi.

In the 50 years since independence, Delhi's population has grown by leaps and bounds. The garden city has expanded to become an unwieldy megametropolis posing a severe strain on civic amenities and the environment.

After partition, the refugees from Punjab were allotted land in compensation for the homes they had to abandon : Karol Bagh, Patel Nagar and Rajendra Nagar in west Delhi, Model Town in north Delhi and Lajpat Nagar in south Delhi. Now they are bustling centres of Punjabi enterprise.

A landscaped park in New Delhi in winter.

The seat of government brought its own changes as the government apparatus grew in size. A certain architectural homogeneity was retained in most of the new government buildings by the use of columns, domes, deep corridors and by

Neem provides dense shade, and its medicinal and germicidal properties have been known and used for centuries.

continuing the use of the familiar pink sandstone from Rajasthan. The manpower needs of the burgeoning bureaucracy accounted for the growth of government housing colonies within New Delhi. Chanakyapuri, named after the master strategist, Chanakya, of the 4th century BC, is the diplomatic quarter.

Leaves of the Kikar.

Expansion continued. As bylaws changed and property values soared, gardens were sacrificed to greed. Soon the city spilled over across the Yamuna in the east, creating a concrete jungle, and south of the border into Haryana which developed self-contained, suburban style housing complexes.

Adjutant storks are becoming increasingly rare.

Parks and Gardens

Some portions of the Ridge have been landscaped and converted into parks. Buddha Jayanti Park was originally conceived as a Japanese garden. A splendid image of the Buddha was installed in 1990. Trees planted by visiting dignitaries in the 1950s have matured and lend variety to the landscaped garden. Mahavir Jayanti Park, near Maurya Sheraton Hotel, was developed more recently.

The city planners had made some provision for park areas other than the Ridge. The necropolis of the Lodi kings was tastefully landscaped around the monuments in the 1960s and called Lodi Garden. The moat around Purana Qila was expanded into a serpentine lake where paddle boats are available. The grounds south of it became the National Zoological Park. Delhi Golf Club incorporates some old monuments creating a picturesque setting. Golfers tee off, often distracted by the unmusical call of peacocks.

In the third week of February, Mughal Garden at Rashtrapati Bhawan is open to the public for about two weeks. The mass of colour is enchanting, the lawns impeccably manicured, the trees magnificent, even if the overwhelming security checks take away quite a bit from their enjoyment.

The nilgai, India's largest antelope can still be seen in the scrub forests around Delhi.

Lodi Garden in winter.

Nehru Park, located near Ashok Hotel in Chanakyapuri, is another well-landscaped garden. The rolling lawns are enlivened with groups of interesting trees and flowering shrubs. A group of three enormous Trees of Heaven (*Ailanthus excelsa*), provides a focus on the lawn near the rather forlorn statue of Lenin.

At the Deer Park in Hauz Khas.

Pink Cassias are popular roadside trees for colour and shade.

Trees

Forest species for avenue trees were selected primarily to provide shade. For instance, Neem is the choice for many of the major roads, including Lodi Road, Sher Shah Marg, Rafi Marg and Sansad Marg leading from Parliament House to Connaught Place. *Arjuna terminalia*, with its distinctive light grey bark, lines Janpath, a major north-south road, and Firoz Shah Road. A group of six stand at the entrance to Safdarjang's Tomb. Tamarind is the choice for Akbar Road, Pipal for Panchsheel Marg, Banyan for Rajaji Marg.

Eugenia jambolana, the Java Plum or Jamun is used extensively : Tughlaq Road, the northern half of Janpath and around India Gate. The dark purple fruit is a seasonal delicacy but messy when it ripens and falls on the ground during the rainy season. Each of these species have many uses besides medicinal properties.

Variety is provided chiefly on the roundabouts or on subsidiary roads. Kanak Champa (*Pterospermum acerifolium*) on Jai Singh Road is a striking tree because of the size of its foot-long creamy flowers surrounded by five curled back sepals of the same length. The leaves of the same size or more are used as wrappings or made into disposable, biodegradable plates. A group of five Ginko trees, a lone Cypress and a clump of Kewra add character to the small masjid on the roundabout at the head of Sunheri Bagh Road.

The kaleidoscope of changing colours and fragrances continues through the year. The older

Bougainvillea overflowing boundary walls.

indigenous trees have insignificant blossoms but provide variety in tints of green as they come into new leaf. Pipal (*Ficus religiosa*) and Kusum (*Schleichera trijuga*) are both delightful, as the young leaves are shades of rust or deep carmine which change gradually into a soft translucent lime green before assuming the deep green. This play of colours characterises spring and early summer.

The Coral leaves.

Then the flowering trees take over. The Coral tree (*Erythrina indica*), with its bright red spike-like blossoms and Jacaranda (*Mimosaefolia*), with its delicate flowers in shades of mauve, is soon followed by Amaltas (*Cassia fistula*), draped in hanging bunches of fragrant bright yellow blossoms offset by the brown foot-long cylindrical seed pods of the last season. Champa or Temple Tree (*Plumeria alba* or *P. rubra*) is a favourite in many homes besides public places and gardens. It grows easily, is attractive, and has exquisitely textured and scented flowers.

The Coral flower.

Chandni, a popular shrub often used in hedges.

Well into summer, Gulmohur (*Delonix regia*), introduced in 1829 from its native Madagascar, comes into its own, its spreading crown a blaze of red shaded with orange. Pride of India (*Lagerstroemia speciosa*), a small-sized tree, blooms in shades of deep pink or mauve, and then, turns to violet. Closer towards winter, the Rusty Shield-bearer (*Peltophorum roxburghi*) stands out with its copper-red oblong seed pods and sprays of yellow-touched-with-rust flowers. By mid September, *Chorissia speciosa* is glorious in its orchid-like blossoms in shades of pink and white, while *Alstonia scholaris*, often called the Devil's Tree, calls attention to itself with its heady fragrance.

The majestic national bird, the peacock.

Birds

Because of trees, gardens and the river, bird life in and around the city is abundant despite the pollution and the teeming population. Late winter and spring are the best time to wander in the gardens and to look out for birds. The winter migrants are still here and the trees, not yet in leaf, provide good viewing. Wagtails begin to lose their winter drabness, the blue throat will have its band of colours, and the red throat too. The warblers flit incessantly. A flock of starlings may alight on the ground and start feeding voraciously.

The brilliant green of the rose-ringed parakeets perching precariously on the soft grey and muted sandstone walls of the tombs at Lodi Garden, tails fanned out, is an unforgettable sight. On the dome, there might be the ponderous white-backed vultures. Flitting through the trees you may glimpse the golden oriole or locate it through its rich flute-like call. A flash of deep turquoise will give away the white-breasted kingfisher. Or you may glimpse the common grey hornbill which is very partial to the *ficus* species. At dusk, the cacophony of mynahs, sparrows, crows, jostling for space in the *putranjivas* or *malsarry* may be punctuated by the sweet song of the magpie robin staking its claim to territory. The harbinger of the monsoon is the pied-crested cuckoo which rides in from Africa on the south-westerlies.

The pariah kite is an efficient scavenger that can negotiate wires and trees skilfully.

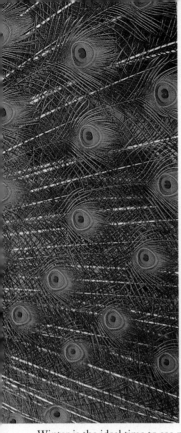

Nesting time for painted storks and cormorants.

Winter is the ideal time to see migratory waterfowl. At the Okhla barrage over the Yamuna in southeast Delhi, you will find herons, barheaded geese and brahmini duck down from their nesting grounds in Ladakh, and from Siberia and central Europe, common pochard, tufted duck, pintails, shoveller, mallard, gadwall, redheaded pochard if you are lucky, besides the comb duck, spotbills and coot. Spoonbills, avocets, painted storks, open-billed storks and the occasional black-necked stork can also be seen.

Another place good for watching water birds is the Sultanpur Bird Sanctuary, about 55 km southwest of Delhi beyond Gurgaon. The Keoladeo Bird Sanctuary near Bharatpur, on the Agra-Jaipur highway, about 120 km from Delhi, is the only wintering ground of endangered Siberian cranes.

Black swans in the Delhi Zoo.

In south Delhi, some areas have been demarcated as wildlife preserves, notably the Asola Wildlife Sanctuary near Tughlaqabad Fort. The area immediately south of Qutb is also worth a wander. Sanjay Van, adjoining the Qutb Institutional Area, is a wilderness within the city and retains the indigenous flora and fauna of the Ridge. Peacocks abound in these parks.

Quwwatul Islam Mosque – sandstone/dholpur.

Entrance arch of Ghiyasuddin Tughlaq's Tomb – red sandstone, white marble.

Yamuna

The Yamuna is under threat. Much of its water is drawn away at the Wazirabad barrage in north Delhi to supply the needs of the metropolis and the rest is subjected to millions of tons of toxic effluents and untreated sewage. The meandering river bed is cultivated to grow water melons in summer but during the monsoon, the river rages in its full glory, reclaiming its bed. The sluice gates are opened allowing the accumulated water hyacinth to be cleared.

Unlike other cities with rivers, Delhi does not have a waterfront, perhaps because of seasonal fluctuations. However, the land created between the eastern wall of the old city and the current riverbed has been developed into massive memorial parks beginning with Raj Ghat, dedicated to Mahatma Gandhi, and later the memorials of Jawaharlal Nehru and other prime ministers of India.

The Stones of Delhi

The basic building material for the older cities of Delhi was the greyish stone quarried in the region. The stucco finish of pre-Mughal and Mughal buildings acted both as a binding plaster and a medium for decorative motifs.

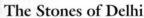

ILLUSTRATIONS OF LEAVES AND FLOWERS BY **BULBUL SHARMA**
ILLUSTRATIONS OF STONES OF DELHI BY **HIMANISH DAS**

Entrance arch of Humayun's Tomb – Jaisalmer stone, white marble, black Cuddapah stone, red sandstone.

Chamber flooring of Humayun's Tomb – white marble, red Cuddapah stone.

Sandstone for exterior facing has been used for over a thousand years. The most spectacular example is the Qutb Minar. Being a soft stone, it lends itself to the chisel and can be worked in intricate detail. The red sandstone comes from Mathura and Agra and the buff-beige from Dholpur, Bharatpur and Alwar.

Red Fort uses a mix of red standstone for the great ramparts and outer walls and the finest Makrana marble, quarried in Rajasthan, gleaming white, for the private palaces and Diwan-e-Am, the hall of public audience. The wall with the built-in throne, has some of the finest examples of *pietra dura* work, using dark grey limestone for the bird panels which are set in shimmering white marble and held together as a composition with coils of delicate floral arabesques. *Kurkura*, a mustard-yellow limestone quarried near Jaisalmer, is used for the borders of the panels, and *abur*, a mottled brown limestone also from Jaisalmer, for branches and stems. For the details of the panels, semiprecious stones are used, including turquoise, cornelian, agate, onyx and lapis lazuli.

Marble and kota stone from Rajasthan, slate from Himachal and black granite from Cuddapah in Andhra Pradesh continue to be used in contemporary buildings.

The many cities of Delhi have been created over the centuries. Its monuments of stone will endure, but its very life-blood, the river Yamuna, is under assault and something must be done immediately to save it.

Inside walls of Diwan-e-Am in Lal Qila – white marble, cornelian.

Jaalis on the parapet of Rashtrapati Bhawan – red and buff sandstone.

Leaves of the Silk Cotton tree.

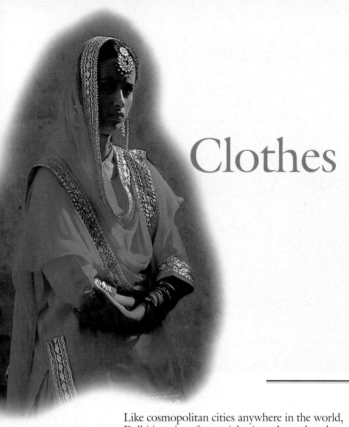

Clothes

Like cosmopolitan cities anywhere in the world, Delhi is a city of sartorial mix and match rather than a bastion of conservatism. This is not a city where one can feast on an oriental vision of traditional Indian attire. Although different clothing traditions do continue here, the general scenario is awash in a sea of synthetics.

As the country's capital, Delhi attracts people from every region, some of whom quietly put away their traditional dress in favour of modern attire, while others retain or adapt it to the climate and culture of the city. At the same time, people of Delhi draw on different regional traditions, reworking them into a national fashion, with the result that appearances can often be deceptive. The flared *lehnga* or *ghagra* (ankle-length skirt), for instance, is usually associated with Rajasthani and Haryanvi women, but in Delhi the person wearing it could just be a college girl flaunting an 'ethnic look'.

The *piece de resistance* of the Indian woman's clothing is the sari, a piece of cloth six yards long, in varied weaves and colours, which is draped around the body. The sari was traditionally worn without a blouse, until the straight-laced Victorian colonialists arrived and insisted that what they considered over-exposed flesh should be covered with the short blouse. Most saris worn in Delhi, however, represent traditions of different parts of the country blended into the standardised sari-blouse combination.

The salwar-kameez was introduced in India by the Mughals and adopted as the daily attire by women in Punjab. Today it is one of the most popular garments among women in Delhi.

Saris are draped around the head in the presence of elders and strangers to show respect and as a mark of family dignity.

Married Hindu women are traditionally distinguished by certain accessories and ornaments. These include *sindoor* (vermilion powder) in the parting of the hair, a *bindi* (small dot, usually red) on the forehead, and bangles (glass or gold) on each arm. These accessories are considered symbols of *suhaag* (the auspicious state of having a living husband). Consequently, a Hindu widow was debarred from using these symbols and made to wear only white. With the march of modernity, the rigidity of such codes has weakened. *Bindis* and bangles, for instance, are today fashion accessories that are worn even by unmarried girls and by women of other religions. In any case, the absence of these symbols does not necessarily signify much in an urban setting.

A bridegroom in traditional attire, complete with headgear and a garland of flowers.

The most distinctive feature of male clothing used to be the headgear. While Sikh men still retain their turbans, and some Muslim men wear *topis* (caps), most Hindu men have abandoned the various forms of headgear which once indicated not only individual styles, but caste affiliations and occupational groups as well. On important occasions like weddings, the groom and senior male members of the family often wear the traditional turban. Gold-embroidered and tinselled turbans can be bought readymade in a number of Delhi markets, of which Kinari Bazaar in Shahjahanabad is the most famous *(see : Bazaars, p.62).*

Traditional men's wear like the *dhoti* and *kurta-pajama* are still worn, but most men in Delhi have taken to shirts and trousers. Way back in 1911 the renowned art critic, Ananda Coomaraswamy, criticised Indian men for wearing 'dingy tubular garments best adapted not to show the dirt of the atmosphere they are content to breathe'. Were he to stand at the Kendriya Bus Terminal next to the Central Secretariat today, he would be reassured to find that trousers and pollution continue to make good companions.

Mannequins dressed in salwar kameez adorn shop windows in markets all over Delhi.

Whether the waiting hordes of grey scissor-legged men outside office complexes represent the march of modernity or the march of mediocrity remains a matter of debate. While government servants stick to a code of respectable dreariness, they are by no means alone in wearing western tailored garments, which have become an established part of the male wardrobe. So has the safari suit, a relic of colonial hunting parties, which is still worn by some senior bureaucrats and staid businessmen.

The fashion industry, which is booming in the metropolis, has reworked different fabrics and styles that were previously associated with particular communities into high fashion. If you have the money and the panache to carry off fabulously embroidered velvets and silks that are reminiscent of the splendour of the Mughal courts, you could drop in at the boutiques of the city where top designers display male and female outfits that are both innovative and outrageous.

A word about the seasonal variations in Delhi. The temperature swings quite wildly in the course of the year, demanding a versatile wardrobe. It is very hot during summer while winter brings to mind silhouettes of shawl-swathed *chowkidars* (watchmen) huddled around a fire in an enveloping mist.

Perhaps the most striking feature of the fashionable urban youth is his or her ability to ignore the weather. Such young trendies think nothing of wearing tight denim jeans and heavy ankle boots in mid-summer temperatures of 40-45°C. University campuses and fashionable shopping centres like the Priya Cinema complex, Defence Colony or South Extension markets are good places for spotting such aspiring and perspiring trendy youths.

Handloom cotton fabrics worn in the form of salwar-kameez, sari, or kurta and jeans, accompanied with leather *chappals* (thongs) or embroidered *juttis* (shoes) are the hallmarks of Delhi's artists and intellectuals. They are often seen in rough cotton *khadi* (hand-spun, hand-woven cloth). Earth-coloured, vegetable-dyed, block-printed fabrics are their favourites, and synthetics are shunned.

The old Gandhian is rarely seen, although his attire (with necessary sophistication) has become the stock-in-trade of politicians. The old Gandhian is recognised by his loose, white *khadi kurta*, a *dhoti* or *pajamas*, and a white boat-shaped Gandhi *topi*. During India's freedom struggle, *khadi* clothes and the Gandhi cap were symbols of self-reliance and represented the quest for liberation from colonial rule while today it is often identified as the politicians' uniform.

Rajasthani women labourers, dressed in colourful *lehnga*, *choli* and *dupatta*, often with thick silver anklets and heavy bracelets are such a common sight for residents of Delhi that they seldom notice them. To foreign tourists, however, the vision of such elegance on construction sites is likely to cause curiosity, if not disbelief.

Burqah-clad Muslim women, seen mainly in the bazaars of old Delhi, are usually dressed in black, although the garments they wear beneath their *burqah* are generally made from bright shiny materials, often with lots of embroidery and sequins. Those who comply with strict codes of modesty wear both a full length cape-like garment and a head-dress which is tied under the chin with a *jaali* or net flap which can be pulled down to conceal the face when necessary. Some women have replaced this headgear with a simple *chaddar* (wrap) which they use to cover their heads, shoulders and sometimes even their mouths.

The traditional Delhi *bania* (trader) may seem a nondescript figure in his shop in the lanes of Shahjahanabad, as he sits cross-legged, propped up by a bolster, but he may well be at the centre of a vast wholesale trading network. Today, most Hindu *banias* have given up their traditional attire of starched *dhoti-kurta* for trousers. Elderly Muslim traders continue to sport white caps, while the younger ones usually tuck them into the pockets of their jeans and bring them out for *namaz* (prayer).

Meena Bazaar, outside Jama Masjid, displays a stupendous variety of velvet, woollen, nylon, cotton and plastic caps. The most popular ones are white crochet caps, known as jaaliwali topis, which are allegedly imported from China.

Coolies at railway stations can be easily spotted by their red kurtas or shirts and white cloth coiled around their head ready to balance large trunks and suitcases.

Cycle rickshawalas and coolies throng the railway station and the bazaars of Shahjahanabad, most of which are too narrow to accommodate motorised vehicles. Although some of them wear trousers, most dress in the more comfortable *lungi* which consists of one long strip of cloth wrapped around the body and tied at the waist. Most popular are the blue checked cotton *lungis* from the Madras area with brand names like Sadaam, Wall Clock, Violin, Abba and 999. They are usually worn with a *ganji* (cotton vest) or a long sleeved shirt.

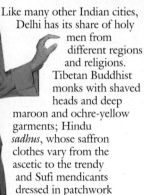

Like many other Indian cities, Delhi has its share of holy men from different regions and religions. Tibetan Buddhist monks with shaved heads and deep maroon and ochre-yellow garments; Hindu *sadhus*, whose saffron clothes vary from the ascetic to the trendy and Sufi mendicants dressed in patchwork garments.

Foreign tourists everywhere are renowned for their lack of awareness or perhaps their lack of concern about how they ought to be dressed. Many young foreign women hang about in décolleté see-through dresses, scarves wrapped around the loins as skirts, skimpy vests, shorts or minis, all of which fuel the imagination of Delhi's male population! Foreign men, though less prone to attract sexual advances, often wear rather outrageous combinations such as a woman's *dupatta* worn as a *lungi* or a priest's saffron scarf topped with a baseball cap made from traditional Tibetan weaves.

COURTESY : NGMA

46

Food

Delhi is a generous city. It has assimilated the cuisines of Banias, Rajputs, Arabs, Afghans, Mughals and the English and more recently, the Punjabis. Sometimes it makes you wonder if what unites the country is not language or religion, but food.

Eating in the Past

People of the early Vedic civilisation ate meat and were fond of *soma rasa* (fermented fruit juice). In the following centuries, the priestly class became vegetarian and so did those who adopted Buddhism and Jainism. The Turko-Afghan invaders of Delhi were fond of lamb and poultry but their food was not very spicy, and peppercorn was used to liven a dish. The Mughals, who came thereafter, favoured various types of meat cooked with *ghee*, curds and spices. They were fond of fruit and they imported grapes and musk melons from Central Asia. What is today termed 'Mughlai' food in Delhi has little resemblance to what the emperors ate. It is a blend of Punjabi and Mughal cuisine, standardised so much it tastes the same all over the city. If anything can be called the original Delhi food, it is probably the vegetarian Bania food which retained its original flavour despite the influence of Mughal cuisine. After the partition of India in 1947, many people from west Punjab moved into Delhi and the city was introduced to Punjab's vegetarian fare which is spicier than the food eaten locally.

Nowhere else in India will you find so many types of cuisines – each with its own pedigree – which have evolved over the years. While Delhi's ethnic specialities can be identified as Bania, Mughal and Punjabi, the European and Chinese food available are of a high standard.

Non-Vegetarian Food

Places that offer authentic Muslim food are the areas around Jama Masjid, Bara Hindu Rao near Sadar Bazaar and Nizamuddin. Some restaurants in the exclusive five-star hotels serve excellent Muslim food.

Jama Masjid is today probably the best place for Mughal cuisine in north India. The variety and the quality are incredible, from the *gola kebabs* of Babu Khan, who sits near the mosque in Matia Mahal, to Kallu's *halim* and *nahiri* at the end of Gali Chitli Qabar. The different types of *kebab* and bread that are available in the Jama Masjid area are mind-boggling. The *kebabs* range from *seekh* and *reshmi* to *kathi* and *kalmi*, and the bread from *naan* and *roomali roti* to *bakarkhani* and *tandoori roti*.

For Punjabi-Mughlai food the most popular places are the restaurants in Pandara Road Market, Karol Bagh and Connaught Place. **Pindi** and **Gulati** in Pandara Road and **Kake da Hotel** in Connaught Place have a large clientele. Every locality in south and west Delhi has one or two good eating places serving this hybrid of Punjabi and Mughlai food. The menu here is predictable, with the ubiquitous *tandoori* chicken, butter chicken and *dal makhani* being favourites.

The most famous non-vegetarian restaurant in the Shahjahanabad area is **Karim** in Gali Kababiyan in Matia Mahal. The restaurant has been run by the same family for over 90 years. Mutton *korma*, *ishtew* and *barra kababs* are musts for the gourmet visiting Karim and the meal should end with *firni*, a milk-based dessert served in an earthenware dish. Karim has a branch near the *dargah* at Hazrat Nizamuddin.

There is an interesting story about how the beef stew, *nahiri*, first came to be made during the reign of Emperor Shahjahan. Delhi's water supply came from the canal in Chandni Chowk. The water in the canal was once found to be unfit for consumption, so the *hakims* of Delhi put their heads together and devised a recipe for a stew, cooked overnight over slow fire, with beef and a large measure of red chillies. The furiously hot chillies were meant to burn any germs present in the polluted water. It is said that the use of chillies and *amchoor* (dried green mangoes) in Bania food started around this time.

In a lane off Chandni Chowk, called Paranthewali Gali, there are three old families which sell paranthas; Gaya Prasad Shiv claims on his signboard that he brings to you 'the expertise of five generations'. Paranthas come with different kinds of fillings, potato, spinach, cauliflower and radish. Also available, though not at Paranthewali Gali, are paranthas with mince meat filling or with eggs poured over them.

Breads: People of Delhi are wheat eaters, though rice, barley and maize are also eaten. There are different kinds of rotis (wheat-based bread) available and eaten in Delhi. These include chapatis, khasta rotis, roomali rotis, tandoori rotis, naans, and so on. Makki ki roti, made of maize flour is a great favourite in the winter months, eaten with sarson ka saag (mustard greens).

Deep-fried Indian bread include puris, kachoris and bhaturas.

Loaves of white bread, available all over the city, are called 'double roti', possibly because when Europeans introduced bread, two slices were eaten together as in sandwiches.

Vegetarian Food

Interestingly, there are no restaurants in Delhi offering the traditional, vegetarian Bania food. Most vegetarian restaurants or *bhojanalayas* offer Marwari food. The better known being **Sakahari** in Chawri Bazaar, **New Soni** on Nai Sarak and **Brijbasi** outside Katra Neel.

In most places the vegetarian food available is basically Punjabi. Unfortunately, most restaurants tend to thrive on *dal makhani* and the eternal *paneer* or cottage cheese. These restaurants give any international fast food chain competition when it comes to standardising the flavour of food!

The mainstay of the restaurant scene is the numerous makeshift eateries or *dhabas*. Originally *dhabas* were located on major highways, catering mainly to the truck drivers. Within the city these modest eateries have acquired a different dimension, serving reasonably priced food ranging from Punjabi to Chinese. The speed and dexterity with which food is splashed out on plates and brusquely placed on rickety tables is commendable.

Special mention must be made of the Punjabi favourite, *chhole bhature* or *chhole kulche*. The best thing about *chhole* is that it tastes different in every household and in every restaurant. One of the best places offering *chhole bhature* is **Kwality** in Connaught Place.

Another Delhi favourite is *rajma-chawal*, kidney beans cooked with spices and tomatoes, and served with rice. *Rajma-chawal* is available outside most office complexes though this is a dish best cooked at home.

An important part of Bania food culture is its savouries, *chaats* and snacks, for which Delhi is famous. The *chaats* available in Delhi include *gol gappas* (flour puffs filled with spiced, tangy, tamarind water), *papris, dahi pakore* and *raj kachoris*. Some old *chaat* stalls survive in the Shahjahanabad area. **Ashok Chaat Bhandar** at Hauz Qazi Chowk is a great favourite as are the shops selling *chaat* in Bengali Market in New Delhi and **Haldiram Bhujiawala** on Mathura Road near Badarpur.

The neighbourhood fruitjuicewala is easily recognised by the mountains of oranges and sweet lime displayed on his makeshift counter. In the winter months he plies his customers with carrot and mixed vegetable juice.

The city would not be the same without its roadside bhuttawalas selling freshly roasted corn on the cob and mungphaliwalas selling roasted peanuts.

The south Indian dosa, served with coconut chutney and sambhar.

Food Today

Satellite TV has made the Dilliwala familiar with international cuisines. The generation that grew up on Archie comics knew what burgers and pizzas were. But only recently did phrases like Fettucine Verde, Quiche Lorraine and Spaghetti Bolognaise start tripping off the Dilliwala's tongue. Apart from restaurants in five-star hotels, Delhi now has a large number of restaurants specialising in food ranging from Mexican, Lebanese and Italian to Indonesian, Japanese and Thai. Also, the small restaurants in Paharganj, where young foreign tourists on shoe-string budgets gather, serve reasonably good European food. Major international fast food chains find a large clientele in Delhi, although the *desi* eateries next door serving spicy *chaat* and hot *masala dosa* with equal efficiency, are just as busy. Delhi's children are as passionate about *chaat* as they are about Chinese noodles and burgers.

Sweets

For those with a sweet tooth, Delhi is the place to be. Apart from the original fare associated with Delhi, popular sweets from all parts of the country are available here, *rasmalai, pakeezah, mohan bhog, kalakand, milk cake, gulab jamun* and all kinds of *burfis* and *laddoos*.

The oldest *mithai* (sweet) shop in the city is **Ghantewala** in Chandni Chowk which has been run by the same family since 1790. They make the traditional sweets of Delhi – *habshi halwa, sohan halwa, pinni*, and all-time favourites like *pista* and *kaju burfis* and *motichur laddoos*.

Rows upon rows of pistachio sweets.

Crowds outside sweet shops in Matia Mahal just before Id.

A platter of Indian sweets.

Other well-known sweet shops in Chandni Chowk are **Haldiram Bhujiawala** and **Annapoorna**. The latter is the oldest authentic Bengali sweet shop in Delhi (authentic because every other shop that sells *rasgullas* is called Bengali Sweets). Annapoorna has branches in Green Park and Chittaranjan Park. Among the best sweet shops in New Delhi are **Kaleva** in Gole Market, **Nathu's** and **Bengali Sweets** in Bengali Market.

One of the best loved sweets in Delhi is *kulfi*, made with thickened milk and topped with saffron and nuts. *Kulfi* is eaten with *falooda*, a type of vermicelli. **Roshan di Kulfi** on Ajmal Khan Road in Karol Bagh serves excellent *kulfis*.

Delhi is also known for various kinds of *halwa – mung dal* (yellow lentils) and *gajar* (carrot) *halwas* are popular. *Jalebis* are another favourite, eaten throughout the year, but especially in winter, when all sweet shops reserve a corner for frying piping hot *jalebis*. The best *jalebis* are to be found at **Old Famous Jalebiwala** at the crossing of Dariba Kalan and Chandni Chowk.

For those with western tastes, Delhi has a host of excellent confectioneries. **Wenger's** in Connaught Place, **Sugar and Spice** and **Nirula's** with branches in different localities are among the best. The bakery at Santushti Complex (opposite Samrat Hotel) makes excellent breads, while the one at Aurobindo Ashram (Aurobindo Marg) is recommended for its variety of biscuits.

Paan is a conically folded betel leaf with a filling of areca nuts, lime and often with extras like cardamom, cloves, nutmeg and grated coconut. Traditionally offered at the end of a meal, paan is said to have digestive properties. The ancient Indian treatise on sex, Kama Sutra, refers to the fragrance and aphrodisiac qualities of paan. Today, more people in India are addicted to paan than to cigarettes or bidis.

Roadside paanwala.

Bazaars

There are countless bazaars in Delhi. But for sheer ambience, few can compare with the ancient bazaars around Jama Masjid and Chandni Chowk - each a world in itself - like the romantic old souks of Baghdad and Damascus.

The best place to begin exploring these bazaars would be Jama Masjid. Built on a rocky outcrop, Jama Masjid gives a kaleidoscopic view of the old city.

The flight of steps on the eastern end of Jama Masjid facing Lal Qila (Red Fort) leads to Meena Bazaar. This bazaar was built in the late 1970s to cater to the needs of pilgrims and tourists. It has rows of small shops selling readymade garments, local cosmetics, embroidered caps in silk, cotton and nylon. There are also many *dhabas*, makeshift stalls where you can get a piping hot meal of meat curry and *rotis* for just a few rupees, or *biryani*, a fragrant, spicy Muslim rice speciality.

Urdu Park with Lal Qila in the distance.

The lane going through the left flank of the bazaar, behind Jama Masjid, will take you to the cotton market which specialises in making and selling quilts, pillows and mattresses. Beyond it is the busy cycle market which has the best range of bicycles and tricycles as well as accessories.

You can also go down the right flank of the Meena Bazaar and head for Kasturba Hospital Marg. Before doing so pause for a while at Urdu Park. Here you can sit under the soft shade of the age-old trees, have your ears cleaned or get a body or head massage. At the far end of Urdu Park you can see the *akharas* where wrestling bouts are held every Sunday evening from 4 pm onwards.

It may be worthwhile to hire a cycle rickshaw at Kasturba Hospital Marg to negotiate the labyrinthine lanes and bylanes of these old bazaars. The perpetual crowd of pedestrians, handcarts, rickshaws and stray buffaloes might intimidate you. The lanes are narrow and winding and in no way conducive to a leisurely stroll. They are a pot-pourri of shops, godowns, eating places, residential quarters, temples and mosques. The rickshawalas are careful navigators who will point out the landmarks to you as they manoeuvre their way. Climb carefully on to the rickshaw and wedge yourself firmly on the narrow seat. Use your feet to push against the foot rest and hold on to the side.

Chawri Bazaar.

A little way down Kasturba Hospital Marg is the meat market. The shops display rows of goats' heads, piles of trotters, chicken in crowded coops waiting to be slaughtered. It is not a pleasing sight and certainly no place for the faint of heart. The fish market across the street is probably more interesting because it is visually vibrant though wet and messy and not as starkly carnal as the meat shops.

On the left, the meat shops give way to the motor parts market. Motoring aficionados claim that this is one of the largest second-hand spare parts market in the world, with over a thousand shops packed into a square kilometre behind Jama Masjid.

Exactly half way down the length of the west wall of Jama Masjid, is a road leading to the heart of the specialised wholesale market. Chawri Bazaar, the paper products market is where one could buy paper by the ream, wedding cards and wallpaper in exquisite shades. The melee is maddening, as cars and rickshaws vie for passage with pedestrians and coolies who rush around with huge bales on their back.

Glass bangles in Churiwali Gali: myriad designs in as many hues to suit every whim and fancy.

If you want a breather, ask the rickshawala to take you down Churiwali Gali. Once upon a time bangles were manufactured here. There were countless, colourful bangle shops. Today, only about a dozen shops remain and the bangles are brought from faraway manufacturing centres.

Turn back now and go to Nai Sarak which specialises in school and college textbooks. At the end of the lane, turn left for Khari Baoli, Asia's largest spice market. The pungent aroma of spices will hit you as the shops display mounds of turmeric, red chillies, cardamom cloves and nutmeg. There are raisins from California, sultanas from Afghanistan, walnuts from Kashmir, and much else. Shopkeepers here claim that this is also the biggest market in Asia for edible oils and dry fruits.

Khari Baoli.

Chandni Chowk.

It is time to return to Chandni Chowk. The historical accounts of this market are legion, of times when merchants came from Turkey, China, Holland and other distant lands, with weapons, exotic birds, pearls and tapestry. There was nothing that was not available here. An amir's son could squander away a ransom during a stroll without affecting the supply of goods!

Travellers wrote of tall trees and a canal running down the centre of the street. Sadly, the trees have long gone and the canal has given way to an unaesthetic road divider painted a bilious yellow. But there is no denying that the charm remains.

A roadside barber's shop.

A professional ear-cleaner outside Town Hall on Chandni Chowk.

Katra Neel.

The *katras* or wholesale markets are sandwiched between the shops, offices, churches, mosques, temples and gurudwaras. One of the most popular is Katra Neel which deals with fabric and there is nothing in textiles that you cannot find here. Silks, cotton, voiles, muslins, brocades from Benaras, and much, much more. It is a fascinating maze of shops, most of which are no more than two feet by five feet.

A tailor at work on the pavements of Chandni Chowk.

Glitz and glitter of tinsel wedding accessories at Kinari Bazaar.

Dariba Kalan, the jewellers' street.

A little ahead is Bhagirath Palace, Asia's largest market for electrical goods. Old and new, outdated or imported, it is all available here. And what is not available, can be especially fabricated for you.

Cross the main street and go down Kinari Bazaar. You will be overwhelmed by an outburst of dense colours. Everything needed for an Indian wedding is available here, garlands of fresh paper currency decorated lavishly with gold and silver tinsel, garments, jewellery, even paper plates and glasses! And if you are in a rush to tie the knot, you can hire clothes and accessories for the occasion. Vishal Chitrashala Dresswala, for example, rents out splendid gold brocade *achkan*, *salwar* and turban for the groom and *lehnga* with *zardozi* work veil for the bride for anything between Rs 300 and Rs 1000. Many of these shops also sell and rent out theatre costumes. If there is a festival in the offing, people come here from all over the city to make their purchases – *gulal* or coloured powder if it is Holi, *rakhis* if it is Rakshabandhan or extra heads of Ravan if it is Dussehra.

The lane ends at Dariba Kalan which is still known as the jewellers' street. There was a time when it used to be lined with gold and silversmiths, but over time most of them have moved away. Those that remain deal largely in silver. It is an interesting place to buy silver jewellery, old or new. But be sure that you have ample time in hand, for it is not possible to rush things here. While in Dariba, look out for Gulab Singh Johrimal, a perfume and attar shop that has been doing business since 1816.

Turn towards Lal Qila and stroll through the flower market. The sharp fragrance of flowers will envelop you as deft fingers weave garlands of roses, jasmine and marigolds. The fragrance stays with you long after you have left the flower market behind.

Across the street, in Lal Qila, beyond the high arches of Lahore Gate is Chhatta Chowk Bazaar. Its long and chequered history goes back to the 17th century, to the days of Shahjahan, when caravan traders displayed their exotic wares for the ladies of the royal household - silks, pearls, precious stones, perfumes, brocades, carpets. Since the ladies were in *purdah*, the traders would lay out their wares and move away to allow the ladies to come out and make their choices. And so it was till the British came and turned the fort into a garrison for its troops.

Lord Ganesha in an antique shop outside Jama Masjid.

Today Chhatta Chowk Bazaar has about forty glass-fronted shops dealing in artificial and semi-precious jewellery, embroidered bags, hand-painted wall hangings and fake 'antiques' from India and Nepal.

Chhatta Chowk Bazaar.

The electrical goods bazaar at Bhagirath Palace.

The modern vies with the traditional for space in Chandni Chowk.

Bazaars at Night

With sunset the ambience of Shahjahanabad
changes. As lights are switched on temple bells
announce the evening *aarti* and *muezzins* call the
faithful to prayer. Shutters are pulled down and the
hectic crowd disappears, as if by magic. Gradually
all activity shifts to the eating places, especially in
and around Matia Mahal Bazaar near Jama Masjid.
The lanes are filled with the aroma of fire and food,
and the sound of Hindi film music. It is time to
celebrate the flavours of traditional Muslim food as
people from all over Delhi find their way to their
favourite restaurants (*see : Food, Where to Eat*).

The act of collective cooking and eating acquires a
special meaning in this cobweb of lanes. Huge pots
simmer on slow fires, infusing flavours and needing
to be stirred frequently with large ladles, often with
both hands. Meat is not only fried, roasted and
cooked in front of you, but outside many
restaurants you may actually see live goats
waiting their turn.

*A roadside
mithai shop in
the bustling
Matia Mahal
Bazaar near
Jama Masjid.*

Haats

*Sunday bazaar
below the ramparts
of Lal Quila*

Traditionally, most villages in India have a *haat* or
weekly bazaar where villagers sell grains, vegetables,
tools, handicrafts and cattle. With urbanisation
most villages in and around Delhi have disappeared
but the *haats* remain, so much so that even an
urban jungle like Delhi has about 50 of them. These
sprawling bazaars cater to diverse needs, from
petticoats, pots and pans, to aphrodisiacs, miracle
oils and exotic herbs and spices.

Many localities in Delhi have their own weekly *haats*.
The biggest is probably the one held in Ajmal Khan
Road in Karol Bagh on Mondays. On Tuesday there
is one in Govindpuri, Wednesday in Bhogal, and so
on. If you are not particularly keen on quality you
can pick up attractive bargains at these weekly *haats*.

An interesting book bazaar is held on the pavements
of Daryaganj every Sunday which is certainly worth
a visit. If you are lucky you may even spot a rare
book among the piles of secondhand books, old
magazines and periodicals.

The Sunday Bazaar below the eastern ramparts of Lal
Qila, on the Ring Road, is variously known as *Chor*
Bazaar, *Kabadi* Bazaar and Lal Qila Bazaar. This is
Delhi's own flea market. Here you can get almost
anything, antiques, alarm clocks, beautiful bottles,
box cameras, typewriters, army shoes and overcoats,
brass lamps, used bullets, and even carpets and
crockery. As with flea markets anywhere, you must
have an eye for the unusual. You could very well
walk away with a crystal decanter, an old prayer
rug, or a priceless first edition.

Crafts

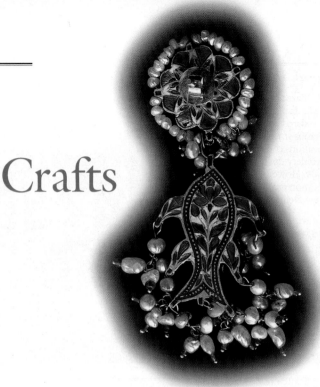

Delhi prides itself in its rich craft tradition that struck root during the reign of Emperor Shahjahan. It was in his new city of Shahjahanabad that arts and crafts proliferated. Artisans and craftspersons were invited, bought, won in battles or gifted by other sovereigns. They settled within the estates, in the *karkhanas* (workshops) of the noblemen and princes, and nurtured their special styles and sensibilities with a finesse developed over years of learning. The evolving Shahjahanabad was a maze of avenues and alleys, dictated by trade and commerce. Specific streets derived their names and character from different crafts and occupations.

Their inheritors, painstakingly, and often against all odds, carried on the secret code of these special knowledge systems, with their fingers, their eyes, mind and soul. Today what we see as meticulously beautiful in craft, design and conception is a real testimony to this inheritance.

Despite modernity and its aggressive onslaught, despite urban sharks and middlemen, many traditional crafts have survived and have evolved new parameters of aesthetic and commercial value.

Craft, unlike so-called 'fine' art, is an expression of functional necessity, directly affecting peoples' daily lives. Design intervention and adaptations have rejuvenated some crafts which are alive and pulsating in the labyrinthine lanes of Delhi.

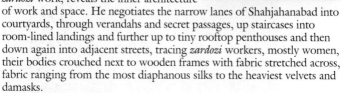

Zardozi

Kinari Bazaar, a narrow lane off Chandni Chowk, displays a dazzling array of gold-embroidered garments. Available in the numerous small shops here are multiple applications of *zardozi* or intricate hand embroidery done with gold and silver threads. However, its sophisticated application is to be seen in the boutiques of New Delhi.

A talk with Gul Mohammed, a national award winner for the best craftsperson of *zardozi* work, reveals the inner architecture of work and space. He negotiates the narrow lanes of Shahjahanabad into courtyards, through verandahs and secret passages, up staircases into room-lined landings and further up to tiny rooftop penthouses and then down again into adjacent streets, tracing *zardozi* workers, mostly women, their bodies crouched next to wooden frames with fabric stretched across, fabric ranging from the most diaphanous silks to the heaviest velvets and damasks.

Nimble fingers pluck away with fine needles at gold, silver and coloured threads, beads and spangles. The patterns are *phool-patti* (flower and leaf). Today, contemporary patterns have been assimilated into the vocabulary. *Gotas*, or woven tapes of gold and silver, are stitched in geometric patterns on *lehngas* (ankle-length skirts), saris and veils. The embroidered fabric could finally end up as wedding garments, temple hangings, bags, shoe-uppers, caps or even decorative cloth for draping a bridegroom's horse.

Delhi Blue Pottery

Behind Asaf Ali Road, as you go in from Turkman Gate into Hauz Suiwalan, one of the little alleys leads to Hazarilal's house. He is the only practitioner of the Delhi Blue Pottery tradition. A special mix of powdered quartz is used to make the stoneware base which is then glazed blue, with ingredients which were used for the blue tiles of pre-Mughal and Mughal domes, a style inherited from Persia.

Hazarilal's grandfather was famous for making the tiniest, lightest little pots with lovely floral designs, for keeping pigeon feed. In earlier times, the connoisseurs of *Kabutarbaazi,* or pigeon-flying, prized such pots which were not more than 6 cm in diameter. Today Hazarilal and his family continue making pickle jars, painted tiles, flower vases and even little animal figurines.

Miniature Painting

The tradition of the Delhi school of miniature painting has continued from the time of Emperor Jehangir, father of Shahjahan.

The Delhi school is an offshoot of the Mughal painting tradition. Mansoor, a painter in Jehangir's court, was apprenticed to the Iranian miniature painters, Mir Ali and Abdul Samer during the 16th century. The Delhi school was distinguished for its dynamism and naturalism in treatment, contrast of colours and strong urban influence. The preferred base for the painting was ivory, but today special handmade paper is used.

In the Zakir Nagar house of Firozbhai, Faridbhai and Akhtarbhai, direct descendants of Mansoor, the ambience is that of a medieval studio. They prepare their own brushes with squirrel hair inserted into quills with specifications for fine single hair lines or thicker strokes. Only herbal and mineral colours are used. The gold-leaf work is the last to be applied before burnishing with agate stones.

These shy artists are willing to arrange a demonstration of their art by previous appointment. Interested persons may contact them on (6842746.

Ivory Carving

Ivory was in Mughal India a symbol of aristocracy. African ivory was coveted as a material for its close grain, though Indian ivory was extensively used. Furniture, screens, lamps, platters and decorative items were inlaid with gold, silver, precious stones and miniature paintings. The carving was delicate, as can be seen in the screens in the Red Fort Archaeological Museum.

Delhi Ivory Palace, a 300-year-old shop at the northern gate of Jama Masjid, attracted the best craftsmen who lived in Shahjahanabad. It has, in its collection an old set of furniture carved by three generations of craftsmen which was intended as a gift for Queen Victoria. Because of the ban on ivory, craftsmen now work on bone for small items such as pendants and earrings, and on sandalwood.

Jewellery

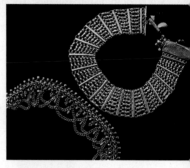

Dariba Kalan near Chandni Chowk, known as the jeweller's street, is famous for Meenakari or the art of enamelling on silver and gold. Setting in gold of *navaratan* (nine precious stones), is a traditional skill of Muslim craftsmen called *Saadegars* who settled in Delhi during Shahjahan's time. Dariba also has Hindu craftsmen from Punjab and Bengal who specialise in gold and silver work.

The *sarafs*, sellers of jewellery, are mostly Hindus and have been around for more than two centuries. Over the years, a lot of work has shifted from gold to silver and gold-plated silver ornaments. Exquisite handcrafted silver ornaments are also available in Dariba Kalan.

Terracotta Pottery

Uttam Nagar and Bindapur in west Delhi are where most potters in the city live. Most of them are originally from Rajasthan and Haryana. A neatly laid-out settlement in Uttam Nagar called Kumhar Colony (*kumhar* meaning potter) was built in the 1970s to suit their specific needs. This is a unique case of group migration and solidarity. Most *kumhars* fan out to various parts of the city and establish pavement stalls from where they sell their wares.

The crafting of objects of everyday use like clay pitchers, cooking pots and small oil lamps continues. Modern adaptations include flower pots and exotic display pots and planters. Quality earthenware is available at the Crafts Museum in Pragati Maidan, Dilli Haat, Lajpat Nagar and along major roads and at the annual Surajkund Crafts Mela.

Puppetry

Opposite the Shadipur Bus Depot in west Delhi, one dips under the flyover and turns left into a deceptively innocuous street marked by a small stall of *dholak* (drum) sellers. This is a settlement of Rajasthani puppeteers, street performers and craftspeople who migrated to Delhi decades ago. Puppets, large and small, are made here as well as big, dramatic sculptures.

Families of the Bhopa community who live here are traditionally storytellers. Their women sing out the stories which are, in turn, painted on horizontal scrolls. The paintings are folk versions of the Rajasthani school of miniature painting. The paintings are adapted to surfaces such as wood and clay, on furniture and decorative pots. The densely packed images are lyrical tales of local heroes.

Women and children of the puppeteer Bhat community make papier mache wall decorations, stuffed toys and lamps. The itinerant Gilahre community make folk instruments like *dug-dugi* (small two-sided drums with slim waists) and *seetis* (whistles). The Bhat women and children are seen in most Delhi markets selling stuffed animals – large and small horses, camels and elephants made of black cloth and decorated with bright gold braids.

Other Crafts

There are a few old shops dealing in **musical instruments**, most of which are brought to Delhi from various parts of India. Here, assemblage work is done, such as fitting of hide membranes of *tablas*, *dholaks* and other drums. Harmoniums are set. String instruments such as *dilruba*, *israj* and *sarod* are fitted, and the single-stringed *ektara* is made. One of the oldest shops dealing in musical instruments is Bina Musical Stores in Nai Sarak ℂ 326395. Rishi Ram at Connaught Circus is known for its sitars. Others shops of repute are Delhi Musical Stores at Jama Masjid and Lahore Music House at Daryaganj. Harshvardhan (House 1799 Ram Gali, Malkaganj ℂ 3263595), an independent craftsman, specialises in making flutes

A variety of **paper crafts** are prevalent, of which *tazia* making is the most spectacular. *Tazias* are commemorative paper structures, intricately cut and pasted on a bamboo frame. Fantastic, colourful images of paper are taken in a procession during the Muslim festival of Muharram.

The same *tazia*-makers also make huge Ravana effigies during the Hindu festival of Dussehra which are packed with fire crackers and burnt with flaming arrows. Their work place is known as *teer ghar* meaning house of arrows. They are also involved in making tazias with flowers for the festival of *Phoolwalon ki Sair* at Mehrauli.

The making of **paper kites** caters to the famous kite-flying mania of Dilliwalas which reaches its height during the monsoons, especially on 15 August, India's Independence Day, and during the spring festival of Basant Panchami. The *patang* or kite market in Lal Kuan Bazaar in Shahjahanabad is then a riot of colours. Kites come in all sizes, ranging from 36 inches to their miniature versions, which are available at the Crafts Museum, Dilli Haat and Central Cottage Industries Emporium. However, the two standard sizes are 12 inches and 15 inches. Kites made of plastic sheets are also available.

Also popular are **paper toys** that do magical tricks, move like snakes and tortoises and quickly disintegrate to be replaced with newer ones. The toy makers do not have a stable market because mainline showrooms prefer expensive western-style toys. A few are stocked at Crafts Museum, Dilli Haat and Central Cottage Industries Emporium.

Festivals

As the capital of a nation, with its pot-pourri of people, Delhi relishes its heterogeneous character and celebrates every festival with gaiety and abandon.

In India everything is celebrated, from harvests to the changing of seasons, from the triumph of a goddess battling evil to the love between a brother and his sisters. Festivals are what give life its richness and colour. Through the sharing of a celebration, society continues with its traditions and, at times, even creates new ones. Through conquests and calamities India has held on to its culture. And inevitably every new generation falls under the spell of this medley of worship and rejoicing.

Dilliwalas brave the cold January morning to watch the Republic Day parade.

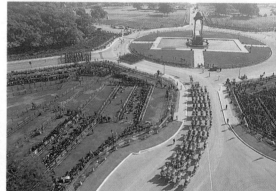

JANUARY TO MARCH

Republic Day : Come 26 January and people line the streets to watch the Republic Day parade. As the President of India takes the salute on Rajpath, marching columns from the armed forces, tanks and missile carriers rumble past. Camels amble along, elephants come swaying, school children turn cartwheels and transform the solemn occasion into a carnival. An exciting folk dance festival follows a day later at Talkatora Stadium. The festivities end with **Beating the Retreat,** a feast of martial music, at Vijay Chowk on 29 January.

On 13 January, a rural festival, **Lohri**, invades the streets of Delhi and is celebrated with bonfires in parks and open spaces. Traditionally, Lohri marks the end of winter.

Basant Panchami : The biting winter winds continue till end January-early February when the Hindu festival of Basant Panchami welcomes spring.

Festivals, especially Hindu and Muslim ones, follow traditional lunar calendars, and their dates vary from year to year. The only way to list them is by season as has been done here. However, with most Muslim festivals, even the seasonal dates vary. Many Hindu festivals are related to *purnima* (full moon) and *amavasya* (new moon) which are significant days in the Hindu calendar. We have included colourful happenings unique to Delhi, as well as some of the more important religious festivals.

Corresponding months in the Hindu Saka calendar.	
January	Pausa-Magha
February	Magha-Phalguna
March	Phalguna-Chaitra
April	Chaitra-Vaisakha
May	Vaisakha-Jyaishtha
June	Jyaishtha-Asadha
July	Asadha-Sravana
August	Sravana-Bhadra
September	Bhadra-Asvina
October	Asvina-Kartika
November	Kartika-Agrahayana
December	Agrahayana-Pausa

Statesman Vintage Car Rally is held in early February on a balmy weekend. Classic cars roll sedately out on to the roads, ambling off on a day trip to Sohna in the bordering state of Haryana.

Surajkund Crafts Mela is an annual fair which is held for a fortnight in February. Just beyond the borders of Delhi, in the state of Haryana, a traditional village fair is recreated with little thatched huts where craftspeople from all over India display exotic artifacts.

Holi : On the day of the full moon in the month of Phalguna, Delhi braces itself for a day of uninhibited revelry as Holi is celebrated with great vigour and joy. All morning people smear *gulal* (coloured powder) often mixed with water on one another and dance to the beat of drums. There is a tradition in north India of consuming *bhang* (a derivative of cannabis) on Holi. *Pakoras* (savoury snacks) and *thandai* (milk-based drink), both laced with *bhang* are consumed with gay abandon in many households and community gatherings.

Holi paraphernalia in pavement shops.

Outsiders are advised not to go into unfamiliar localities on the morning of Holi and to play only with those they know well as the revelry could get out of hand and rowdyism is known to creep in. The festivities end with lunch and is often followed by long hours of gambling.

The night before Holi bonfires are lit at street corners, symbolically burning the demon Holika and celebrating the triumph of good over evil.

Mahashivratri is celebrated on the *amavasya* night of Phalguna. It is said Lord Shiva danced the *tandava nritya* (cosmic dance) on this dark night. He is worshipped at temples with all night vigils and prayers. Unmarried women keep day long fasts so that Shiva may grant them good husbands.

As summer moves in with its unrelenting heat and cloudless days, the energy for festivities begins to flag.

In north India, the Hindu New Year is celebrated on **Baisakhi** in mid-April just as the sun begins to get fierce and the dusty winds herald summer.

Baisakhi is particularly important for Sikhs, because it was on this day that Guru Gobind Singhji, the tenth guru, organised the Sikhs into a powerful brotherhood and called them Khalsa. Gurudwaras commemorate the day with the singing of *shabad kirtan*.

The faithful at prayer in Jama Masjid.

Traditional celebrations, prayers and hymns in the many churches across the city marks **Easter**.

Id-ul-Fitr is most often celebrated in this season. It marks the end of Ramzan, the month of fasting for Muslims. This day is also called *meethi* Id (sweet Id), because of a special sweet delicacy, *sevaiyyan* (a kind of vermicelli), which is cooked on this day.

The **Urs** of Hazrat Nizamuddin is celebrated with fervour at his *dargah*. Devotees put flowers and *chaddars* on his grave. The nights sway to the singing of *qawwalis*, especially those composed by the medieval poet, Amir Khusro, a friend and disciple of the saint.

Ramnavami, the birth of Lord Rama, is celebrated on the ninth day of *Shuklapaksh* (waxing moon) in Vaisakha with readings from the Hindu epic, *Ramayana,* at temples, both large and small.

Buddha Purnima in the month of Vaisakha, commemorates not just Lord Buddha's birth, but also his Enlightenment and Nirvana.

Mahavir Jayanti, the birth of Lord Mahavira who founded Jainism, is celebrated around this time with prayers and processions.

Muharram is observed with processions of emotionally charged devotees wailing and beating their breasts. Others recount the story of Husain and carry elaborate paper, pith and tinsel replicas of the tomb at Karbala called *tazias*.

JULY TO SEPTEMBER

On 15 August, India celebrates **Independence Day** with the Prime Minister addressing the Nation from Lal Qila's sandstone ramparts. On this day, a tradition has evolved of people flying kites and the breezy evening sky is dotted with soaring squares of fragile, coloured paper.

By July everyone is dreaming of the monsoons and the benediction of the rains.

On Sravana *purnima* **Rakshabandhan** is celebrated. Sisters tie *rakhis* or woven bands of tinsel and thread on their brothers' wrists as a pledge of love and receive their promise of protection and normally a gift or money.

Janmashtami is the celebration of the birth of Lord Krishna on the eigth day of *Krishnapaksh* (waning moon) in Sravana. Temples across the city are decorated with fairy lights and colourful exhibits on Krishna's life. Laxmi Narayan Mandir (Birla Mandir) has a special display which atracts huge crowds.

Id-ul-Zuha is popularly known as *bakr* Id, the 'feast of sacrifice'. This is time for celebration for meat-eaters and a spirit of general bonhomie pervades among Muslims.

Phoolwalon ki Sair (flowersellers' walk) is a festival unique to Delhi. It is celebrated in September in Mehrauli *(see : Qutb Minar and Mehrauli, p.190)*.

Some of the most important festivals take place in early autumn and winter as the sun mellows to an easy warmth, the breeze is gentle and celebration is on everyone's minds.

Navaratrey, literally nine nights, commemorates the victory of goddess Durga over the demon Mahishasur. Navaratrey ends with Dussehra, also called **Vijay Dashami,** or the tenth day of victory. Through the nine days diligent Hindus in north India keep fasts all day long. The tenth day, **Dussehra,** is celebrated in different ways by people from different parts of country.

On Vijay Dashami, Rama is believed to have defeated Ravana. Huge effigies are made of Ravana, his brother Kumbhakarna and son Meghnath, filled with fire crackers and set on fire in community gatherings in open spaces all over the city.

Night after night, people watch the story of *Ramayana* re-enacted, and the magic never fades. **Ram Lilas** are organised in most neighbourhoods all through the nine days of Navaratrey.

Durga Puja is celebrated by Bengalis on the last four days of Navaratrey. Images of the mother goddess, Durga, all fiery power and exquisite beauty, are worshipped with flowers, incense and the beating of drums. On Vijay Dashami the idols are taken out in a procession to be immersed in the Yamuna.

79

Around the same time, the vibrant **Balloon Mela** at Safdarjang Airport celebrates adventure with huge exotic hot air balloons lazily floating across the sky.

Diwali, the festival of lights, falls on *Amavasya*, the darkest night of Kartika. It is believed that on this day Lord Rama came home to his kingdom after a fourteen year exile and the city of Ayodhya lit oil lamps to welcome him. As dusk falls, streets turn into fairylands with shimmering garlands of lamps and candles strung across balconies and windows. Sweets and gifts are exchanged between families and friends amidst the bursting of crackers. Doors are left open on Diwali because goddess Laxmi is supposed to enter homes and bring prosperity and good luck. With many small business establishments in north India, the financial calendar begins on Diwali when the new *khata* (ledger) is inaugurated.

Guru Purab is the celebration of the birth of the first of the ten Sikh gurus, Guru Nanak. *Nagar kirtans* (processions) are taken out through the streets and in the gurudwaras, *granthees* recite verses from the Guru Granth Sahib, the holy book of the Sikhs.

Delhi's year of festivities end with **Christmas** and **New Year's Eve** when there are special programmes at most hotels and restaurants across the city. In Connaught Place, people step out at midnight to welcome the New Year with noise and revelry.

Ahinsa Sthal
Mehrauli- Gurgaon Road

Arya Samaj Mandir
Greater Kailash I

Ayyappa Temple
Sector 2, R.K. Puram

Baha'i House of Worship (Lotus Temple) Near Nehru Place

Baptist Church Chandni Chowk

Bhairon Mandir
Behind Purana Qila

Cathedral Church of the Redemption Church Road

Chinmaya Mission Lodi Road

Chhatarpur Mandir Chhatarpur

Church of Holy Trinity
Turkman Gate

Dargah Hazrat Nizamuddin
Nizamuddin West

Dargah Chiragh Dehlvi
Chiragh Delhi

Dargah Qutbuddin Bakhtiyar Kaki Mehrauli

Devi Mandir D. B. Gupta Road

Fakr-ul-Masajid Kashmere Gate

Fatehpuri Masjid
Khari Baoli Road

Gauri Shankar Mandir
Chandni Chowk

Gurudwara Bangla Sahib
Baba Kharak Singh Marg

Gurudwara Majnu ka Tila
Outer Ring Road

Gurudwara Moti Bagh
Moti Bagh

Gurudwara Nanaksar
Sir Ganga Ram Hospital Marg

Gurudwara Rakab Ganj
Near Sansad Bhawan

Gurudwara Sisganj
Chandni Chowk

Hanuman Mandir
Baba Kharak Singh Marg

Jain Mandir Chandni Chowk

Jain Mandir Jain Mandir Road

Jain Mandir Dada Bari Mehrauli

Jama Masjid Opposite Lal Qila

Jogmaya Mandir Mehrauli

Kalibari Mandir Mandir Marg

Kali Mandir Chittaranjan Park

Kalkaji Mandir Near Nehru Place

On 14 November, **India International Trade Fair** begins its annual show at Pragati Maidan, Delhi's sprawling exhibition ground.

Ladakh Buddhist Vihar
Near ISBT, north of Kashmere Gate

Laxmi Narayan Mandir (Birla Mandir) Mandir Marg

Malai Mandir
Sector 7, R.K. Puram

Parsi Anjuman
Opp. Firoz Shah Kotla Stadium

Radha Swami Satsang Bhawan
Prasad Nagar, Opp. Rajendra Place

Ramakrishna Mission
Panchkuian Road

Sacred Heart Cathedral
Bangla Sahib Road

Sai Baba Mandir Lodi Road

Sant Nirankari Satsang Bhawan
Near Coronation Memorial

Sri Parthasarthi Mandir (ISKCON) East of Kailash

St. James Church Kashmere Gate

St. Martin's Church
Church Road, Delhi Cantonment

St. Stephen's Church
Church Mission Road

St. Thomas Church Mandir Marg

In all places of worship except Christian churches, shoes are not permitted and it is impolite to enter with uncovered legs.

Most mosques do not allow women inside, so check before entering.

If you are entering a gurudwara (a Sikh temple of prayer), it is customary to cover the head. A large handkerchief, corners tucked behind the ears to hold it down, is the easiest way to cover your head if you are not carrying a scarf. But no hats please!

Silhouettes

Littering the rocky, arid plains below the humped Aravalli hills to the west of the Yamuna river are the remains of seven cities, from where chieftains, sultans and emperors ruled Hindustan. One can wander past the ornate victory tower, the Qutb Minar, built some eight hundred years ago, and the magnificently carved mosque next to it in the citadel of the sultans of the Slave dynasty. Walk down the modern road northwards to the massive walls of Siri, the great 14th century city, which were reputedly so wide that two chariots could be driven abreast along them; and go eastwards a few miles to the mighty fortifications of Sultan Ghiyasuddin's capital city, Tughlaqabad, now desolate, overgrown with thorn bushes, its broken walls and fallen pillars baking in the heat of the sun, the few remaining rooms oppressively dark and silent. The river has moved far eastwards, leaving it dry and parched. Closer to the river, further upstream are the battlements now sadly ruined, of the elegant yet sturdy fort called the Purana Qila, the Old Fort, citadel of Humayun, the second Mughal Emperor.

of a Capital *City*

Further upstream, and closer to the river, are the ravaged remains of Firozabad, another city, plundered and vandalised over three hundred years ago when the vast, splendid city of Shahjahanabad, the city of the Mughal Emperor Shahjahan, was built next to it: this was the seventh city, and the greatest, most vibrant and varied, a city whose energy swelled and poured far into the night, amidst flaming torches, laughter and the never ending sounds of people conversing, of hawkers calling, and, ever so often, the muezzin's call to prayer, from the great mosque, the Jama Masjid, floating over the city almost like a benediction. Even today, long after the Emperor and his court have gone, the vitality of the city lives on, renewed by successive generations, in different ways. The sapphire blue sky is often dotted with brightly coloured kites, while flocks of pigeons wheel and swoop across it as the citizens play the games that were played centuries ago by their forefathers, with the same enthusiasm and gaiety.

The British built two cities when they came here as colonial rulers. The first of these was not the capital of India, but the administrative centre of the region, built north of Shahjahanabad, for the British had grown to distrust the city and also to see themselves as rulers, who consequently had to distance themselves from the ruled. This area, Civil Lines, was once no different from the district towns the British built elsewhere, with large bungalows set in dusty compounds.

The capital city the British built is to the southwest of Shahjahanabad, the gracious imperial city of New Delhi. The focal point is the low Raisina Hill, from where what was then called the Viceregal Lodge gazes proudly, in regal splendour, at the two buildings flanking it, the Secretariat, formal, with ramrod straight pillars, austere and yet with an elegance which can only be called royal. This was true imperial splendour, meant to overawe the subjects: a metaphor of the benign, if always stern paternalism the British fancied they had brought to India. Above one on the imposing entrances to the North Block of the Secretariat they carved what could be their message to the subject masses:
'Liberty will not descend to people; people must raise themselves up to liberty'. *Sic transit gloria mundi.*

To the south of the Viceregal Lodge are the cool bungalows of the satraps of the Raj, with deep verandahs, patios and pillars, set in acres of green gardens. All is hushed and quiet, except for the birds singing, and the occasional swish of cars. A second metaphor, perhaps a little more private, of the Raj.

Independence has made only a little difference to the ambience of this gracious, sanitised city. It still is the seat of power, but the symbols have changed. There are the cars, usually white Ambassadors with winking red lights and an array of antennae followed by jeeploads of men in khaki, or, depending on the stature of the person in the car, in black, who journey the wide roads sirens wailing, at an astonishingly high speed. These are the people, the power mendicants themselves, seen usually in official receptions or 'functions' as they are called, each surrounded by scads of men in khaki, or as mentioned, in black, all of them carrying fearsome looking weapons of indeterminate make and character.

There is actually yet another city, which has grown around the city Lutyens built, a city which is brash, tumultous, chaotic, violent and also very warm, lovely and engaging – this is the city which stretches from Rohini in the north, through Janakpuri in the west to Vasant Kunj and Sangam Vihar in the south and across the river to Patparganj and Shahdara. Here slums live cheek by jowl with steel and glass high-rise buildings, the nightmarish traffic flows and eddies past loud bazaars, the most sophisticated departmental stores and pavement shops. It skirts, noisy and murderous, the sylvan quietness of institutions like Indian Agricultural Research Institute, National Council of Education Research and Training, Jawaharlal Nehru University and Indian Institute of Technology.

North of the narrow *galis* of Shahjahanabad, beyond the wider streets and more obviously laid out spaces of the first city the British built, is the University of Delhi where the frenzy of the traffic which is so much a part of the metropolis fades as one enters the tree-lined roads which go past buildings of mellow brick, set in gardens. The centre of this very laid-back ambience is the old Viceregal Lodge, now the University offices where the Vice Chancellor and other dignitaries have their offices.

To the east of the University, running through the city almost to its southern outskirts is a rocky outcropping, covered for the most part with low trees and thorn bushes, called the Ridge. It provides blessed relief from the city, and takes one away to a different time frame, to a world of quietness broken only by birdsong and the occasional voices of people strolling through the trees. This too, is Delhi, and an integral part of it, as it has been since the city was first established.

There can be no categorisation of the city. It does not fit into any one pattern. From the crowded bazaars of Karol Bagh, saris and textiles spilling in brightly coloured profusion on to the pavements, to the sophisticated glitter of the markets in South Extension or Greater Kailash, the prodigal display of wares in Lajpat Nagar, to the classically clean lines of Lutyens' New Delhi, and the dense throng of people, vendors, cobblers, hawkers, tailors, silversmiths and sellers of sweets and other eatables in the *galis* of Shahjahanabad, there is a variety that few cities in the world can match. There is something for everyone here – as indeed there ought to be in one of the greatest capitals of the world.

A complex city with many faces, with a gravitas of historical tradition and the brashness of the *arriviste*, sensitive and violent, a vortex of political and economic power, and of academic enquiry and a growing richness in the arts. There is a vitality – often a raw vitality – which informs life here. That is what persists through the ages, and it is this which will take it through the century that is coming, and to many others.

Delhi's perspective is not of a mere century. It has seen emperors, kings, courtiers, generals, prime ministers and party leaders. It will see so much more, in the years when the present day splendour of the magnificent buildings designed by Lutyens, the modern steel and glass towers and the dreadful new houses with their pastel colours and curlicued balconies crumble and become part of the ruins that are all around, half-destroyed landmarks in an even greater capital city, with new contemporary symbols of its strength and power. For buildings are, for all their splendour, evanescent – what ultimately remains is the vitality and the strength. That is what Delhi hands down from generation to generation.

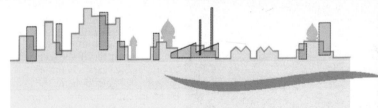

India Gate to Lodi Garden

Connaught Place

Shahjahanabad

Firoz Shah Kotla to Nizamuddin

Qutb Minar and Mehrauli

DELHI
Area by Area

Tughlaqabad to Surajkund

Hauz Khas to Lotus Temple

Kashmere Gate to Coronation Memorial

Rashtrapati Bhawan.

India Gate
TO
Lodi Garden

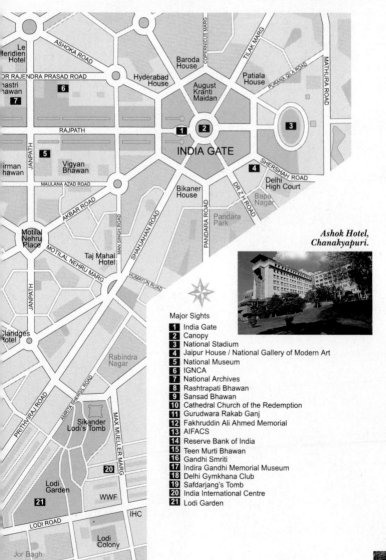

Ashok Hotel, Chanakyapuri.

Le Meridien Hotel

ASHOKA ROAD

DR RAJENDRA PRASAD ROAD

Shastri Bhawan

6

7

COPERNICUS MARG

Baroda House

TILAK MARG

Hyderabad House

August Kranti Maidan

Patiala House

PURANA QILA ROAD

MATHURA ROAD

RAJPATH

1 **2**

3

INDIA GATE

Nirman Bhawan

JANPATH

5

Vigyan Bhawan

MAULANA AZAD ROAD

SHERSHAH ROAD

4

Delhi High Court

AKBAR ROAD

Bikaner House

DR Z H ROAD

Bapa Nagar

Motilal Nehru Place

MAN SINGH ROAD

SHAHJAHAN ROAD

PANDARA ROAD

Pandara Park

MOTILAL NEHRU MARG

Taj Mahal Hotel

HUMAYUN ROAD

Claridges Hotel

JANPATH

Rabindra Nagar

PRITHVIRAJ ROAD

AMRITA SHERGIL ROAD

Sikander Lodi's Tomb

MAX MUELLER MARG

20

Lodi Garden

WWF

21

IHC

LODI ROAD

Lodi Colony

Jor Bagh

Major Sights

1 India Gate
2 Canopy
3 National Stadium
4 Jaipur House / National Gallery of Modern Art
5 National Museum
6 IGNCA
7 National Archives
8 Rashtrapati Bhawan
9 Sansad Bhawan
10 Cathedral Church of the Redemption
11 Gurudwara Rakab Ganj
12 Fakhruddin Ali Ahmed Memorial
13 AIFACS
14 Reserve Bank of India
15 Teen Murti Bhawan
16 Gandhi Smriti
17 Indira Gandhi Memorial Museum
18 Delhi Gymkhana Club
19 Safdarjang's Tomb
20 India International Centre
21 Lodi Garden

A huge garden exists in the heart of Delhi, its layout and the design of the buildings around it conceived by the architect, Edwin Lutyens. In 1912 it was decided that the capital of British India be shifted from Calcutta to Delhi. At that time the area from Willingdon Crescent to National Stadium, and from Connaught Place to Lodi Garden was covered by villages. Lutyens and his associate Herbert Baker planned the buildings of the new capital on a monumental scale. The Viceroy's House and the twin secretariat buildings were put on top of a hill at the apex of a grand vista called Kingsway, with large lawns and water channels lining its sides. Carefully chosen trees were planted along the miles of avenues to mitigate the summer heat.

Within sixteen years of its completion in 1931, India won independence, and Delhi became the capital of the new nation. Kingsway is now Rajpath. The Viceroy's House is Rashtrapati Bhawan – the official residence of the President of India. The secretariat buildings are the offices of the Indian government and the Indian Parliament meets in the Sansad Bhawan nearby.

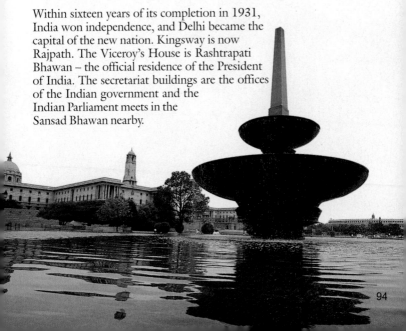

After 1947, other buildings, in equally grand
proportions, were built in the vicinity to house
new institutions and ministries. Despite this
and the increasing traffic, the area maintains a
stately calm because most of the green areas
have been retained and hardly any high-rise
buildings permitted.

Lutyens was not familiar with India when he was appointed Chief Architect in 1912. He was flooded with suggestions as to the style to be adopted, European, Renaissance, Gothic, Islamic, Hindu....

In an interview to *The Times of India* in January 1914, he said, 'There has been a very strong desire expressed in certain quarters for the adoption of the pointed arch in modern Indian buildings.... All I can say is that when God created India, he did not show his sympathy with this movement by making the Indian rainbow pointed.... You could not build Westminster Abbey in India. It would be a frying pan; and the lead work in the windows would melt and run down. And there is not only the heat to be thought of. There is light. The violence of light in India is tremendous'.

India Gate

1 MAP 22DI The 42 metre high, free standing arch, popularly known as India Gate, was designed by Lutyens and built in 1931. It was originally called All India War Memorial in memory of the 90,000 soldiers of the Indian Army who died in World War I. The names of the soldiers are inscribed all along the walls of the arch. In 1971, an eternal flame was lit here to honour the *Amar Jawan* (Immortal Soldier).

At night India Gate is dramatically floodlit while the fountains nearby are lit with coloured lights. India Gate stands at one end of Rajpath, and the area surrounding it is generally referred to as India Gate.

It was under the red sandstone roof of the beautiful **Canopy 2** MAP 22DI designed by Lutyens in 1936, that the marble statue of George V stood, looking westward at the magnificent residence of his viceroy. The statue has since been removed from its decorative surroundings to the Coronation Memorial Park beyond Kingsway Camp *(see : Kashmere Gate to Coronation Memorial, p.224)*.

The Canopy is, at present, bereft of any occupant. It is a pleasant counterpoint to the bulk of India Gate.

National Stadium **3** MAP 22E1 was built in 1931 at the insistence of the domineering wife of the viceroy, Willingdon. It blocked the view of Purana Qila which had been intended to crown the eastern end of Rajpath. The first Asian Games were held here in 1951.

Hyderabad House.

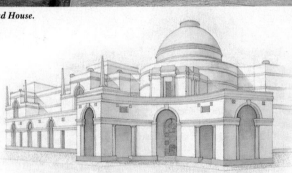

The Princes' Area

In 1931, Lutyens began work on India Gate – at the far end of Kingsway (Rajpath). It had earlier been decided to surround the hexagonal space around the arch with the palaces of the most important Indian princes – all of whom needed to have a residence in New Delhi. They had been recently inducted into the Chamber of Princes by the colonial government.

The entire area from Jantar Mantar to Rashtrapati Bhawan and beyond belonged to the Maharaja of Jaipur and was known as Jaipuria. In 1912 when this site was chosen for the new capital, the Jaipur *durbar,* then headed by a minor, was forced to sell the land to the government. As a gesture of appeasement, it was decided to invite the Jaipur state to build a royal residence in the new city. Thereafter 36 sites were allocated to various other Indian princes in an area measuring approximately 250 acres.

As relative precedence among the leading Indian states – then numbering 149 – was determined by the number of gun salutes a ruler received on ceremonial occasions, the states (Hyderabad, Jaipur, Bikaner, Baroda) with a higher number of gun salutes were given prominent sites closer to the hexagon around India Gate.

The architectural style of many of these princely houses was influenced by Lutyens' and Baker's buildings. Lutyens himself designed Hyderabad House and Baroda House. Hyderabad House was the biggest and the grandest of all the princely houses. Built at the cost of about £ 200,000 and completed in 1928, it did not please the Nizam's two sons who found its appearance too western for their taste.

After 1947, most of these palaces were taken over by the Indian government. Two palaces which retain some of their original splendour are Hyderabad House and Jaipur House. The former is the State Guest House for important foreign dignitaries, and the latter houses the National Gallery of Modern Art **4** MAP 22E1 *(see : Art Galleries, p.240).*

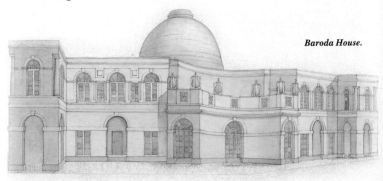

Baroda House.

The Supreme Court of India MAP 15C5 functioned from the Parliament House until 1958 when it moved to its present, and equally magnificent, building on Tilak Marg. This is one of the most impressive structures built by the Central Public Works Department (CPWD). It has a 37.6 metre high dome and a spacious colonnaded verandah. One may obtain a visitor's pass from the front office to go inside.

National Museum 5 MAP 21B1 At the intersection of Rajpath and Janpath are three important institutions – National Archives, National Museum and IGNCA. Lutyens had planned a set of four buildings, a library, a records office and two museums at this intersection. However, only the Imperial Records Department was built in the

1920s. This later became the National Archives 7 MAP 14E6 The National Museum was built in 1956 by CPWD. Until it was built, the collection that is now exhibited here was kept in the Durbar Hall of Rashtrapati Bhawan *(see : Museums, p.227).*

Indira Gandhi National Centre for the Arts (IGNCA) 6 MAP 14E6 Presently housed in the Central Vista Mess on Janpath, IGNCA is an important centre for the study of the arts. It has a vast collection of manuscripts and books on a wide range of art forms. In 1998, IGNCA is moving to a new building designed by Ralph Lerner.

Mati Ghar, an exhibition hall at IGNCA.

Central Government Offices

Visible from Rajpath are many prominent
government *bhawans* (buildings) – Shastri Bhawan
MAP 14D6, Krishi Bhawan MAP 14D6, Nirman Bhawan
MAP 21A1, Udyog Bhawan MAP 21A1 and many more.
In the 1950s and early 1960s, CPWD
constructed these buildings to accommodate
the growing number of government offices.
The *chhattris* on top of the buildings, and
the use of sandstone base were CPWD's
attempts at maintaining continuity with
Lutyens' buildings. You need a visitor's pass
and a purpose to visit these buildings.

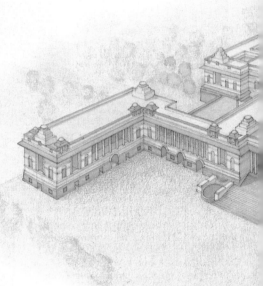

Rashtrapati Bhawan

8 **MAP 13A6** The site chosen for the
Viceroy's House, now the Rashtrapati Bhawan,
was on Raisina Hill which was seen as an
Indian acropolis.

The building, designed by Lutyens, has a large court
to its front and a Mughal style garden at the back.
It is not like the garden at Humayun's Tomb, but
is a terraced garden like the ones the Mughals built
in Kashmir. The garden is open to the public in
February.

The most magnificent room in Rashtrapati Bhawan
is the Durbar Hall which lies directly
under the main dome. This
ceremonial hall is the venue for
all official functions of the
President of India. The
columns at the front entrance
to the Durbar Hall have bells
carved into their capitals.
Lutyens reasoned that 'the
ringing of bells sound the end of
an empire and stone bells
never sound'. Despite this, the empire
came to an end a brief sixteen years later.

Rashtrapati Bhawan has 340 rooms. Lord Irwin, its first occupant, 'kept losing his way'. It is big and grand – everything, stairs, ceilings and furniture is designed to reinforce the sense of the importance of its occupant. After India became independent, the sheer size of the building overwhelmed its new keepers. Mahatma Gandhi suggested it be turned into a hospital. The Durbar Hall served as a museum for several years till the building which now houses the National Museum was completed.

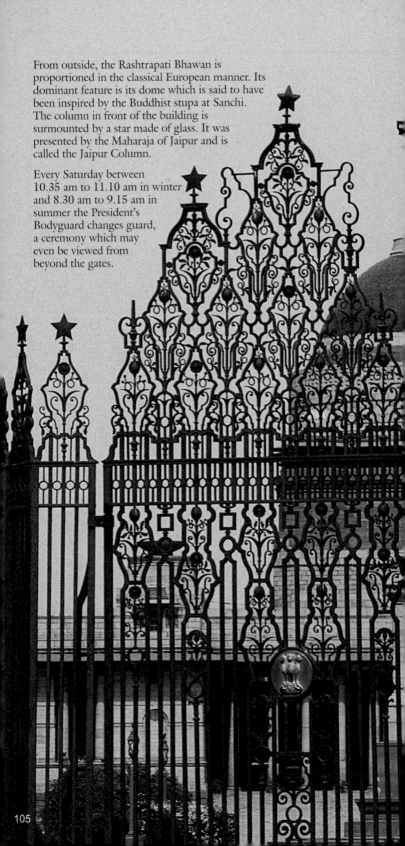

From outside, the Rashtrapati Bhawan is proportioned in the classical European manner. Its dominant feature is its dome which is said to have been inspired by the Buddhist stupa at Sanchi. The column in front of the building is surmounted by a star made of glass. It was presented by the Maharaja of Jaipur and is called the Jaipur Column.

Every Saturday between 10.35 am to 11.10 am in winter and 8.30 am to 9.15 am in summer the President's Bodyguard changes guard, a ceremony which may even be viewed from beyond the gates.

It is possible to arrange a visit to the
Rashtrapati Bhawan, by appointment
with the Deputy Military Secretary to the
President. Only the following are open to
the public : Durbar Hall, Ashok Hall,
the Dining Room and
the Mughal Garden.

The Secretariat

Lutyens intended Kingsway to slope right up to the Viceroy's House, but Baker felt it necessary to level the space between the two secretariat buildings, North Block and South Block, and create a plaza, thus ending the slope prematurely and steeply. As you approach Rashtrapati Bhawan from India Gate, the dome disappears when you reach the foot of the slope and rises again as you go up.

The plaza between the two secretariat buildings may be approached either by taking the office-goers' short cut and entering North Block from the Kendriya Terminal, or by making a grand entry up the Rajpath slope. The latter is far more exciting, especially in a slow-moving vehicle.

The secretariat buildings are raised on a plinth so as to be level with Rashtrapati Bhawan. The high plinths and the use of red sandstone relates them to the monuments in the city, though they are basically European in style. At the foot of the slope, the plinths have alcoves that contain stone tablets commemorating all those who built the city.

Between the two main entrances, are four sandstone columns, each surmounted by a bronze ship – these were gifts from the dominions of the empire, and are called the Dominion Columns.

The secretariat buildings are now offices of the Government of India and you need a visitor's pass to enter. The Home Affairs and Finance ministries are in the North Block, while the External Affairs ministry is in the South Block.

The great open space at the base of the slope is called Vijay Chowk (victory square). Beating the Retreat ceremony takes place here on 29 January each year.

Sansad Bhawan
(Parliament House)

9 **MAP 13C6** On the northwest of Vijay Chowk, is a huge circular, colonnaded building, Sansad Bhawan, where the Indian Parliament meets. This imposing building does not occupy as prominent a position as the other buildings of Lutyens and Baker because the legislature was originally planned to be located in a semicircular extension on the north face of the Viceroy's House.

Parliament House has a domed, circular central hall and three semi-circular structures which were designed for the Chamber of Princes, the Council of State and the Legislative Assembly. Today they house the chambers of the Lok Sabha (House of the People), Rajya Sabha (Upper House) and the library. A verandah with 144 columns surrounds the three chambers. The boundary wall has blocks of sandstone carved in geometrical patterns that echo the Mughal *jaalis*.

An entry pass to the library can be obtained from the Visitor's Reception on Raisina Road by providing a letter of introduction from a Member of Parliament. The library working hours are from 10 am to 6 pm. To obtain a visitor's pass to Sansad Bhawan, Indian nationals should apply to the Parliament Secretariat. Foreign nationals should apply through their embassies or high commissions.

10 MAP 13B6 **Cathedral Church of the Redemption** located north of the Jaipur Column, looks uncannily like a birthday cake. It is not innovative in design or construction, but the interior is very pleasant. The glare of the sun is filtered (with the help of small and recessed openings) into a soft light. The Cathedral has a fine organ and a silver cross donated by Irwin. There is a striking stained glass window as well.

11 MAP 13B6 **Gurudwara Rakab Ganj** stands where there once was a neighbourhood of stirrup-makers (*rakab* - stirrup, *ganj* - market). It was built in 1732 by Lakkhi Banjara, the man who performed the last rites of the martyred Sikh Guru, Tegh Bahadurji. The style is characteristic of Sikh gurudwaras. With typical arrogance, Edwin Lutyens' team could only describe the building as a 'Sikh shrine impossible to remove'.

12 MAP 13C5 **Fakhruddin Ali Ahmed Memorial** is on the roundabout where Parliament Street meets the north entrance to Parliament House. This memorial to a former President of India is an elegant, open-to-the-sky tomb enclosure with marble screens, designed by Habib Rahman. The best time to visit it is early morning when the sun is in the east and the marble screens form intricate patterns on the floor.

Gurudwara Rakab Ganj.

13 MAP 14D6 **The All India Fine Arts and Crafts Society,** AIFACS, as the building is popularly known, has galleries for art exhibitions and the society's office. It also has a large auditorium.

14 MAP 14D5 **Reserve Bank of India** on Parliament Street has two remarkable sculptures of Yakshas (Hindu mythological figures who guard the wealth of the gods) at the entrance to the building by the famous sculptor from Santiniketan, Ram Kinkar Baij.

All India Fine Arts and Crafts Society.

15 MAP 20D3 **Teen Murti Bhawan**, built as the residence of the British commander-in-chief in India, became the official residence of Jawaharlal Nehru, the first Prime Minister of independent India. After he died it was converted into a memorial. The library within the compound is probably the finest resource centre of modern Indian history. The three statues (*teen murti*) on the roundabout outside the building give the building its name.

Kushk Mahal, a hunting lodge built during the reign of Firoz Shah Tughlaq is on a mound just behind the main building. The Nehru Planetarium is also in the same compound.

16 MAP 21A3 **Gandhi Smriti**
Mahatma Gandhi was assassinated by a Hindu fanatic on 30 January 1948 in the Birla House, as he was coming out into the lawn for a prayer meeting. The building is now a national museum.

The residence of former Prime Minister Indira Gandhi on 1 Safdarjang Road has also been converted into a national memorial called **Indira Gandhi Memorial Museum 17** MAP 20E4.

The Prime Minister of India now lives on Race Course Road. All the bungalows on this road have been linked up to the PM's residence. In which of these bungalows he actually lives is not supposed to be known.

Gandhi Smriti.

18 MAP 20E4 **Delhi Gymkhana Club** was established in 1913 by the British for senior government and military officials. It remains to this day an exclusive club, though its membership has widened over the years. After New Delhi was built the club was housed in a typical Lutyens' bungalow.

All avenues in New Delhi are lined with trees. Most of these avenues are named after a national hero or one of the many emperors who have ruled Delhi over the centuries. Why certain roads have a certain name is usually difficult to say. People who decide never explain, but it is a good way to know about people who figured prominently in our history.

Midway along Willingdon Crescent, which is the quickest and greenest way to go from Talkatora Garden to Teen Murti House and further south to the embassies and state government houses, is a sculpture well worth a visit. The sculpture, by Devi Prasad Roy Choudhary, depicts the famous Dandi March led by Mahatma Gandhi in 1931, against the oppressive salt taxes imposed by the colonial regime.

Getting Lost, Bus Stops and Road Signs

You will not find too many bus stops in this part of the city but look for a frame of iron tubes painted black and supporting a yellow bordered roof with the location neatly stencilled in black.

This part of the city is full of roundabouts, many of which have more than four roads meeting them. They are so large that you lose track of which way to go. This is not unusual even for Dilliwalas. Look for poles with small blue and silver pointers showing which road is what. If you are in your own car it is fun to lose your way and find it again, but in a taxi the diversion means paying extra money.

Safdarjang's Tomb

19 MAP 20F6 Safdarjang's Tomb is the last enclosed garden tomb in Delhi in the tradition of Humayun's Tomb, though it is far less grand in scale. It was built in 1753-54 as the mausoleum of Safdarjang, the viceroy of Awadh under the Mughal Emperor, Mohammed Shah. It has several smaller pavilions with evocative names like Jangli Mahal (Palace in the Woods), Moti Mahal (Pearl Palace) and Badshah Pasand (King's Favourite). The complex also has a *madarsa*. The Archaeological Survey of India maintains a library over the main gateway.

J.A. Stein on Lutyens' Delhi : *The architecture of Lutyens is magnificent in concept and the gardens are superb. Nowhere in the entire British Delhi is a single bad stone to be seen. The quality of stone, the workmanship of the lanterns and lampposts is perhaps superior to what is seen in Agra....*

J.A. Stein's buildings in Lodi Estate :

India International Centre
1962
Ford Foundation
1968
Memorial Plaza
1970
Lodi Garden Greenhouse
1971
UNICEF Headquarters
1981
World Wide Fund for Nature - India
1990
India Habitat Centre
1994

India Habitat Centre.

India International Centre

20 MAP 21B5 India International Centre(IIC) was visualised as an international centre for exchange of ideas among scholars. What is most attractive about the buildings is the soft quality of light which the architect, J.A. Stein, captured so well. The buildings have a very down-to-earth scale and meticulous detailing, and extensive use of traditional *jaalis*. There is a library, an auditorium, conference rooms, restaurants and a beautiful garden.

Lodi Garden

21 MAP 21B5 Lodi Garden is the favourite garden in Delhi for picnickers, mothers with small babies, joggers with mobile phones, and it is large enough to provide a quiet corner for all of them.

It is laid out around the beautiful tombs of the Lodi and Sayyid sultans who ruled north India in the 15th and 16th centuries. There used to be a village where the garden is now, which was relocated in 1936, and the garden, then called Lady Willingdon Park, laid out. It was named Lodi Garden in 1947. It was relandscaped by J.A Stein and Garrett Eckbo in 1968.

The tomb of Mohammed Shah (1444) is also called Mubarak Khan ka Gumbad. Originally an enclosed tomb, it has an octagonal chamber in which are the graves of Mohammed Shah and his relatives. It has features typical of octagonal tombs - the stone *chhajjas* along the verandah arches and the sloping buttresses and *guldastas* (bouquets) along the corners.

The tomb of Sikander Lodi (1517) resembles Mohammed Shah's tomb, except that the battlements enclosing it survive and there are no *chhattris* along the dome.

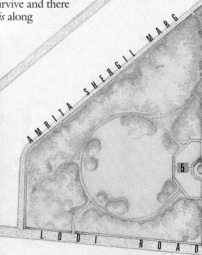

Athpula is said to have been built in Akbar's time. The bridge gets its name from its eight piers.

Bara Gumbad and Masjid (1494), as the name indicates, has a large dome. The tomb's layout resembles that of the Alai Minar in the Qutb complex. Likewise, the masjid adjoining it has minarets that are replicas of Qutb Minar. The masjid has bays with arched entrances, features later adopted in Mughal structures. The room opposite the masjid may have been used as a resting place by travellers. An open court links the three structures.

Sheesh Gumbad shares many features of the Bara Gumbad. It is decorated with tiles in two shades of blue giving it a glazed appearance.

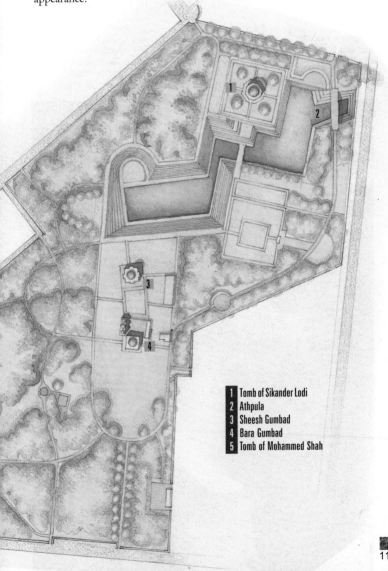

1 Tomb of Sikander Lodi
2 Athpula
3 Sheesh Gumbad
4 Bara Gumbad
5 Tomb of Mohammed Shah

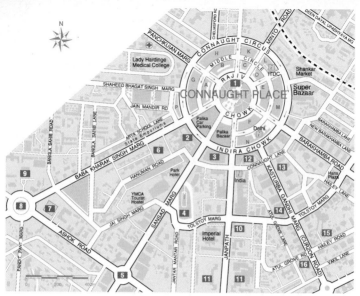

Major Sights

1 Central Park	**6** Hanuman Mandir	**11** Eastern & Western Courts
2 Regal Building	**7** Gurudwara Bangla Sahib	**12** Scindia House
3 Jeevan Bharati Bhawan	**8** Gole Dak Khana	**13** American Center
4 Jantar Mantar	**9** Sacred Heart Cathedral	**14** British Council Division
5 Patel Chowk	**10** Central Cottage Industries Emporium	**15** Ugrasen ki Baoli
		16 Max Mueller Bhawan

Connaught Place

Edwin Lutyens, when drawing up the plans for British New Delhi, meant the new city to lie southwest of the walled city of Shahjahanabad. In the true spirit of colonial rule, the interface between this new imperial city and the older 'native' settlement was intended to be a market, where Lutyens imagined the Indian traders would invest in 'the grand shopping centre for the residents of Shahjahanabad and New Delhi'. Thus, the idea of the 'market at D-Circle' was born. This might also have been a security device. The British were housed south of Kingsway (now Rajpath), and so the market and the spacious bungalows of the Indians lay between them and the crowded Shahjahanabad, where excited political meetings and demonstrations took place.

The market got the name Connaught Place in honour of the Duke of Connaught who visited Delhi in 1921. By this time, R.T. Russell (formerly assistant to Lutyens on the New Delhi project), Chief Architect in the Central Public Works Department was ready with an exciting plan for Connaught Place.

Connaught Place is like a large doughnut with a garden in the centre. The outer and inner faces of the doughnut are the spacious colonnaded verandahs, which give CP its unique identity.

In 1995, the Indian government legislated for the market's name to be changed. Connaught Place was renamed Rajiv Chowk, and Connaught Circus became Indira Chowk. However, it is still popularly referred to as Connaught Place or CP.

The concentric buildings are reached by the inner, outer and middle circles and eight roads radiate from this concentric arrangement. There are commercial establishments on the ground floor of the buildings and also on the upper floor, which once had residential apartments. Prior to 1947, CP was the shopping centre for Europeans and rich Indians. Clerks and Indian officials shopped at the nearby Gole Market and Bengali Market.

CP was the most important business and shopping centre of the city for many years after Independence, until its pre-eminence was challenged by newer entrants like South Extension, Ajmal Khan Road, Rajendra Place and Nehru Place. CP, however, remains very popular with Dilliwalas. It is an explorer's paradise which comes with a safety net. No matter where you start, you go round in circles and are brought back to square one.

Central Park

I MAP 2D2 The gulmohur trees, the fountain, the fencing and the light posts are recent additions to Central Park. Used as a short cut across the shop blocks, this park is popular with regular loungers, including office-goers. It is a place where

you can find all sorts of curiosities, watch snake charmers, get a quick body massage or have your ears cleaned.

Parliament Street
(Sansad Marg)

Parliament Street was laid out along the imaginary line connecting Jama Masjid and Sansad Bhawan (Parliament House). Where Parliament Street enters Connaught Place there is an open space where no shopping blocks are built. This open space was meant to serve as a symbolic 'gateway' to British New Delhi. There used to be a popular coffee house where today you will see Palika Bazaar, an underground shopping centre.

Regal Building **2** MAP IC4 is one of the earliest buildings in CP. There is a popular cinema hall, Regal, here. In its early days there used to be a bar in the lobby for gentlemen and a special matinee show for ladies.

One of the first shops in Regal Building was the Army and Navy Stores which has now closed down and in its place stands the Khadi Gramodyog Bhawan (*see : **Where to Shop***). The most striking feature of Regal Building is its porch which is forever dressed in a riot of film posters. The pavement here is a celebration in total chaos, with booksellers, icecream vendors, curio shops, music shops and lottery ticket booths vying for space.

Regal Building.

Built in the 1980s, the Life Insurance Corporation headquarters, **Jeevan Bharati Bhawan** **3** MAP 2D4 is Connaught Place's proud sculpture in glass and stone. Architect Charles Correa drew a lot of flak for being too modernist and not in keeping with the ambience of Connaught Place. The fact is that CP is today cluttered with numerous high-rise structures, with the DLF Centre and New Delhi Municipal Corporation's Palika Bhawan, on Sansad Marg, designed by Kuldip Singh, competing for attention with Jeevan Bharati.

Jeevan Bharati Bhawan.

Jantar Mantar

4 MAP I C6 Jantar Mantar (*yantra* - instruments, *mantra* - formulae) was constructed in 1724. Maharaja Jai Singh of Jaipur who built this observatory, went on to build other observatories in Jaipur, Ujjain, Varanasi and Mathura. Jai Singh had found the existing astronomical instruments too small to take correct measurements and so he built these larger and more accurate instruments.

The instruments at Jantar Mantar are fascinating for their ingenuity, but accurate observations can no longer be made from here because of the tall buildings around. Jantar Mantar is a popular place for staging *dharnas* (protests) and hunger strikes, and one is sure to come across one group of protesters or another permanently parked here.

The statue of Sardar Vallabhbhai Patel stands on a pedestal at the roundabout known as **Patel Chowk** `5` MAP 14D4. Sardar Patel, a prominent nationalist leader, is remembered for bringing together the many princely states into the Indian Union during1947-48. Across the road from Patel Chowk is Dak Bhawan which has a post office with an outlet for philatelists interested in Indian stamps and houses the National Philatelic Museum.

Baba Kharak Singh Marg

Along a tree-lined path, on the right side of Baba Kharak Singh Marg, are the state emporia - showcases of handicrafts and handlooms from all corners of India (see : *Where to Shop*).

Hanuman Mandir.

Hanuman Mandir `7` MAP 1B4 was built by Maharaja Jai Singh at about the same time as he built Jantar Mantar. Since then, many additions have been made to the original structure. A colourful *mela* is held in the compound every Tuesday and Saturday. Maharaja Jai Singh also built a Jain temple on his vast property in Delhi. This temple is on Jain Mandir Marg.

Gurudwara Bangla Sahib `6` MAP 13C4 is built at the site of the house in which Guru Harkrishan Dev, the eighth Guru of the Sikhs, stayed when he visited Delhi in 1664. His host was Mirza Raja Jai Singh (father of the Jai Singh who built Jantar Mantar). It is said that the water from a tank, blessed by the Guru, cured people suffering from small pox and cholera. The tank exists to this day, and continues to be revered by Sikhs. A museum of Sikh history called Baba Baghel Singh Museum is also within the Gurudwara complex.

Gurudwara Bangla Sahib.

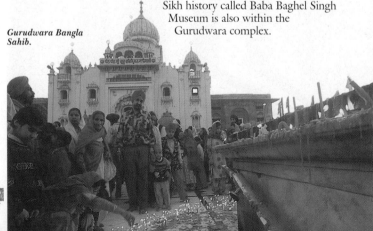

Gole Dak Khana 8 MAP 13C4 which means round post office, was formerly known as Alexandra Place. It was the office of the Central Public Works Department till the 1960s. Plans to convert this roundabout into a garden have never materialised. However, this remains the only post office in Delhi where, thanks to its being located in the centre of a traffic intersection, you have the excitement of dodging traffic in order to post a letter.

Sacred Heart Cathedral 9 MAP 13B3 is across the road from Bangla Sahib Gurudwara. The Cathedral stands between two prominent schools, St. Columba's and Convent of Jesus and Mary.

Mandir Marg

Mandir Marg gets its name from **Laxmi Narayan Mandir** MAP 13A2 which was built in 1938 and is among the most popular Hindu temples in Delhi. It is known as Birla Mandir since it was built by the well known industrialist B.D. Birla. The temple is dedicated to Laxmi (goddess of wealth) and Narayana (the preserver). The annual festival of Janmashtami, commemorating the birth of Lord Krishna, is celebrated with great gaiety and attracts thousands of devotees.

Laxmi Narayan temple was inaugurated by Mahatma Gandhi on condition that people of all castes be allowed to enter the temple. He had fought against the ostracism of 'untouchable' castes, whom he called Harijans (children of God). At the entrance, there is a plaque welcoming people of all faiths and classes, including Harijans.

Kali Bari Mandir MAP 13A3 is next to the Birla Mandir and is almost as old. It is especially revered by the Bengali community. Durga Puja is celebrated here every October and a carnival-like atmosphere pervades during the four days of the festival.

St. Thomas Church MAP 13B1 was built in 1930-32 for Indian converts to Christianity. The church is built in red brick, the favourite material of the architect Walter George. He designed many other prominent buildings in Delhi including Scindia House, St.Stephen's College and the first multi-storeyed apartments in Delhi, Sujan Singh Park, near Khan Market.

Janpath

Janpath, literally the road of the people, was the Queensway of British New Delhi till it got its more down-to-earth name. It runs from north to south connecting Connaught Place to the south end of British New Delhi near Lodi Garden. Janpath is best known for its colourful market.

The market on Janpath just happened after 1947. Thousands of refugees came to Delhi from

Pakistan and, suddenly, Connaught Place and its verandahs were full of people who had become small time traders and entrepreneurs. Janpath was one of the many markets that took root in the lanes and roads of Delhi around that time.

Central Cottage Industries Emporium

10 MAP 2D6 is an excellent place to shop for Indian crafts and textiles. It is located in Jawahar Vyapar Bhawan, a building that is easily identified by its many cantilevers and octagonal windows (*see : **Where to Shop***).

Eastern and Western Courts

11 MAP 14E5, 14E4 with the grand columns of their verandahs, were designed by R.T. Russell. Western Court is now a hostel for Members of Parliament and Eastern Court is the Central Telegraph Office.

Kasturba Gandhi Marg

Scindia House 12 MAP 2D4 was designed by Walter George for the Maharaja of Gwalior. Today it is a warren of small offices belonging to travel agents and tour operators. The state-run Delhi Transport Corporation also has an office here. Outside Scindia House there is a bus stand for tourist buses, luxury or otherwise, travelling to diverse destinations.

American Center 13 MAP 2F4 was built in the 1960s. The building is reminiscent of the spirit of the cold war, with its virtually windowless facade. It has an excellent library which is open to short term membership as well.

British Council Division's 14 MAP 2F6 building is designed by Charles Correa. The British Council has an art gallery, an auditorium and an extremely good library, of which one can also become a short term member.

Ugrasen ki Baoli  MAP 14F4 was built in the 14th century, probably by Maharaja Ugrasen, the supposed progenitor of the Aggarwals, a prominent trading community in India. *Baolis* (step wells) were public places that were carefully maintained to provide travellers and residents with water and a cool place to rest. This *baoli* is a tranquil oasis in an area dominated by high-rise buildings.

Max Mueller Bhawan
16 MAP 14F4 the German cultural centre, is named after the famous 19th century German Indologist. It is housed in one of the British bungalows that has survived the onslaught of property developers who have changed the area into a concrete jungle. Among Max Mueller Bhawan's many activities are regular film shows and music concerts.

Mandi House

The buildings at Mandi House circle MAP 15A4 were built in the 1950s to house national cultural institutions. The Mandi House area is the informal cultural hub of Delhi with its array of cultural centres and auditoria built around an extremely busy roundabout *(see : Music, Dance, Theatre and Cinema, p.253)*.

Mandi House circle.

Rabindra Bhawan, designed by Habib Rehman, houses the Lalit Kala Akademi (Academy of Fine Arts), Sangeet Natak Akademi (Academy of Music and Dance) and Sahitya Akademi (Academy of Literature). Rabindra Bhawan has a good library of music and Indian literature.

The National School of Drama and the Kathak Kendra are located in **Bahawalpur House.**

The **Federation of Indian Chambers of Commerce and Industry (FICCI)**, one of the major industry associations in the country, has its headquarters in the Mandi House area. The building also houses the **National Museum of Natural History.**

Triveni Kala Sangam is a prominent cultural centre. It has exhibition galleries, an open air theatre and a bookshop. The café here is very popular with artists and intellectuals who frequent this area.

Shri Ram Centre, an important cultural venue, is an attractive exposed concrete building designed by Shivnath Prasad in the late 1960s.

Kamani Auditorium, also in the Mandi House area, is a popular auditorium for plays and concerts.

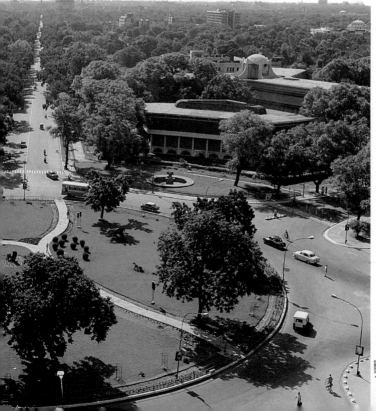

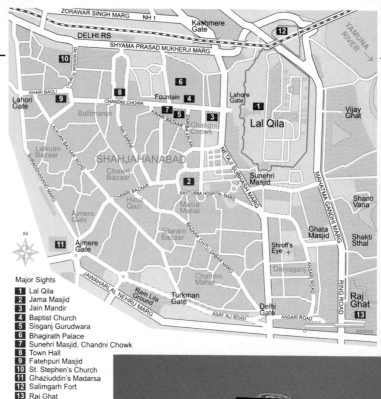

Major Sights

1. Lal Qila
2. Jama Masjid
3. Jain Mandir
4. Baptist Church
5. Sisganj Gurudwara
6. Bhagirath Palace
7. Sunehri Masjid, Chandni Chowk
8. Town Hall
9. Fatehpuri Masjid
10. St. Stephen's Church
11. Ghaziuddin's Madarsa
12. Salimgarh Fort
13. Raj Ghat

*Lahore Gate,
Lal Qila.*

Shahjahanabad

The only historic settlement in Delhi which can still be 'read' clearly is Shahjahanabad, the city established by Emperor Shahjahan in 1648. It has to be experienced as a city as well as seen in terms of its architecture. Shahjahanabad today is a thriving commercial and trading centre and more people work here than ever before.

Jama Masjid.

The town planners call it 'the walled city' but there are only very small parts of the wall left. Scholars call it 'Shahjahanabad' but there is no statue or portrait of the founder. The people of Delhi call it 'Purani Dilli' (Old Delhi) but there are many other areas of Delhi which are older. Migrants from elsewhere recognise it as 'Dilli 6', but how many residents of this city understand the logic of Delhi's postal code?

Shahjahanabad is the only part of Delhi which can boast that great Urdu poets, Mir, Zauq, Ghalib, have written verses about it. Today's sceptical visitor might, at first glance, wonder why. But if he allows himself time to wander through the city for a few leisurely hours, he will begin to understand why. Shahjahanabad is that magic mix of planned elements and individual initiative which makes a beautiful city. In countries which can afford it, such cityscapes have been carefully tended as 'conservation areas'. Delhi's Master Plan would like to do the same; this would call for sensitive measures to retain its vitality and recover its beauty.

Daryaganj by night.

Shahjahanabad beyond the north gate of Jama Masjid.

With the expansion of Delhi on all sides of Shahjahanabad, the city has ceased to be a focal point for routes and has become a thoroughfare.

Delhi Main Railway Station has the charm and stateliness of 19th century railway stations in Britain.

Time was when the names of the city gates conjured up visions of other cities, Lahore, Kabul, Ajmer…. Today, the names remain, though most of the city wall and many gates have been demolished. A south-north road from Delhi Gate (named for the older Delhi, that is, Mehrauli) to Kashmere Gate slices through the city, separating the Jama Masjid from the fort.

Lal Qila or Red Fort is set back from the city, though it was not always so. After the Rising of 1857 a vast area around it was cleared of buildings, and the fort itself occupied by the army (which it still is). If nature abhors a vacuum, so do Indian towns… and this vast maidan is perennially covered with camps of travelling circuses, with fairs, or with rows of buses carrying pilgrims on tours. There is a north-south bisection made by the railway line and the Gothic railway station, Delhi Main Railway Station, built in 1867 by the British.

Shahjahanabad has changed over its 350 years. Which city has not? But it remains as distinctive a piece of landscape as Mughal food is a distinctive cuisine or the Mughal salwar kameez a distinctive costume. And the most reassuring fact for visitors to understand is that it is so compact and its people so friendly that it is impossible to get lost in it - the chief charm of a pre-automobile city.

Delhi Gate.

Intricate designs on the cusped arch of Khas Mahal.

Lal Qila

MAP 10D3 So much has altered in Lal Qila, or Red Fort as it is also called, that the visitor does not get a sense of what it was like before 1857. He has access to less than a quarter of the fort, the rest of it being the territory of the Indian Army, who continue the occupation begun after the Rising of 1857 was suppressed. In 1858, a large number of palaces in the fort were demolished, many of the *taikhanas* (basement rooms) sealed and massive barracks constructed for the soldiers.

Before 1857, the fort was a mini-city, with palaces, offices, workshops and halls of audience, where about 3,000 people lived. Today, more than 10,000 visitors stream through the open areas every day. They get to see some of the public and some of the private realms of the palace complex.

The Lahore Gate of the palace is veiled by the barbican added by Aurangzeb. It is from here that the Prime Minister of India addresses the country and unfurls the national flag every year on 15 August, Independence Day.

Khas Mahal.

1	Lahore Gate
2	Chhatta Chowk
3	Naqqar Khana
4	Diwan-e-Am
5	Mumtaz Mahal
6	Rang Mahal
7	Khas Mahal
8	Diwan-e-Khas
9	Hammam
10	Hira Mahal
11	Shah Burj
12	Bhadon Pavilion
13	Zafar Mahal
14	Sawan Pavilion
15	Moti Masjid

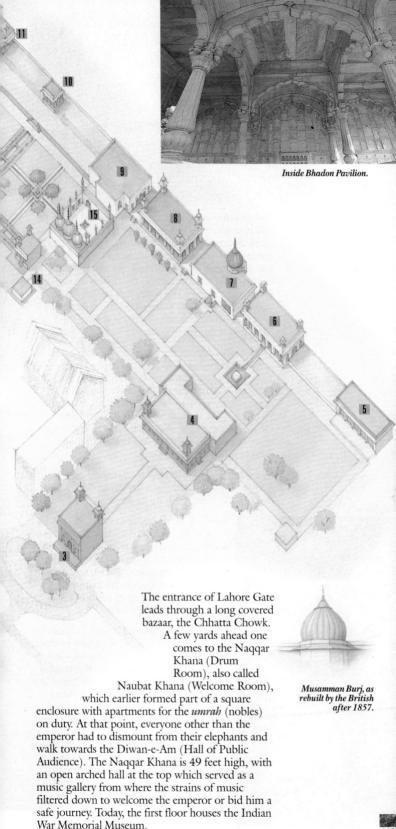

Inside Bhadon Pavilion.

Musamman Burj, as
rebuilt by the British
after 1857.

The entrance of Lahore Gate
leads through a long covered
bazaar, the Chhatta Chowk.
A few yards ahead one
comes to the Naqqar
Khana (Drum
Room), also called
Naubat Khana (Welcome Room),
which earlier formed part of a square
enclosure with apartments for the *umrah* (nobles)
on duty. At that point, everyone other than the
emperor had to dismount from their elephants and
walk towards the Diwan-e-Am (Hall of Public
Audience). The Naqqar Khana is 49 feet high, with
an open arched hall at the top which served as a
music gallery from where the strains of music
filtered down to welcome the emperor or bid him a
safe journey. Today, the first floor houses the Indian
War Memorial Museum.

Diwan-e-Am.

Diwan-e-Am is built of red sandstone and sits atop an impressive plinth. The pavilion is articulated by small *chhattris* on its northwest and southwest corners. An ornamental panel depicting Orpheus was dismantled after 1857 and restored at the beginning of this century on the British viceroy Curzon's initiative. The entire hall was originally gilded with elaborate stucco work. Today one can only experience the shell of what was once the handsomest theatre of public audience.

The private realm of the emperor was distributed along the eastern wall and commanded a view of the Yamuna, which in those days flowed past the walls. What remains of these palaces are, from south to north, Mumtaz Mahal, Rang Mahal, Khas Mahal, Diwan-e-Khas, the *hammam* and the Shah Burj. Originating at the Shah Burj, the Nahar-e-Bihisht (Canal of Paradise) flowed in a channel through these buildings.

Mumtaz Mahal now houses the Museum of Archaeology, which has artefacts salvaged from the royal palace.

Rang Mahal.

Rang Mahal (Palace of Colours) derives its name from its painted interior. Its northern and southern sections were called Sheesh Mahal (Palace of Mirrors) because of the wedges of mirror embedded in the ceiling which reflected lights in fascinating multiplicity. This, with its basement, was the palace of the royal ladies.

Khas Mahal (Emperor's Palace), was small and elegant, with special rooms for private worship and for sleeping. A fine marble screen at the north end carries the motif of the scales of justice, which can be found in many miniature paintings of Shahjahan's reign. There is also a marble balcony which once projected over the river bank. In later centuries when the river had changed course, this was the place from where the emperors used to present themselves to their subjects in the traditional *darshan* (public appearance).

Diwan-e-Am.

144

Diwan-e-Khas.

Diwan-e-Khas (Hall of Private Audience), the most beautifully ornamented building in Lal Qila, is bound up with the history of the Mughal empire. In 1739 it saw Nadir Shah receiving the submission of Emperor Mohammed Shah, and depriving him of his most valuable treasures including the Peacock Throne. And it was here, in May 1857, that Indian soldiers declared Bahadur Shah Zafar, the Emperor of Hindustan.

Set on a high, impressive plinth along the rear wall, this building was the setting for the Peacock Throne. Its flat ceiling, supported by a series of engrailed arches, was gilded in silver and had some of the finest *pietra dura* work and paintings. Over the corner arches is inscribed the beautiful couplet,

> *Agar firdaus bar rue zamin ast*
> *Hamin ast o hamin ast o hamin ast.*

> If there is a paradise on earth,
> it is here, it is here, it is here.

The *hammam* (bathing area) consists of three chambers with a fountain in the middle of the central one, and *pietra dura* work on the walls.

Shah Burj, a favourite eyrie of the emperors, was a conveniently secluded point where the rulers could hold private conclaves and also, on occasion, dream away the hours in a 'monarch of all I survey' haze.

Marble pillar in Bhadon pavilion.

Moti Masjid (Pearl Mosque), an addition by Aurangzeb, was a private masjid. The three domes and the perfect proportions give this pearl-white building a great sense of beauty and dignity.

To the north of Moti Masjid is the Hayat Baksh Bagh, a typical Mughal *chahar bagh* (garden), built by Shahjahan. At the centre of the garden stands the Zafar Mahal, while the Sawan and Bhadon pavilions are on the southern and northern ends.

Lal Qila addresses the citizens of Shahjahanabad through two arched gateways – Lahore and Delhi – which determine its two cardinal axes. The east-west axis through Lahore Gate became Chandni Chowk. The north-south axis, through the Delhi Gate of Lal Qila, was Faiz Bazaar, now called Daryaganj (*darya* - river, *ganj* - market). It was through the Delhi Gate that the emperor led his ceremonial procession every Friday to the Jama Masjid.

Inside Shah Burj.

146

Jama Masjid

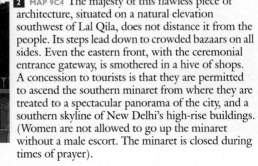

2 MAP 9C4 The majesty of this flawless piece of architecture, situated on a natural elevation southwest of Lal Qila, does not distance it from the people. Its steps lead down to crowded bazaars on all sides. Even the eastern front, with the ceremonial entrance gateway, is smothered in a hive of shops. A concession to tourists is that they are permitted to ascend the southern minaret from where they are treated to a spectacular panorama of the city, and a southern skyline of New Delhi's high-rise buildings. (Women are not allowed to go up the minaret without a male escort. The minaret is closed during times of prayer).

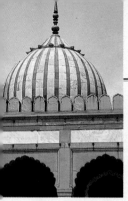

Ghata Masjid (Cloud Mosque).

The three-dome Mughal mosque, of which the most noble example is Jama Masjid, is repeated on a smaller scale in many other places in Shahjahanabad. Perhaps the most beautiful ones are Ghata Masjid MAP 10E5 in Daryaganj, Sunehri Masjid 7 MAP 9B3 in Chandni Chowk and Fakhr-ul-Masajid MAP 9B1 near Kashmere Gate. There is another Sunehri Masjid MAP 10D4 which is just south of Lal Qila, not to be confused with the mosque in Chandni Chowk.

Fakhr-ul-Masajid.

Sunehri Masjid, south of Lal Qila.

Shahjahanabad abounds in mandirs, gurudwaras and churches as well. The main Jain Mandir opposite Lal Qila is very beautiful, and has a charming Birds' Hospital **3** MAP 9C3 attached to it. Baptist Church **4** MAP 9C3, founded in 1814, is the earliest Christian mission in Delhi. The stately Sisganj Gurudwara **5** MAP 9C3 on Chandni Chowk is hallowed as the site of the Sikh Guru Tegh Bahadurji's martyrdom. St. Stephen's Church **10** MAP 9A3 is a small and attractive church built in 1865 as a memorial to the British who died in 1857. The coexistence of all these places of worship within yards of each other makes Chandni Chowk a unique thoroughfare.

Baptist Church.

Jama Masjid.

Jain Mandir.

Chandni Chowk

The golden domes of Sisganj Gurudwara.

Chandni Chowk (Moonlight Square) refers to the open space in front of the modern Town Hall that had been laid out by Jahanara, Shahjahan's daughter and where the water in a pool reflected the moonlight, and then flowed on into a channel that ran down the length of the avenue. Today the name is used to indicate the avenue. Agra has a more spectacular fort, but Delhi is distinguished by this wide street that links the Lahore Gate of Lal Qila with the Fatehpuri Masjid. The visitor has to switch on his imagination to maximum strength to allow the moving ramp of vehicles that is today's Chandni Chowk to become blurred. He has to go back in time at least a couple of hundred years to picture a quieter view of this street made up of bazaars, with a row of banyan trees down the centre, the silver ribbon of the canal, flanked by a wide platform where people sat and talked; horse-driven carriages, *palkis* (palanquins) and an occasional elephant would have moved along the avenue which overflows with buses, scooters and cycle rickshaws today.

Swami Shraddhanand's statue outside the Town Hall.

North of the avenue were vast gardens – one surrounded the magnificent Jahanara Sarai, which had a plinth as spacious as that of Jama Masjid; another set off the stately home of Begum Samru, an unusual woman with an incredible 'rags to riches' career. The Begum's palace is today north India's biggest electrical goods wholesale market and is called Bhagirath Palace **6** MAP 9C3. And, the Italianate Town Hall **8** MAP 9B3 built in 1864, stands where the Sarai did.

At the western end of Chandni Chowk is the attractive Fatehpuri Masjid **9** MAP 9A3. Built by one of Shahjahan's wives, it was the venue of public debates between Muslim theologians and Christian missionaries in the last century.

Fatehpuri Masjid.

Galis

Kaun jaye Zauq / Par Dilli ki galian chhorkar (who would want to leave / forsaking the *galis* of Delhi) is one of the best known lines of the Urdu poet Zauq. Many other poets have written with affection of the *galis* (narrow lanes) of this city. The network of lanes behind the avenues is typical of the landscape of many Indian towns. Each *gali* used to – and many still do – specialise in some particular merchandise, silver, stationery, textiles, spices *(see : Bazaars)*.

Also, along the *galis*, hidden behind misleadingly ordinary gates and blank walls were oases of tranquility, town-houses built round a courtyard which filtered in the sunshine and were often green with trees and shrubs. Few of these remain. Many have decayed because of the owners' poverty, many sold and partitioned into pocket-size homes, and many used for small workshops.

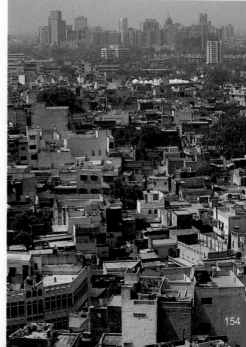

Ghaziuddin's *Madarsa*

11 MAP 9A6 Ghaziuddin's *madarsa*, though part of Shahjahanabad, lies beyond its walls near Ajmere Gate. It is well worth a visit, but may have to be seen on a separate outing, since to cover it along with the rest of Shahjahanabad would involve travelling some distance through the narrow *galis* of the city.

Ghaziuddin's *madarsa* (also called the Anglo-Arabic School after English classes were added in 1824) was built in 1692. The two storey building is one of the few surviving examples of *madarsa* architecture in Delhi. Near it is a beautiful mosque and the tomb of Ghaziuddin, who was a minister in the court of the Mughal emperor, Aurangzeb.

Salimgarh

12 MAP 10D2 About 1.5 km north east of Lal Qila, on the right side of the busy Ring Road, are the ruins of the small fort of Salimgarh. It was built by Salim Shah, son and successor of Sher Shah Suri, in 1546, as an island fort on the Yamuna.

Aurangzeb made Salimgarh a state prison, and the British continued using it as such. The leaders of the Indian National Army, Shah Nawaz, Prem Kumar Sahgal and Gurbaksh Singh Dhillon were imprisoned here in 1945, before their public trial in Lal Qila. Salimgarh has now been renamed Swatantrata Senani Smarak (Freedom Fighters' Memorial).

Raj Ghat

13 **MAP 16E1** To the southeast of Lal Qila, between the Ring Road and the Yamuna, lies Raj Ghat. The historic name refers to the *ghat* (stepped embankment) at the edge of the river, but today it means only one thing, it is the memorial to the Father of the Nation, Mohandas Karamchand Gandhi - Mahatma to millions of Indians.

Mahatma Gandhi was cremated on the banks of the Yamuna on 31 January 1948. He had been assassinated the day before while walking to his customary prayer meeting at Birla House (Gandhi Smriti on Tees January Marg). Raj Ghat was later made into a national memorial, the design for which was proposed by Vanu Bhuta. A stone footpath flanked by well-kept lawns leads to a walled enclosure, open to the sky, with a simple stone platform in black marble which marks the site.

Prayer meetings are held here every Friday at 5 pm. Gandhi Darshan, a small museum on the life of Mahatma Gandhi, is across the road and Gandhi National Museum a little further down, on Ring Road.

Thereafter, a trend has set in of honouring former Prime Ministers, by building for them memorials on the banks of the Yamuna. Incidentally, Hindus consider it auspicious to be cremated on the banks of sacred rivers, particularly on the *ghats* along the Ganga, the Yamuna, as well as other major rivers.

Over the years many memorials have been built around Raj Ghat. These are set in acres of beautifully landscaped gardens, where people can pay homage to their leaders and for which the grounds are kept open throughout the year. The memorials along the Yamuna, on the Ring Road, are Shanti Vana for Pandit Jawaharlal Nehru, India's first Prime Minister (1947-64); Shakti Sthal for his daughter, Prime Minister Indira Gandhi (1966-77, 1980-84); and Vir Bhumi for her son, Prime Minister Rajiv Gandhi (1984-89). There is also Vijay Ghat for Lal Bahadur Shastri (1964-66) and Kisan Ghat for Chaudhary Charan Singh (1979), both of whom have served as Prime Ministers of India.

COURTESY: THE HINDUSTAN TIMES

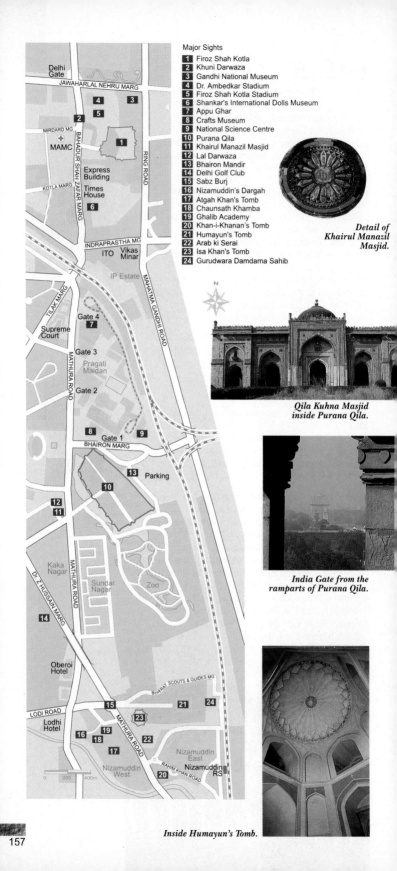

Major Sights

1. Firoz Shah Kotla
2. Khuni Darwaza
3. Gandhi National Museum
4. Dr. Ambedkar Stadium
5. Firoz Shah Kotla Stadium
6. Shankar's International Dolls Museum
7. Appu Ghar
8. Crafts Museum
9. National Science Centre
10. Purana Qila
11. Khairul Manazil Masjid
12. Lal Darwaza
13. Bhairon Mandir
14. Delhi Golf Club
15. Sabz Burj
16. Nizamuddin's Dargah
17. Atgah Khan's Tomb
18. Chaunsath Khamba
19. Ghalib Academy
20. Khan-i-Khanan's Tomb
21. Humayun's Tomb
22. Arab ki Serai
23. Isa Khan's Tomb
24. Gurudwara Damdama Sahib

Detail of Khairul Manazil Masjid.

Qila Kuhna Masjid inside Purana Qila.

India Gate from the ramparts of Purana Qila.

Inside Humayun's Tomb.

Firoz Shah Kotla
TO Nizamuddin

The area south of Delhi Gate up to Nizamuddin, bordering the river Yamuna, has seen capital cities of several dynasties over the last one thousand years. Within the area there are two ancient forts, Firoz Shah Kotla and Purana Qila, India's prime exhibition complex, Pragati Maidan, the National Zoological Park, the *dargah* of Sheikh Nizamuddin Auliya and Humayun's Tomb, a World Heritage monument. The area includes Bahadur Shah Zafar Marg, the centre of Delhi's newspaper industry, which has the offices of many major national newspapers.

Inside Humayun's Tomb.

Talaqi Darwaza, Purana Qila.

Firoz Shah Kotla

MAP 16D2 Firoz Shah Tughlaq, a nephew of Ghiyasuddin Tughlaq, built the enormous city of Firozabad in 1354. It extended from the Ridge in the north, where there is a hunting lodge of Firoz Shah, to Hauz Khas in the south, where Firoz Shah built a *madarsa* and his own tomb enclosure.

Approached from Bahadur Shah Zafar Marg, nothing much survives of Firoz Shah Kotla, the citadel of Firozabad, apart from the Ashoka Pillar, the remains of the Jama Masjid and a circular *baoli* (step well), two floors deep, with rooms on each level.

Ruins of Jama Masjid inside Firoz Shah Kotla.

Ashoka Pillar, a monolith over 12.8 metres in height and 27 tonnes in weight, was installed here by Firoz Shah. It dates to Emperor Ashoka who ruled a vast empire stretching from Taxila, near modern Rawalpindi in the north, to Orissa in the south, two hundred years before Julius Caesar. The Ashokan edicts on this column were deciphered in 1837, yielding the key to the ancient Brahmi script.

Detail of Ashoka Pillar

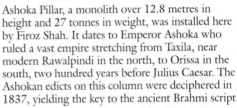

The domed gateway and the south and west walls are the only vestiges that remain of Jama Masjid or the congregational mosque. Made of local quartzite stone, it was originally covered with lime plaster giving it a milk-like whiteness. The plaster is now covered with a layer of black fungus. On all four sides of the mosque are underground rooms which are today inhabited by hundreds of bats.

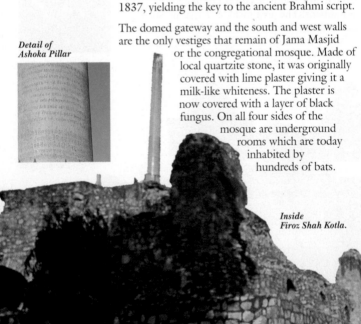

Inside Firoz Shah Kotla.

Khuni Darwaza

2 MAP 15C2 Khuni Darwaza (blood-soaked gate) is the imposing gateway on Bahadur Shah Zafar Marg, opposite Maulana Azad Medical College. It is believed to have been the northern gateway of Sher Shah's capital, Shergarh. The intrepid tourist may still reach the top of the three-storeyed gateway using the staircases within the walls. It is believed that Dara Shikoh's head was displayed here after he was beheaded by his brother, Aurangzeb, in their battle for the throne of Delhi. It was also here that the two sons and a grandson of the last Mughal emperor, Bahadur Shah Zafar, were shot by the British in 1857, and their bodies displayed for public viewing. Local folklore has references to blood dripping from the ceiling of the gateway. The story acquires added colour because during the rainy season, rainwater collects the rust from the iron joints resulting in a reddish dribble.

3 Gandhi National Museum
(see : Museums)
4 Dr. Ambedkar Stadium
5 Firoz Shah Kotla Stadium
6 Shankar's International Dolls Museum
(see : Museums)
7 Appu Ghar
8 Crafts Museum
(see : Museums)
9 National Science Centre

Bara Darwaza.

Purana Qila

10 MAP 23A2 In the year 1538, Emperor Humayun, son of the first Mughal, Babur, laid the foundations of a city he named Dinpanah, or the Refuge of the Faithful. The inner citadel of this city is today known as Purana Qila (Old Fort). Within six years, Humayun was ousted by Sher Shah Suri who promptly renamed the city Shergarh and added many buildings to it.

A Sound-and-Light show is organised by Delhi Tourism at Purana Qila every evening.
For details contact :
✆ *4629365 / 4603178.*

The location of Purana Qila is not new to history, as the earliest reference to this site is made in the Hindu epic, *Mahabharata*, which states that the Pandavas founded a city called Indraprastha beside the river Yamuna. Recent excavations at Purana Qila have yielded Painted Grey Ware pottery, which is dated to *c.*1000 BC.

Detail of
Talaqi Darwaza.

Similar remains have also been found in other sites associated with the *Mahabharata*. The fact that till 1913 there was a village within the fort walls called Indrapat adds credence to the theory that Purana Qila is built on the remains of Indraprastha.

The magnificent walls of the fort reach 18 metres in places. There are groups of holes arranged in interesting patterns on the walls which were apparently meant to be nesting spaces for birds. Hundreds of parrots and pigeons continue to make these walls their homes.

Purana Qila has three gates – Humayun Darwaza, Talaqi Darwaza and Bara Darwaza. One may enter the fort today through the Bara Darwaza. The south gate is known as Humayun Darwaza not because Humayun built it, but probably because Humayun's Tomb is visible through it.

Inside Purana Qila is Qila Kuhna Masjid built by Sultan Sher Shah in 1541, and certainly one of his finest architectural statements. The builders must have attempted to complete the central portion in white marble but the scarcity of this material seems to have led them to use deep red sandstone which gives the building a pleasing character. The inner west wall of the building has five arched openings which are richly ornamented in white and black marble. On a marble slab within the mosque is an inscription which translates, 'As long as there are people on this earth, may this edifice be frequented and people be cheerful and happy in it'.

Sher Mandal

Sher Shah built Sher Mandal, a two-storeyed octagonal pavilion in red sandstone. The building has acquired historical importance as Emperor Humayun, after he regained the throne of Delhi, tripped on its tortuous staircase and fell to his death in 1556.

Qila Kuhna Masjid.

Khairul Manazil Masjid.

Khairul Manazil Masjid

☐ MAP 22F2 Khairul Manazil Masjid, opposite the Delhi Zoo entrance, was built in 1561 by Maham Anga, one of the wet nurses of Akbar, and the mother of Adham Khan, whose tomb is in Mehrauli.

Detail of enamelled tile work on Khairul Manazil Masjid.

Delhi Zoo

MAP 23A3 National Zoological Park, as Delhi Zoo is officially known, is next to Purana Qila. It has an early 17th century Kos Minar, which was one of the many put up by Jehangir, son of Emperor Akbar, at every *kos* (roughly four miles) between Agra and Lahore (*see : Children's Delhi*).

Lal Darwaza

12 MAP 22F2 Also known as Sher Shah Gate, the imposing Lal Darwaza(red gate), is believed to have been the southern gateway of Sher Shah's city, Shergarh.

Bhairon Mandir

13 MAP 23A1 On the northeast end of Purana Qila, there are two Hindu temples dedicated to Bhaironji. In one the offering made to the reigning deity is milk while in the other it is liquor. The belief that the temple complex dates back to the Pandava period lends it great sanctity. However, if this is true, then the buildings show no sign of historicity and have, in all probability, been renovated several times. While there, do notice the concrete cow whose udders serve as water taps!

14 Delhi Golf Club has a 27 hole course spread over 200 acres around several Lodi period monuments.

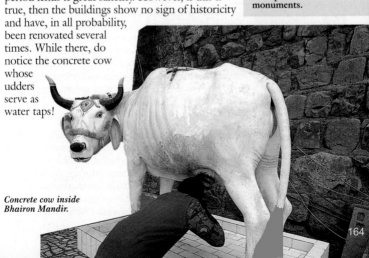

Concrete cow inside Bhairon Mandir.

Hazrat Nizamuddin

About 2 km south of the Purana Qila, on Mathura Road, is Hazrat Nizamuddin, one of the many historic village settlements which still continue to exist within modern Delhi. Nizamuddin gets its name from the Sufi saint, Sheikh Nizamuddin Auliya, who was born in Budaun in Uttar Pradesh in 1236, and lived most of his life in Delhi until his death in 1325. Among his illustrious disciples were the sultans, Alauddin Khilji and Mohammed bin Tughlaq, and the celebrated poet, Amir Khusro.

Sabz Burj

15 MAP 23A5 The entry point to Nizamuddin is marked by a traffic island with an exquisite blue-domed Mughal tomb known as Sabz Burj (*sabz* - green, *burj* - dome). The blue tiles are a recent restoration effort by the Archaeological Survey of India, but some of the original green, yellow and blue tiles can still be seen on the walls. The British used this building as a police station for many years till the beginning of the century.

Nizamuddin's *Dargah*

Nizamuddin's Tomb and Jamaat Khana Masjid.

16 MAP 22F6 Nizamuddin West, as the area around the *dargah* is formally called, is characterised by crowded lanes, jerry-built houses, innumerable small shops, tombs and mosques and the pleasant aroma of kebabs. The constant crowd of devotees outside Nizamuddin's *dargah* is testimony to the devotion the saint commands. The religious fervour and frenzy of the mystics lends a very special character to the *dargah*. Every Thursday, after sunset, qawwals sing the lyrics of Amir Khusro.

Many big and small tombs have been built over the centuries in and around the *dargah* complex, since it is considered auspicious to be buried near a saint's grave. To the south of Nizamuddin's grave is the tomb of Amir Khusro. Nearby are marble screen enclosures around the tombs of Jahanara, the daughter of Shahjahan and a later Mughal emperor, Mohammed Shah Rangila.

An interesting legend associated with the *dargah* is of the war of wits between the saint and the first Tughlaq king, Ghiyasuddin. Sheikh Nizamuddin was getting a *baoli* constructed at about the same time as the king was engaged in building Tughlaqabad. The king forbade his construction workers from working elsewhere, and so they decided to work for the Sheikh at night. This made Ghiyasuddin prohibit the sale of oil for earthen lamps, but the workers found that the lamps could be lit with the water of the *baoli!* The faithful believe that the water of the *baoli* has healing powers.

1 TOMB OF SHEIKH NIZAMUDDIN
2 TOMB OF AMIR KHUSRO
3 JAHANARA'S TOMB
4 TOMB OF MOHAMMED SHAH RANGILA
5 JAMAAT KHANA MASJID
6 TOMB OF ATGAH KHAN
7 ENTRANCE

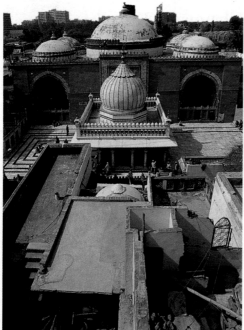

Nizamuddin's Dargah.

Nizamuddin at night.

Atgah Khan's Tomb

**Detail of
Atgah Khan's Tomb.**

17 MAP 22F6 The tomb of Atgah Khan, the husband of one of Akbar's wet nurses, Jiji Angah, is an impressive structure in red sandstone thickly inlaid with marble and coloured tiles. Small in size and sandwiched between two modern buildings, its original grandeur is still visible.

Chaunsath Khamba

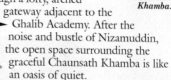

**Jaalis on
Chaunsath
Khamba.**

18 MAP 22F5 The tomb of Mirza Aziz, built in 1623 of white marble, is known as Chaunsath Khamba, because, as its name indicates, it has sixty-four pillars supporting the roof. It is entered through a lofty, arched gateway adjacent to the Ghalib Academy. After the noise and bustle of Nizamuddin, the open space surrounding the graceful Chaunsath Khamba is like an oasis of quiet.

Chaunsath Khamba.

Ghalib Academy

19 MAP 23A5 In Nizamuddin West is also buried the famous 19th century Urdu poet, Mirza Ghalib. Ghalib Academy has a large library and an interesting museum which, besides some paintings, also has a large collection of rocks. Mirza Ghalib's tomb is kept locked within the precincts of the Ghalib Academy.

Khan-i-Khanan's Tomb

20 MAP 23B6 The tomb of Abdur Rahim Khan, who had the title of Khan-i-Khanan, is on the opposite side of Mathura Road. Abdur Rahim Khan (d.1626) was the son of Bairam Khan, Akbar's loyal protector during his early years, and an influential courtier in the courts of both Akbar and Jehangir. Today Rahim is remembered as a popular Hindi poet whose couplets every Hindi-speaking child in India is familiar with.

A modern Hindu temple on the outskirts of Nizamuddin West.

The now dilapidated tomb was an architectural landmark in its time. Built of red sandstone, it followed the design of Humayun's Tomb and also had a marble dome. The dome was stripped of its marble slabs which were later used on the dome of Safdarjang's Tomb.

Khan-i-Khanan's Tomb.

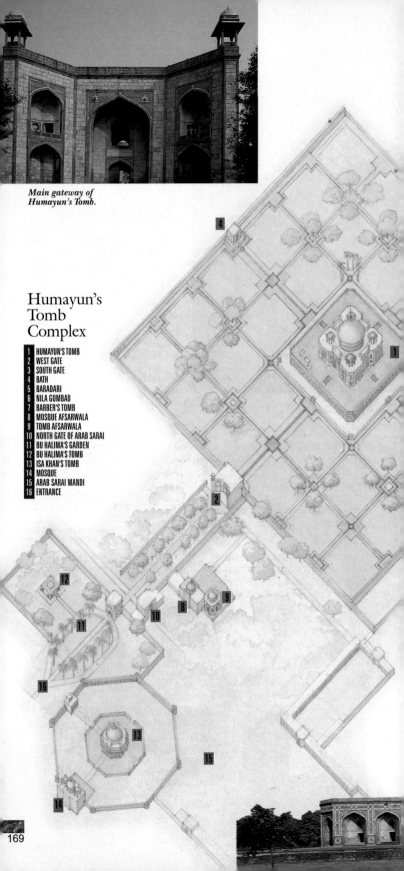

Main gateway of
Humayun's Tomb.

Humayun's Tomb Complex

1 HUMAYUN'S TOMB
2 WEST GATE
3 SOUTH GATE
4 BATH
5 BARADARI
6 NILA GUMBAD
7 BARBER'S TOMB
8 MOSQUE AFSARWALA
9 TOMB AFSARWALA
10 NORTH GATE OF ARAB SARAI
11 BU HALIMA'S GARDEN
12 BU HALIMA'S TOMB
13 ISA KHAN'S TOMB
14 MOSQUE
15 ARAB SARAI MANDI
16 ENTRANCE

Humayun's Tomb

21 MAP 23B5 Taj Mahal is known to have been inspired by Humayun's Tomb, and in many ways this magnificent red and white building is as spectacular as the famous 'monument to love' at Agra. Humayun's Tomb is a memorial by a grieving wife – it was built by his widow Haji Begum in 1565-66, nine years after his death. She is said to have spent one and a half million rupees on the building.

Intricate jaalis (lattice work in white marble) inside Humayun's Tomb.

The splendour of this grand monument becomes overpowering on entering through the lofty double-storeyed gateway. It is set in the centre of a large square garden enclosed by high walls on three sides, while the river would have been the fourth boundary. The *chahar bagh* is divided into four parts by wide causeways and water channels, and each square divided into smaller squares by pathways as in a typical Mughal garden. The fountains were worked with simple yet highly developed engineering skills quite common in India during that period.

Humayun's Tomb stands on a 8 metre high platform.

Humayun's Tomb is built in local stone and faced with red sandstone and white marble.

Visible from the terrace of Humayun's Tomb, towards the southeast is Nai ka Gumbad or the barber's tomb. Outside the complex, again on the southeast, is a blue domed building known as Nila Gumbad, a late Mughal tomb.

Emperor Humayun's tomb chamber is entered through the south entrance, while the other three sides are blocked with *jaalis* in white marble. In the serene central chamber lies the tomb, though the actual resting place of Humayun is directly beneath in an underground chamber.

Several members of the Mughal royal family lie buried in the mausoleum, and many tombstones can be seen on the terrace.

Arab ki Sarai

22 MAP 23A6 On the south of the main pathway leading to Humayun's Tomb is a picturesque gateway which leads to a walled enclosure called Arab ki Sarai. This was built by Humayun's widow for the 300 Arab merchants she is said to have brought from her pilgrimage to Mecca. Afsarwala Tomb and Masjid, built by a nobleman in Emperor Akbar's court, are within this complex.

Further west on the main pathway is the gateway to the Garden of Bu Halima. Not much is known of this lady and the gateway and two very ornamental *chhattris* are all that remain of the garden.

Tomb of Isa Khan

23 MAP 23A5 On the southwest end of Bu Halima's garden is the octagonal tomb of Isa Khan, a nobleman in the court of Sher Shah. In this early gardentomb built in 1547-48 are found some of the basic architectural ingredients which were to be developed to great excellence in Humayun's Tomb. The structure follows the pattern of the Lodi tombs.

Afsarwala Tomb inside Arab ki Sarai complex.

Isa Khan's Tomb.

Gurudwara Damdama Sahib

24 MAP 23C5 On the northeast of Humayun's Tomb is the white building of Gurudwara Damdama Sahib, a typical Sikh shrine.

174

Qutb Minar.

Major Sights

1 Quwwatul Islam Masjid
2 Iron Pillar
3 Qutb Minar
4 Tomb of Iltutmish
5 Alai Darwaza
6 Bhulbhulaiyan (Adham Khan's Tomb)
7 Gandak ki Baoli
8 Jogmaya Mandir
9 Dargah of Qutbuddin Bakhtiyar Kaki
10 Hathi Gate (of Zafar Mahal)
11 Hauz-i-Shamsi
12 Jamali Kamali Masjid and Tomb
13 Jain Mandir Dada Bari
14 Madhi Masjid
15 Ahinsa Sthal
16 Chhatarpur Temple

St. John's Church in Mehrauli, an early 20th century building with a Mughal gateway and a Hindu temple shikhar.

Qutb Minar AND Mehrauli

The picturesque area around the Qutb complex and Mehrauli, where the rocky outspur of the Aravalli Ridge is scattered with ruins, is the site of the oldest of Delhi's many cities. Here one can see the ramparts of Qila Rai Pithora, the city built by the Rajput king, Prithviraj Chauhan. Prithviraj expanded Lalkot, the citadel of another Rajput clan, the Tomars, who moved here from Surajkund. The road-pierced walls of Qila Rai Pithora can be seen by anyone approaching Qutb Minar from Aurobindo Marg. Mehrauli is dominated by the Qutb, a star destination of any visitor to Delhi.

Jahaz Mahal.

In the late 18th century, the Mughal emperors, enticed by the cool and fresh air of Mehrauli, used it as a summer retreat. When a British Resident was appointed at the Mughal court, he and his officials also discovered the pleasant charms of Mehrauli and converted the tombs into weekend retreats.

After 1857, the British sold off the *havelis* of the Muslim royalty and nobility to the traders of Delhi, and Mehrauli became a *mandi* or a market town for the agricultural hinterland. The agricultural land has now been swallowed by palatial 'farm houses' of Delhi's rich and famous and the narrow bazaar lanes of Mehrauli are today congested with scooters and trucks. But some of the erstwhile charm of Mehrauli can still be discovered if you probe a little deeper and are prepared for a long walk.

Qutb Minar with Quwwatul Islam Masjid in the foreground.

Qutb Complex

1   Quwwatul Islam Masjid
2   Iron Pillar
3   Qutb Minar
4   Alai Darwaza
5   Imam Zamin's Tomb
6   Tomb of Iltutmish
7   Alai Minar

The dome over the gateway to Quwwatul Islam Masjid.

The richly ornamented columns of Quwwatul Islam Masjid.

Quwwatul Islam Masjid

⬛ MAP 40D2 Sultan Qutbuddin's mosque, Quwwatul Islam or Might of Islam (1192-1198), within the Qutb complex, is the earliest extant mosque in north India. Passing through the main gateway, you find yourself standing under an intricately carved temple ceiling with richly ornamented pillars on both sides. These were taken from 27 Hindu temples of Qila Rai Pithora, as recorded by Qutbuddin in an inscription on the main eastern entrance. Some of the pillars with motifs of bells and garlands are still resplendent in their pristine glory.

The small attractive tomb of Imam Zamim who came to India from Turkestan during the reign of Sikander Lodi (1488-1517). The Imam was said to have been an important functionary at the Quwwatul Islam Masjid.

Details of carvings on the columns of Quwwatul Islam Masjid.

The Iron Pillar draws hundreds of visitors because of the popular belief that if you encircle the pillar with your arms behind you, your wishes will come true!

Iron Pillar

2 MAP 40D2 The Iron Pillar bears a Sanskrit inscription which records that it was set up as a *dhvaja stambha* (flagpole) of a Vishnu temple of the 4th-5th century AD. A deep hole on the top of the pillar indicates that an additional member was fitted into it. No one really knows how the Iron Pillar got here. However, what is really remarkable about this 7.2 metre tall pillar is that it has

Qutb Minar

3 MAP 40D2 Qutb Minar was built to celebrate the victory of Mohammed Ghori over the Rajputs in 1192, and erected by his viceroy, Qutbuddin Aibak (1192-98), the first sultan of the Slave dynasty (so called because the sultans had been royal slaves).

Qutb Minar towers just outside the central courtyard of Quwwatul Islam Masjid, and following the Arabic tradition, it was probably meant to function as a *minar*, for the use of the *muezzin* to call the faithful to prayer. But surely no *muezzin* could expect to be heard from a height of 72.5 metres on the top floor of Qutb Minar, even if he were to climb the 379 steps each time. The Minar was visualised as something more : a symbol of the military might of the Turko-Afghan Slave dynasty, and the *qutb* or pole of justice and Islam.

The first storey of Qutb Minar was completed during Qutbuddin's lifetime, while the next three storeys were added by his son-in-law and successor, Iltutmish. When lightning knocked off the topmost floor in 1368, Firoz Shah Tughlaq restored it and added two floors, which introduced white marble in the otherwise red and buff sandstone exterior. The circular tower with its pronounced taper to a narrow point, which increases the illusion of height, has a base diameter of 14.3 metres, while the top floor measures 2.7 metres in diameter.

In early 19th century, an earthquake destroyed the crowning cupola. An English engineer, Major Smith, replaced it, but it looked so out of place that it was removed on the orders of Governor-General Hardinge. It now stands on the lawns of the Qutb complex and has acquired the sobriquet Smith's Folly.

The tomb of Iltutmish is now bereft of its dome. It must have fallen because the local masons were not skilled in the technique of building domes. However, in the upper corners are the remains of supports which once held the dome.

Tomb of Iltutmish

4 MAP 40D2 The tomb of Iltutmish (1211-36), son-in-law and successor of Qutbuddin Aibak, was built in 1235, and has an exquisite sculptural character. It has inscriptions from the Qoran on its walls which have been delicately carved giving the appearance of fine lacework in stone.

The three niches of the tomb of Iltutmish facing the entrance. The central one in highly polished marble is the mihrab.

Alai Darwaza

5 MAP 40D3 By the time Alai Darwaza was built by Alauddin Khilji in 1311, Indian workmen had mastered the art of constructing the dome. By a system of squinches (a series of arched brackets), the square chamber was converted first into an octagon and then a circle, on which the round dome could solidly sit.

Alauddin's celebrated gateway to the Quwwatul Islam Masjid, built of red sandstone, is 17.2 metre square, with arched openings on all sides. It is profusely carved with inscriptions in the Naksh script, and has other decorative details in red sandstone and white marble.

The patterned surface of Qutb Minar creates an exquisite play of light and shade.

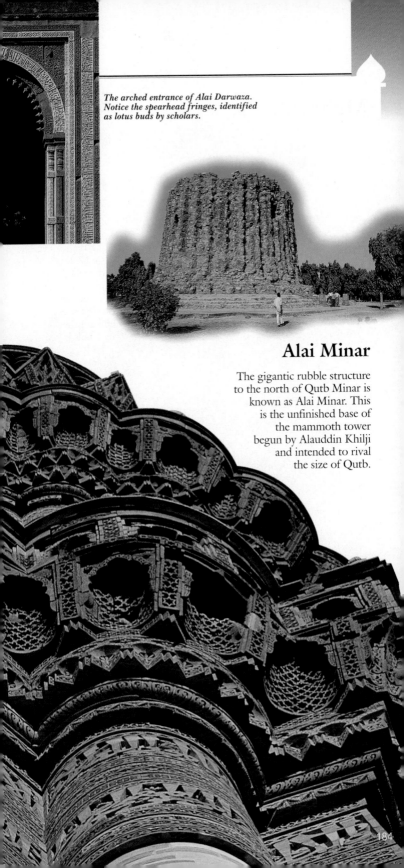

The arched entrance of Alai Darwaza. Notice the spearhead fringes, identified as lotus buds by scholars.

Alai Minar

The gigantic rubble structure to the north of Qutb Minar is known as Alai Minar. This is the unfinished base of the mammoth tower begun by Alauddin Khilji and intended to rival the size of Qutb.

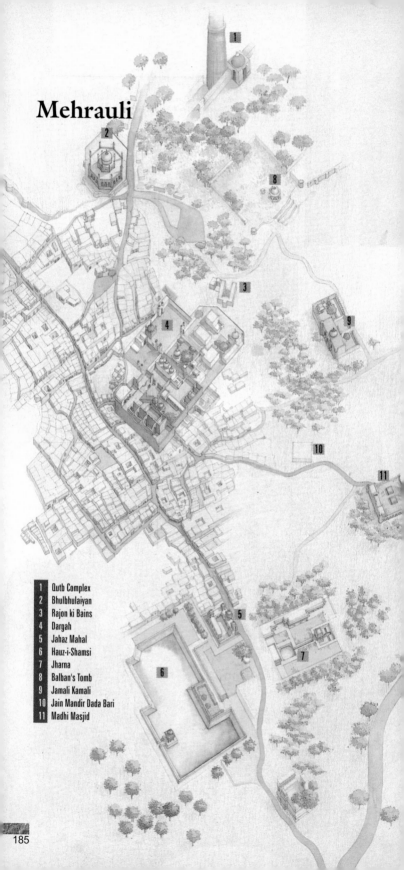

Mehrauli

1   Qutb Complex
2   Bhulbhulaiyan
3   Rajon ki Bains
4   Dargah
5   Jahaz Mahal
6   Hauz-i-Shamsi
7   Jharna
8   Balban's Tomb
9   Jamali Kamali
10   Jain Mandir Dada Bari
11   Madhi Masjid

Bhulbhulaiyan.

Bhulbhulaiyan

6 MAP 40D3 As you enter Mehrauli village, on the right, is the octagonal tomb of Adham Khan, locally known as Bhulbhulaiyan because of the labyrinthine maze inside. It stands on the ramparts of Lalkot, and from the roof towards the rear there is a good view of the walls of this first citadel of Delhi.

Adham Khan and his mother Maham Anga, a wet nurse of Emperor Akbar, were jealous of the influence of Atgah Khan, the husband of another of Akbar's wet nurses and had him murdered. Akbar, in a fit of fury, had Adham Khan flung from the ramparts of Agra Fort, not once, but twice. His grieving mother joined her son soon after and, in penitence, Akbar built this tomb for them in 1562.

An Englishman called Blake, of the Bengal Civil Service, converted this tomb into his residence in the 1830s and removed the grave to make way for his dining table. To this desecration was attributed his sorry end, for he died soon after. Adham Khan's ghost seems to have left other British officials alone for the tomb was later used as a rest house for many years.

Baolis (step wells)

Rajon ki Bains, an early 16th century step well.

7 MAP 40D3 Across the road, a lane to the left leads to Gandak ki Baoli, a five-tiered step well built in the 13th century. Its water comes from a *gandak* (sulphur) spring. A dirt track leads to Rajon ki Bains, a much larger step well, built during the time of Sikander Lodi.

Jogmaya Mandir

8 MAP 40D2 The lane to Jogmaya Mandir is on the right as you enter Mehrauli. It is a modern building within a walled compound built on the site of an ancient *yogini* (semi-divine females) temple. In fact, a 12th century Jain text refers to Delhi as Yoginipura.

Dargah of Qutbuddin Bakhtiyar Kaki

9 **MAP 40D4** Opposite Gandak ki Baoli, a lane turns right and brings you to the *dargah* (shrine) of the Sufi saint, Khwaja Qutbuddin Bakhtiyar Kaki. There are many graves within this *dargah* complex. The graves of the later Mughal emperors, Bahadur Shah I, Shah Alam and Akbar II are in an adjacent marble enclosure.

One can glimpse through the marble *jaali* screens the grave of Khwaja Sahib. Only men may enter it and see the rather garish marble and mirror studded domed pavilion built over the simple grave only fifty years ago. In the 19th century, an Englishwoman on being told that women may not go inside, naively concluded that 'this worthy Musulman must have been crossed in love'.

On the marble *jaalis* surrounding Khwaja Sahib's grave there are many coloured threads tied by pilgrims – both Hindu and Muslim – to mark a wish that they have made. If their wish is fulfilled they will return to the shrine to untie the thread.

Moti Masjid is to the left of the *dargah's* Ajmere Gate. It is a small mosque for private prayer built by Aurangzeb's son, Bahadur Shah I in 1709, in imitation of his father's grander Moti Masjid in Red Fort *(see: Shahjahanabad, p. 145)*.

Hathi Gate

10 MAP 40D4 A few yards from the *dargah* is the tall and graceful Hathi Gate (*hathi* - elephant) added by the last Mughal emperor, Bahadur Shah Zafar, to the summer palace of his father, Akbar II. This magnificent red sandstone gate with the curved Bengal roof, finely carved *jharoka* windows and marble inlay is as fitting a legacy as his more famous Urdu *ghazals* which continue to be popular. Unfortunately, the palace, Zafar Mahal, has been converted into houses and shops, and has lost its grandeur.

Hauz-i-Shamsi

11 MAP 39C5 On the southern end of Mehrauli, after the narrow crowded lanes of the bazaar, is Hauz-i-Shamsi, a reservoir built by Iltutmish in 1230. It was considered a sacred place and visited by fakirs and mystics. Recently, a park has been laid out around Hauz-i-Shamsi.

Jahaz Mahal (*jahaz* - ship) is on the banks of Hauz-i-Shamsi. It is an unusual building with blue-tiled *chhattris*. It probably gets its name because it is located on the banks of the Hauz. Stylistically, it belongs to the Lodi period (mid 14th to mid 15th century).

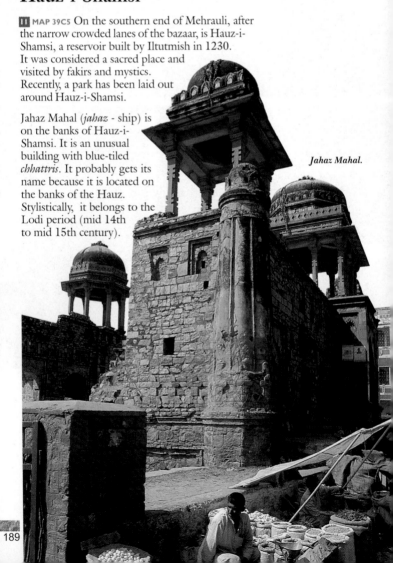

Jahaz Mahal.

At the Hauz-i-Shamsi.

Mehrauli has its own annual festival, *Phoolwalon ki Sair* (flower-sellers' walk). Large *pankhas* or fans made of flowers are ceremonially presented at the *dargah* and at the Hindu Jogmaya Mandir. This old festival was revived after 1947 by Prime Minister Jawaharlal Nehru because it symbolised the traditional ties binding Hindus and Muslims.

Flower bazaar at Mehrauli.

The ornate interiors of the tomb of Jamali Kamali.

Jamali Kamali

12 MAP 40E3 The southern end of Mehrauli is dotted with a number of monuments. Going from Qutb Minar, the first on the right is a dilapidated rubble structure, which is the tomb of Balban (died 1287), the last of the major Slave dynasty sultans.

Jamali Kamali Masjid.

The tomb of Jamali Kamali lies immediately to the north of the masjid. It has a flat roof and its ceilings and walls are highly ornamented with coloured tiles and patterns in painted plaster.

The gravelled path to the right brings you to Jamali Kamali Masjid and Tomb set within a beautiful park. The mosque's simple lines give it an air of elegance and quiet contemplation. Through a door on the right lies the small chamber in which Jamali and Kamali are buried. Jamali was the *nom de plume* of Sheikh Fazlullah, a saint and poet who was a favourite of Sultan Sikander Lodi and Emperor Humayun, but no one really knows who Kamali was. The tomb chamber is usually closed to the public.

Jain Mandir Dada Bari

13 MAP 40D4 Coming back to the main road, a little further down on the right is the turning to Jain Mandir Dada Bari, which is a richly ornamented, modern marble building. The *samadhi* of Guru Jinchanda Suruswarji Maharaj within the complex is said to be 800 years old.

Jain Mandir Dada Bari.

Madhi Masjid

Madhi Masjid

14 MAP 40D5 Coming out, on the right side of the narrow lane is Madhi Masjid. The courtyard is enclosed by strong walls with turrets in each corner giving the mosque the appearance of a miniature fortress. Stylistically this mosque appears to be an early Mughal building.

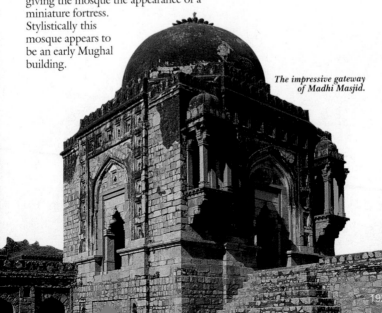

The impressive gateway of Madhi Masjid.

Ahinsa Sthal

15 MAP 40E3 As you reach the main Mehrauli Road, on the other side, on top of a small hill is the large statue of Mahavir which was put up in the 1980s on what used to be the Metcalfe Battery, a small lighthouse erected by Thomas Metcalfe in the nineteenth century. The area around the statue has been made into a park and is called Ahinsa Sthal or area of peace.

Chhatarpur Temple

16 The popular Hindu temples at Chhatarpur are less than 4 km from Qutb Minar. The main temple is dedicated to goddess Durga. What modern Hindu temples have lost in style and grandeur, they have attempted to recreate through ostentation – the Chhatarpur temples, like other modern Hindu temples are massive structures with copious use of white marble.

Sultan Ghari's Tomb

On the road from Andheria More to Delhi Airport, half way down Vasant Kunj, just beyond the Spinal Injuries Centre, is a narrow lane leading to Sultan Ghari, the tomb built by Iltutmish in 1231 for his son Nasiruddin who died waging wars for his father. Though some miles away from the Qutb complex, Sultan Ghari is certainly worth a visit. It is one of the first funerary monuments built by Islamic rulers in India. As with the Quwwatul Islam Masjid, there are many architectural elements in Sultan Ghari which are taken from earlier Hindu temples. The octagonal tomb chamber is housed under a rubble-built platform. Approached from the raised courtyard, the tomb chamber assumes the character of a crypt (*ghar*). With massive walls and domed bastions on the corners, Sultan Ghari looks more like a fortress than a tomb from outside.

The fortified tomb of Sultan Ghari.

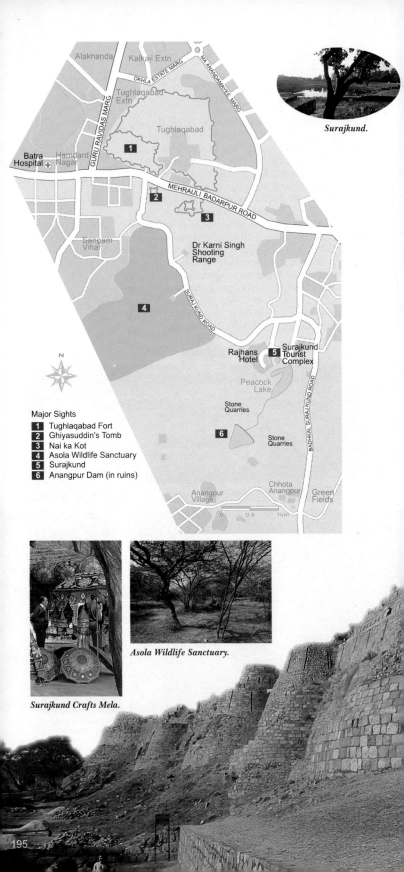

Surajkund.

Major Sights

1. Tughlaqabad Fort
2. Ghiyasuddin's Tomb
3. Nai ka Kot
4. Asola Wildlife Sanctuary
5. Surajkund
6. Anangpur Dam (in ruins)

Surajkund Crafts Mela.

Asola Wildlife Sanctuary.

Tughlaqabad
TO Surajkund

On the southeastern edge of Delhi lies the eerie
remains of the sprawling Tughlaqabad Fort, once
an impregnable city, built by Sultan Ghiyasuddin
Tughlaq in 1321. According to local legend,
while travelling with the Khilji Sultan, in whose
army he was a commander, Ghiyasuddin said,
'O Master, it would be fitting if a city is built
here'. The Sultan mockingly replied, 'When you
become king, build it'. Later, Tughlaq seized the
throne and erected this architectural testimony of
his power on the rocky hills, from where he
could watch the fading horizons of the plains
of Delhi.

*The walls of
Tughlaqabad Fort.*

196

Tughlaqabad Fort

■ MAP 42E4 Tughlaqabad Fort stands on a high outcrop of rocks, with walls which reach to over 27 metres in places, stretching across a perimeter of almost 6.5 km. The sprawling fortress was built in less than four years to guard against the fierce attacks by Mongols from central Asia.

To enter the fortress one has to walk over a causeway which was originally supported by 27 arches, some of which are still visible. Inside, there is a huge depression towards the north, which was one of the tanks built to store rain water. Today, peacocks and partridges rummage in the wild undergrowth.

At the southern edge of the citadel, adjacent to the high three-tiered outer wall, is an escape route leading downwards and out of the fort. Do not try to enter this, because it could be dangerous. West of the main entrance are ruins of a palatial building, where once stood a thousand pillared hall. Further west, within the citadel, is a 15.5 metre deep water tank nicknamed *Jahannum ka Rasta* or the road to hell. Even the hordes of monkeys who inhabit the fort and its surroundings keep away from this tank!

Inside Tughlaqabad Fort the tallest structure is the Vijay Mandal or Victory Tower. This opens up an exceptional view of the fort walls and Tughlaqabad village. Vijay Mandal is not to be confused with Bijai Mandal built by Mohammed bin Tughlaq.

Tughlaqabad was fated to be abandoned soon after its construction. According to legend, Ghiyasuddin had been cursed by the Sufi saint, Nizamuddin Auliya, with whom he had quarrelled. Nizamuddin had prophesied that one day Tughlaqabad would be inhabited only by jackals and Gujjars, a nomadic tribe.

Ghiyasuddin died in 1325 when a pavilion erected in his honour crashed on him. The accident was allegedly engineered by his son, Mohammed. With Ghiyasuddin's death the short-lived glory of the bustling city also came to a tragic end.

Ghiyasuddin's Tomb

2 **MAP P42D6** Ghiyasuddin's Tomb is south of the main fortress and was originally separated from it by a huge water body, but today it is across a very busy road.

The tomb itself symbolises the turbulence and uncertainty of the times. Its grandeur lies in the expression of strength of its sloping walls. It is an excellent example of a warrior's tomb, distinctly different from the garden tombs built by the Lodis and the Mughals in the subsequent centuries.

On coming out from Tughlaqabad Fort, it is worthwhile to drive eastwards to get an idea of the vast dimension of this enormous fortress.

Ghiyasuddin's Tomb is clad in red sandstone and roofed with a white marble dome. It is an exquisite building with a striking mihrab. In the centre is the grave of the emperor, flanked by the graves of his wife and son.

Nai ka Kot

3 **MAP P42F6** The small fortress of Nai ka Kot (barber's fort) is about ten minutes drive away from Tughlaqabad. No one knows how Nai ka Kot got this name, but Ghiyasudddin is said to have stayed here while he was supervising the building of Tughlaqabad. To the west of Nai ka Kot are the ruins of the small fort of Adilabad built by Mohammed bin Tughlaq.

Asola Wildlife Sanctuary

4 Towards the west, immediately after Ghiyasuddin's Tomb, a road leads towards the south. This road is one of the most beautiful drives in Delhi with lush greenery and pink bougainvillea bushes on both sides. Along the road are the entrances to Dr. Karni Singh Shooting Range and Asola Wildlife Sanctuary which covers an area of 26 sq km. Though not much wildlife exists in Asola, the sanctuary is full of all kinds of birds and smaller animals.

Surajkund

5 Further along the road, just beyond the Delhi-Haryana border, set amidst the barren and rocky landscape, is Surajkund. It is an ancient water tank which gets its name from a temple of the sun god believed to have existed here. It is also the site of the oldest city of Delhi, built in early 11th century by the Tomar Rajput, Surajpal. This city was probably occupied for a century before the Tomar kings moved northwards to build Lalkot *(see : Qutb Minar and Mehrauli, p.176)*.

The beauty of this large circular tank lies in its simplicity. The tank has stepped embankments and the receding water level is forever accessible. At one corner of the tank, there is a huge ramp, presumably to make access easy for elephants.

There is a man-made lake nearby, where boating is popular with tourists. It is an ideal place for a picnic, and is a favourite with Dilliwalas – away from the city and yet so close to it.

Surajkund is the site of an annual crafts fair held every February.

Ruins of Anangpur Dam

6 To the southwest of Surajkund are the ruins of a 18 metre high dam said to have been erected by Anangpal Tomar. This amazing structure made of rubble masonry is located beyond Anangpur village. The dam was used to control the flow of water till quite recently. In fact, during the rainy season a steady stream of water can be seen flowing out of the dam. If you climb the hill on the right-hand side of the bund, Surajkund lake can be seen at a distance. On the hill you can also see the scattered remains of an old canopy dating to Anangpal Tomar's time.

Through Anangpur village.

To get to Anangpur, you have to go south on the Badhkal-Surajkund Road and take a right turn at Anangpur village. Follow the village road to a small bus stand and then turn right through farmland, which could be rather slushy during the monsoons. It is a 15 minute walk over rocky terrain to the dam, recommended only for the adventurous. For directions to the bund, ask the local cowherds.

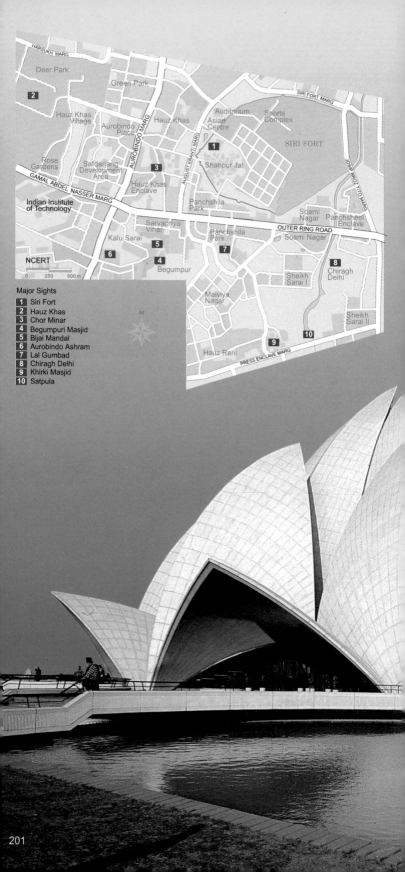

Deer Park

Green Park

SIRI FORT MARG

2

Hauz Khas Village

Aurobindo Place

Hauz Khas

Auditorium
Asiad
Centre

Sports
Complex

SIRI FORT

1

Shahpur Jat

JOSIP BROZ TITO MARG

Rose
Gardens

Safdarjang
Development
Area

3

AUROBINDO MARG

Hauz Khas
Enclave

AUGUST KRANTI MARG

Panchshila
Park

GAMAL ABDEL NASSER MARG

Indian Institute
of Technology

Sarvapriya
Vihar

Panchshila
Park

Soami
Nagar

Panchsheel
Enclave

OUTER RING ROAD

Soami Nagar

Kalu Sarai

5

7

NCERT

6

4

Begumpur

Malviya
Nagar

Sheikh
Sarai I

Chiragh
Delhi

8

0   250   500 m

10

9

Sheikh
Sarai II

Hauz Rani

PRESS ENCLAVE MARG

Major Sights

1 Siri Fort
2 Hauz Khas
3 Chor Minar
4 Begumpuri Masjid
5 Bijai Mandal
6 Aurobindo Ashram
7 Lal Gumbad
8 Chiragh Delhi
9 Khirki Masjid
10 Satpula

N

Hauz Khas
Lotus Temple

In south Delhi, scattered among Nehru Place and other commercial complexes, upmarket shopping malls and posh residential colonies, are remains of what were once flourishing cities of early medieval times. Many of these monuments were architectural landmarks during their times but are now poor shadows of their earlier glory. As you move through an overwhelmingly modern landscape, you will actually traverse layers of historical time and of successive empires.

Siri Fort

1 MAP 35C3 A few outer walls are all that remain of Siri, the city built in 1303 by Sultan Alauddin Khilji, north of Mehrauli. The fragmented ruins of Siri can be seen in sections near Siri Fort Auditorium MAP 35A2, most of it having disappeared or been devoured by real estate development. Some old structures can be spotted in Shahpur Jat village MAP 35A3, further along the road.

Hauz Khas

2 MAP 33C2 The south Delhi neighbourhood of Hauz Khas (royal tank) gets its name from the tank which Sultan Alauddin Khilji excavated in 1300, to supply water to his new city of Siri. Fifty years later, Firoz Shah Tughlaq repaired the tank and established a *madarsa* or college on its banks and also built the enclosure for his own tomb.

It is difficult for the contemporary visitor to comprehend the layout of the college buildings but medieval Islamic education was centred around small group discussions while sitting on the floor, which were said to be covered with 'carpets from Shiraz and Damascus'. The long pillared halls were the lecture rooms and the small cells were probably assigned to the holy men.

The austere tomb of Firoz Shah Tughlaq is next to the madarsa complex. It is a simple square room bare of the painted plaster which enlivened the interiors of many other tombs. The Sultan who built the city of Firozabad next to the river Yamuna, said of himself, 'the great gift that God has bestowed on me is the desire to erect public buildings'.

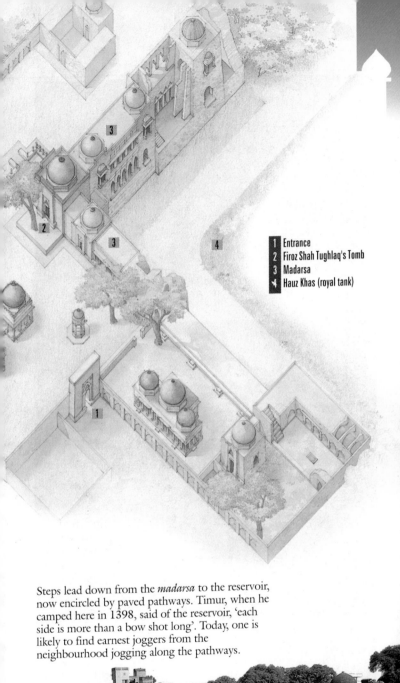

1 Entrance
2 Firoz Shah Tughlaq's Tomb
3 Madarsa
4 Hauz Khas (royal tank)

Steps lead down from the *madarsa* to the reservoir,
now encircled by paved pathways. Timur, when he
camped here in 1398, said of the reservoir, 'each
side is more than a bow shot long'. Today, one is
likely to find earnest joggers from the
neighbourhood jogging along the pathways.

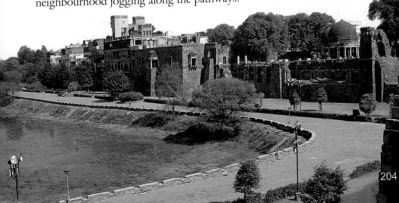

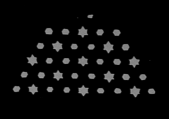

From the tank there is a beautiful view of latticed windows and projecting balconies. Once upon a time it was surrounded by the Tarab Abad, where the musicians and singers lived. In recent years the viewer is confounded by the strange jumble of buildings along the western bank - the shops and restaurants which have made the old village an elite shopping centre, its architectural metaphors as eclectic as its conception.

Hauz Khas Village

MAP 33C2 Inhabitants of this 'urban
village' no longer sit out-of-doors on
their string cots, chatting and
smoking *hookahs*, but the mandatory
buffaloes and cows are around for
authenticity! The shops sell silks and
brocades that would satisfy the
richest medieval sultan and
ethnic hand-blocked, vegetable-
dyed, mirror-worked and
embroidered clothes, transformed
by designers beyond the dreams of
any village girl. In Hauz Khas
village, aggressive ethnicity does not
always match rural rusticity. A mud
and dung plastered shop sells the
collections of India's famous haute
couture designers with prices that
are definitely exorbitant
(*see: Where to Shop*).

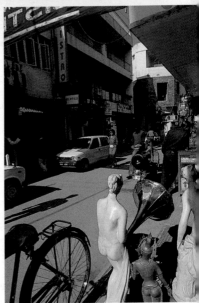

Chor Minar

3 MAP 34E3 Just off Aurobindo Marg,
in Hauz Khas Enclave is Chor
Minar or Thieves' Tower which was
built during the Khilji period. This
is a rubble-built tapering tower set
on a platform with a staircase inside.
There are holes sunk in the walls
where allegedly severed heads of
criminals were displayed as a
deterrent, a practice also known in
medieval Europe.

Begumpuri Masjid

4 MAP 34E5 The remains of the stone walls of Jahanpanah, the grand capital of Sultan Mohammed bin Tughlaq (1325-1351), son of Ghiyasuddin Tughlaq who built Tughlaqabad, have almost entirely been destroyed as the expanding suburbs of south Delhi continue to encroach upon traces of the past. The medieval walls were enormously thick at places, with rooms built into them to store provisions and war equipment. Stray portions can still be seen at Satpula, near Khirki village. Jahanpanah was said to be larger than the old *shahar* (city), Qutb Dilli, and to have had 13 gates.

Begumpuri Masjid stood at the centre of the Sultan's new capital. The masjid had a distinct presence due to its elevated position and bold silhouettes. More than a place for prayer, it formed the locus of community life – it housed a *madarsa*, a treasury, and was a place for meeting and transacting business. Sultans often decreed that the city's grain market and bazaars be situated just outside the mosque's portals.

The masjid is raised on a high plinth, which allowed it to catch the breeze and escape the dust and noise of the city below. Its vast rectangular courtyard is a space totally at rest, conducive to contemplation.

Crowning the prayer hall is a large, pointed dome not visible from the ground level as it is masked by the tall portal. Forty-four smaller domes, some of which have fallen or are in a state of disrepair, crown the *riwaq* (cloister), all around the courtyard above the arcades, imparting to this mosque its unusual skyline Its majesty can best be appreciated from the heights of the Sultan's palace adjacent to it.

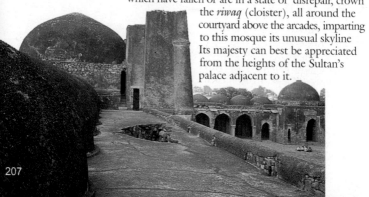

Bijai Mandal

5 MAP 34E5 Within walking distance of the Begumpuri Masjid, to the north, lie the ruins of the royal palace, known as Bijai Mandal. The Arab traveller, Ibn Batuta, also a *qazi* at the Sultan's court, describes the series of gates within the palace.

The palace had a hall where the Sultan, seated on a raised cushioned seat, placed on a white carpeted dias, held public audience and reviewed his troops. Ibn Batuta writes, 'They bring in 60 horses... with bridles and girths of black silk gilded fabric and some with the same in white.... Next, 50 elephants are brought in, adorned with silken and gold cloths, and have their ivory shod with iron for service in killing criminals.... Each elephant is trained to make obeisance to the Sultan and to incline their heads, and when they do so the chamberlains cry in a loud voice, *Bismillah!*' (*The Travels of Ibn Batuta : 1325-1354*, translated by H.A.R. Gibb, Cambridge, 1958).

Standing atop Bijai Mandal, one can only fantasise about the splendour and drama once witnessed here. The kaleidoscopic skyline of the modern city spreads out before you, where the dome-lined Begumpuri Masjid, Qutb Minar, the lotus-shaped Baha'i House of Worship and the marble dome of Humayun's Tomb coexist with the congested towers of Nehru Place and the dense masses of south Delhi's housing complexes.

Lal Gumbad

7 MAP 35A5 About a kilometre and half from the Bijai Mandal, in Malviya Nagar, is an isolated tomb known as Lal Gumbad. This is possibly the burial chamber of the Sufi saint, Kabiruddin Auliya, a disciple of Sheikh Roshan Chiragh Dehlvi. The severity of its facade is relieved by the elegant tall portal surmounted by a *jaali* that evokes the memory of the Alai Darwaza in the Qutb complex.

Aurobindo Ashram

6 MAP 34D5 A branch of the main Ashram at Pondicherry, Aurobindo Ashram is a centre for meditation and yoga. The Ashram shop retails handmade paper, incense sticks and other items made with natural ingredients.

Chiragh Dehlvi's *Dargah*

8 MAP 35C5
Nasiruddin Mohammed (died 1356) also known as Roshan Chiragh Dehlvi (Lamp of Delhi) was a disciple of Nizamuddin Auliya, whom he succeeded as the head of the Chishti sect. The village, Chiragh Delhi, now an urban settlement, grew around his *dargah*. Some *chhattris* and a rather beautiful gateway are all that survive. However, these are encompassed by shops and houses.

Khirki Masjid

9 MAP 35B6 Jahanpanah continued as the capital city for about three years under Mohammed bin Tughlaq's successor, Firoz Shah Tughlaq, who built another mosque about two kilometres south of Begumpuri Masjid in the village of Khirki. Khirki Masjid, as it has come to be known, is just off Press Enclave Road. It is now engulfed by the mushrooming structures of the modern village.

Khirki Masjid rests on an elevated plinth. *Jaalis* in the arched windows of the upper storey of the mosque allow for effective cross ventilation and break the light into patterned forms. The inner courtyards reveal another interesting experiment - two covered passages traverse it on both axes, intersecting each other at right angles in the centre, thus dividing the courtyard into four square courts. This was perhaps in response to the intense heat of north India and intended to provide shade.

Khirki Masjid

Satpula

10 **MAP 35C6** Satpula embankment is about half a kilometre east of Khirki village. Forming part of the enclosure wall of Jahanpanah, this magnificent structure was a sluice gate thrown across a rivulet to control its flow and retain a sheet of water within the city walls. As its name suggests, the embankment is made up of seven arches and contains a mechanism whose grooves suggest a system of sliding shutters for regulating the level of water.

Water was scarce in medieval south Delhi, given the distance from the Yamuna. During the Tughlaq period, Hauz Rani, a reservoir predating the Sultanate, was tapped as the main source of water for the growing population of Jahanpanah.

Satpula is fast becoming inaccessible to the interested visitor as its surroundings are degenerating into a garbage dump.

Satpula.

Moth ki Masjid

MAP 29B6 The 16th century Moth ki Masjid, also known as Masjid Moth, is hidden behind the concrete jungles of South Extension Part II. The easiest way to get to this secluded mosque would be from Khel Gaon Marg, through the residential neighbourhood of Uday Park **MAP 29B6**. Now decaying, the three-domed mosque assumes an elegance which is reflected in its red sandstone gate and its prayer chamber.

Moth ki Masjid.

There is an interesting story associated with Moth ki Masjid. While on a walk with his minister, Mian Buhwa, Sultan Sikander Lodi (1488-1517) picked up a grain of moth (a kind of lentil) and presented it to his minister. Mian Buhwa, honoured by the gift, planted the seed, which in time, flourished and multiplied. When he had earned enough from this miraculous crop, he built a masjid, which he called Moth ki Masjid.

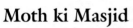

Kalkaji Mandir

MAP 38D3 Four kilometres from the Chirag Delhi flyover, beyond Nehru Place, is the Hindu temple of Kalka Devi. Thousands of pilgrims throng the temple, especially in October during the nine days of Navaratrey, when a large *mela* is held here (*see: Festivals*).

The oldest portion of the building dates to 1764. Raja Kedarnath, Peshkar of Emperor Akbar II, made additions to the original structure in the mid 19th century. A substantial part of the present building is not more than 50 years old. It does not express any aesthetic quality and is covered with marble and granite tiles as is common with most modern Hindu temples. In the 19th and early 20th centuries many merchants and bankers of Delhi constructed *dharamshalas* (rest houses for pilgrims) near the temple.

According to local legend, long years ago a farmer was surprised to find that his cow had stopped giving milk. So he trailed the cow and discovered that she gave all her milk to the goddess Kalkaji. He is said to have built the temple in her honour and bathed her in milk everyday.

Lotus Temple

MAP 38D2 Almost opposite Kalkaji Mandir is the Baha'i House of Worship, popularly called Lotus Temple. The petals are made of concrete clad with white marble which gives freshness and transparency to its surface. In subtle contrast, local red sandstone has been used for the walkways and stairs. Around the blooming petals, there are nine pools of water, which light up in natural light. The idea is to create an illusion of a lotus floating on water.

Fariburz Sahba, the architect, explained that by designing the Lotus Temple he had not discovered anything new. 'Brahma was born in a lotus, Buddha's Boddhisatva was born in a lotus, in Jainism the lotus is a crucial symbol, as it is in Islam; the Taj Mahal is, after all, a bud of the lotus… The lotus is part of the dream of all cultures'.

Major Sights

1. Kashmere Gate
2. Residency/Delhi College of Engineering
3. St. James Church
4. Tilak Park
5. Qudsia Bagh
6. Mother Teresa's Children's Home
7. Metcalfe House
8. Old Secretariat
9. Flagstaff Tower
10. Pir Ghaib
11. Ashoka Pillar
12. Mutiny Memorial
13. Roshanara Garden
14. Vice-Chancellor's Office
15. St. Stephen's College
16. Gurudwara Majnu ka Tila

Gurudwara Majnu ka Tila.

Indraprastha College.

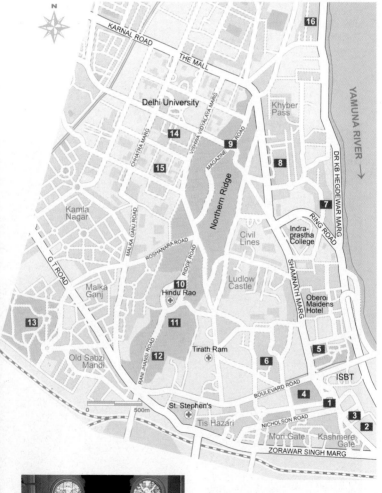

Stained glass windows inside St. James Church.

Kashmere Gate
TO Coronation
Memorial

The walls of Shahjahanabad beyond Kashmere Gate.

Mughal Delhi stretched well beyond the walled city of Shahjahanabad. It included the residential area of Paharganj and the market of Sabzi Mandi in the west, while the area north of the walls, as far as Wazirpur and Azadpur, contained gardens and pavilions of the nobles. This was the extent of Delhi when the British arrived as a colonial force in 1803 after defeating the Marathas, led by a French commander, at the Battle of Patparganj. This event has been commemorated in a memorial column in what is now the NOIDA Golf Course.

Early 19th century Delhi saw some wonderfully individualistic British characters, far from the administration in Calcutta and its attendant conventions and gossip. They settled in the Kashmere Gate area of Delhi which had earlier accommodated Mughal palaces and gardens, or they built themselves large estates north of Shahjahanabad. After 1857, the whole complexion of Delhi changed. The British area, known as Civil Lines, became more populated, but it was and still is comparatively green and quiet. Kashmere Gate became the fashionable and commercial centre of Delhi, a position it lost only after the building of New Delhi.

Kashmere Gate.

Kashmere Gate

I MAP 9BI When the British moved into Delhi in 1803 they found the walls of the city in a poor state of repair and after the siege by the Maratha Holkar in 1804, decided to reinforce the walls. Kashmere Gate was strengthened in 1835, an act the British must have regretted in 1857, when they had to blow up the Gate with gunpowder, killing some of their own forces. In 1965 a section of the wall around Kashmere Gate was demolished to allow faster movement of vehicular traffic.

Residency

2 MAP 9CI The building that was taken over by the British in 1803, to be used as the Residency, or official house of the Resident of the East India Company in Delhi, was known as Dara Shikoh's Library and once formed part of the palace of Dara Shikoh, the favourite son of Emperor Shahjahan. The British added a classical western facade around the original Mughal structure. Traces of the original building can still be seen at the rear and in the interior.

Shops in the Kashmere Gate area.

For many years the building has been part of Delhi College of Engineering. It was slated for demolition in the 1980s but was saved due to the efforts of conservationists. It also houses an office of the Archaeological Survey of India.

Painter at work on film hoardings.

The old Residency.

St. James Church

3 MAP 9B1 Built by James Skinner and consecrated in 1836, St. James is the oldest surviving church in Delhi. James Skinner was the son of a Scottish father and a Rajput mother. He founded a troop of irregular cavalry known as Skinner's Horse which has now been absorbed in the Indian army.

St. James Church is of a western classical design with a Greek cross plan. Three of the arms of the cross have porticoes, while the eastern arm contains the altar. The central area of the church is covered by a dome which bears some resemblance to the dome of the Florence Cathedral by Brunelleschi.

Inside St. James Church.

In 1865 some restoration work was done on the church which had been badly damaged in 1857. Among other things, the original ball and cross over the dome, which was used for target practice in 1857, was replaced by the present ball and cross. The fine stained glass windows, which had been added in the 1860s, were restored in 1996. The grave of James Skinner is in front of the altar, while the graveyard of the Skinner family, with a number of interesting marble monuments, is to the north of the church.

The church is normally kept closed except for services on Sundays, but it can be opened on request.

Detail of stained glass window inside St. James Church.

St. James Church

Behind St. James Church, it is possible to see a large building with a dome, surrounded by newer buildings, which is at present an administrative office of the Indian Railways. This was once the home of William Fraser, who came to Delhi in 1805, and lived a life more Indian than British. He was not popular with his compatriots in Delhi because of his dislike of British social life and his preference for his Indian friends. He was appointed Agent to the Governor General in 1823 and was Resident for a short while in 1828.

Later Fraser decided to build a house on the Ridge, north of the city walls. His was, almost certainly, the earliest British house on the Ridge.

Fraser was murdered in 1835 by the Nawab of Ferozepur because of a personal quarrel, and was buried in the St. James Church compound. After his death, his house on the Ridge was bought by Hindu Rao, a brother-in-law of Scindia of Gwalior. It later became a hospital for wealthy Europeans and is now a large government hospital, still known by the name of Hindu Rao.

William Fraser's house in Kashmere Gate.

218

Tilak Park

4 MAP 9A1 Outside Kashmere Gate is the Nicholson cemetery with its Gothic gateway, where John Nicholson, hero to the British for his part in the recapture of Delhi in September 1857, is buried. Opposite the cemetery is the Nicholson Garden, where once there was an elaborate bandstand. It has been renamed Tilak Park, and is surrounded by dense traffic as Delhi's Inter State Bus Terminus (ISBT) is just across the road.

Outside Inter State Bus Terminus.

Qudsia Bagh

5 MAP 4F6 This garden, north of Kashmere Gate, was built by Qudsia Begum, first the mistress and then the wife of the Mughal emperor, Mohammed Shah (1719-1748). The greater part of the garden was destroyed to make way for the Inter State Bus Terminus and the adjacent tourist camp site. What remains of Qudsia Bagh is quiet and rather beautiful. There is an attractive gateway and a couple of pavilions in carved red sandstone. Many of the structures in the garden are now used by the Masonic Lodge.

Oberoi Maidens Hotel

MAP 4E5 One of the earliest hotels in the Civil Lines area was the Maidens Hotel which was built as a single storey structure in 1900. Edwin Lutyens stayed in this hotel when he first came to Delhi to decide on the site for the new capital of British India. A white plastered classical building, it is now called Oberoi Maidens, and continues to breathe the air of the Raj.

Metcalfe House

7 **MAP 4F3** Thomas Theophilus Metcalfe was unlike most of the early British in Delhi. He sold his family estates in England and brought all his possessions to Delhi where he built an extensive house on a thousand acres of land on the Ridge, just north of the city walls. His daughter Emily wrote a journal of her life in Delhi, which was edited by M.M. Kaye and published with the title, *The Golden Calm*. The book also contains a facsimile reproduction of an illustrated manuscript, the *Delhee Book*. Thomas Metcalfe was poisoned to death in 1853, possibly on the orders of Zeenat Mahal, the young wife of the Mughal emperor, Bahadur Shah Zafar, because he did not support the succession rights of her young son.

Metcalfe House was completely ransacked and left in ruins in 1857. It was rebuilt in 1913 with Gothic arches and is now used as a government office. It is not open to the public but one can see it on the left when leaving Delhi by the Delhi-Chandigarh bypass road.

Metcalfe House.

Mother Teresa's Home

6 **MAP 4D6** Run by the Missionaries of Charity this children's Home is situated in the Civil Lines, north of Qudsia Bagh. The way to the Home is through narrow roads but there are signs indicating the

Old Secretariat

8 **MAP 4E2** The old temporary Secretariat was designed by E. Montague Thomas, and built in only a few months in 1912. After the offices shifted to North and South blocks, it served as a government office. It now houses the offices of the Government of the National Capital Region of Delhi and the Delhi Assembly.

Flagstaff Tower

9 MAP 4D2 Flagstaff Tower, situated on the highest part of the Northern Ridge, was one of the first substantial buildings to be constructed by the British on the Ridge. It was probably built when the army cantonment was moved in 1828.

Ruins of Pir Ghaib.

Pir Ghaib

10 MAP 3C5 The remains of the hunting lodge of Firoz Shah Tughlaq on the Ridge known as Kushk-i-Shikar or Kushk Jahan Numa, built around 1630, is now known as Pir Ghaib (meaning disappearing saint). It is so called after a mystic who suddenly disappeared while meditating at the site. Some believe it was an observatory because of its height and also because of the hollow masonry cylinder through the floor and the roof, allowing the sky to be seen from the ground floor, but it could also have been a tower for viewing animals. Pir Ghaib is now in the grounds of the Hindu Rao Hospital.

There was an elaborate *baoli* nearby which also formed part of the same complex but very little of it remains, only a deep depression in the ground and a small portion of a stone arched construction.

Mutiny Memorial

12 MAP 3B6 Mutiny Memorial, the Gothic memorial to those British and Indian soldiers who were listed as killed, missing or wounded during 1857 was erected in 1863 on the Ridge, 200 metres south of Ashoka Pillar. The Indian soldiers listed were those who fought alongside the British and were not counted as mutineers. In its time, it was considered to be a very poor imitation of the Albert Memorial in London. Its only similarity is the mock Gothic effect of the detailing which is in red sandstone and marble. It now has a new plaque mentioning the fact that Indians died in 1857 fighting the first war of independence.

Ashoka Pillar

11 MAP 3C5 Firoz Shah Tughlaq erected an Ashoka Pillar in 1356 near Pir Ghaib. It was broken into five pieces in an explosion around 1713. Hindu Rao gave the pieces to the Asiatic Society of Bengal and the piece with the inscription was sawn off and sent to Calcutta. It was returned to Delhi and the whole column re-erected on its present platform in 1867. It is one of the original columns of Emperor Ashoka but is not in as good a condition as the one at Firoz Shah Kotla.

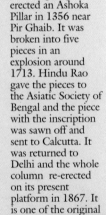

Mutiny Memorial, now called Ajitgarh.

Roshanara Garden and Club

13 **MAP 3A5** Emperor Shahjahan's younger daughter, Roshanara, built a pleasure garden and the enclosure for her own tomb, north of Shahjahanabad in 1650. When she died in 1671, she was buried here. The garden, at that time, was typical of other Mughal gardens and had a number of pavilions.

In 1875, the garden was modified by Colonel Cracroft, Commissioner of Delhi Division. He demolished all the buildings except the tomb, the east tank and the gateway. In 1923, a part of the garden was leased for a European club called Roshanara Club. The Club still exists but with wider membership and has a good cricket ground. The garden is quite well maintained but only the tomb pavilion is in a reasonable condition.

Sunday cricket at Roshanara Club.

Roshanara Begum's Tomb.

Vice-Chancellor's Office

14 **MAP 3C2** University of Delhi campus has some elegant early British buildings. The vice-chancellor's office in Delhi University was the original Circuit House or official guest house for British officers in the Civil Lines area. It was one of the buildings proposed to be used as the Viceroy's residence at the time the new city was being planned for the area north of Shahjahanabad. Incidentally, it was in a room in this building that Mountbatten, the last Viceroy of British India proposed to Edwina, the future Countess Mountbatten. There is a plaque in the room to commemorate the event.

The vice-chancellor's office in Delhi University remains an attractive building surrounded by beautiful gardens.

*The chapel at
St. Stephen's College.*

St. Stephen's College

15 MAP 3B2 When the new campus of the
University of Delhi was opened in Civil Lines,
St. Stephen's College moved to its new buildings
designed by Walter George in red brick and local
Delhi quartzite. It is one of the finest college
buildings in the campus.

The old building of St. Stephen's College, designed
by Samuel Swinton Jacob in 1891, now used by the
Election Commission, is in the Kashmere Gate area.

Majnu ka Tila

16 The gurudwara at Majnu ka Tila commemorates
the visit of the founder of the Sikh religion, Guru
Nanak, to Delhi in the 15th century. For
many years there was a small hutment on
the site which served as a gurudwara. In
the 1980s it was enlarged and elaborated
and is now in the typical style of Sikh
gurudwaras in Delhi – in white marble
with a cusped dome.

*Gurudwara Majnu
ka Tila.*

The area around the gurudwara is
inhabited by Tibetans who fled Tibet
after the Chinese aggression and came to
India with the Dalai Lama. The refugees were
moved here from a temporary camp in 1964. By
now, most of the houses are of brick and many are
two storeyed with shops on the ground floor.

There are also a number of
Buddhist temples.
The area is popular
with Delhi
University students
who come here to
eat and drink in the
many Tibetan
dhabas serving fairly
authentic Tibetan
food and *chaang*.

*Ornate icon inside a
Buddhist temple,
Majnu ka Tila.*

Coronation Memorial

MAP 5A1 Durbars had been held in Delhi by the British since 1877 when Queen Victoria was proclaimed Empress of India. Another Durbar in 1903 celebrated the accession of Edward VII. Both were held in the same area north of the Civil Lines, beyond Kingsway Camp. The same site was used for the Durbar of 1911 for the accession of George V at which the king was present. At this grand Durbar, he announced that the capital of India would be moved from Calcutta to Delhi.

The site for the new capital city originally envisaged was near the Durbar site and the foundation stone was laid accordingly. The stone was moved secretly at a later date and was embedded in the walls of the forecourt of the Secretariat. A memorial column was erected at the site, which has now been made into a refuge for the British statues which originally stood in Delhi and New Delhi. The area is popularly known as Coronation Memorial.

Coronation Memorial has the statue of King George V, which once stood under the Canopy near India Gate. The king is attired in the coronation robe he wore for the Durbar of 1911. King George is surrounded by other statues, including those of Lord Willingdon and Lord Hardinge, all standing on red sandstone plinths.

The statues and a few empty plinths are inside a neglected walled garden, about 5 km from Majnu ka Tila along the Ring Road.

Shalimar Bagh

Shalimar Bagh was built by Emperor Shahjahan in 1653. His son, Aurangzeb, was crowned here in 1658. After the British came to Delhi, it was used by the British Residents as a holiday retreat. A couple of pavilions set in a dry pool are all that remain of the Mughal garden. Today it lies hidden behind dull government housing estates, over 7 km from Majnu ka Tila.

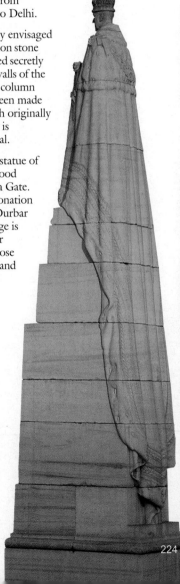

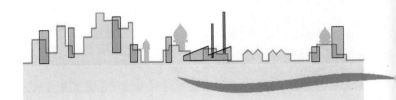

Arts and Entertainment

Museums

Art Galleries

Music, Dance, Theatre and Cinema

Sports

Children's Delhi

Pragati Maidan

Museums

National Museum

The National Museum has a remarkable collection of Indian art and sculpture which dates from the prehistoric era through the late medieval period. The nucleus of this priceless collection was formed from the exhibition of Indian art which was displayed at Burlington House, London, in 1947-48. On their return to India, the exhibits were displayed at the Durbar Hall in Rashtrapati Bhawan till they were moved to the present building in 1960. The rich and varied collection is spread over three spacious floors and at least one full day is required to see all the objects on display.

Begin on the ground floor with an exploration of the prehistoric age. In these galleries are displayed rare pieces from the Palaeolithic and successive periods. There are stone age tools as well as terracotta pieces from the later Chalcolithic period. There is a good collection of archaeological finds from the Indus Valley sites of Harappa and Mohenjodaro which include beautiful pieces of terracotta pottery from 2700 BC. The famous bronze dancing girl from Mohenjodaro, on display in this gallery, shows the high artistic and technical skills the people of this ancient civilisation had achieved. Another notable sculpture in this gallery is the elegant male torso from Harappa in red

Gautama Buddha in Gandhara style, 2nd-3rd century AD.

Janpath. ℂ 3019272.
Open 10 am to 5 pm.
Entry 50paise.

Film shows on art heritage of India weekdays at 2.30 pm, Saturdays and Sundays at 11.30 am, 2.30 pm, 4 pm. Free guided tours 10.30 am, 11.30 am, 12 noon, 2 pm, 3.30 pm. There is a library and sales counter on the ground floor.

Bronze dancing girl from Mohenjodaro, 2500 BC.

sandstone carved in a flowing, realistic style which anticipates later styles of Indian sculpture.

The next four galleries are a treasure house of sculptures in stone. The graceful busts from the Mauryan period (3rd century BC) and majestic sculptures of the Sunga period (2nd century BC) are displayed here. The high point of Indian sculptural art continues through the Gandhara period with its elegant stucco heads of exquisite beauty which show the influence of Hellenic art on Buddhist sculpture. Figures of Buddha stand like Roman senators in toga-like robes.

The change in sculptural styles as different dynasties rose and fell is visible as you walk through the ground floor galleries. The terracotta figures from the Gupta period (4th-6th century AD) move away from the uncluttered Hellenic lines and display a more ornamental style with full figures and doe-eyed female heads. We move on to the medieval period and encounter bejewelled stone figures from the Pala and Sena dynasties and carved lintels from Hampi in south India.

Kubera, god of wealth, in red sandstone, 2nd century AD.

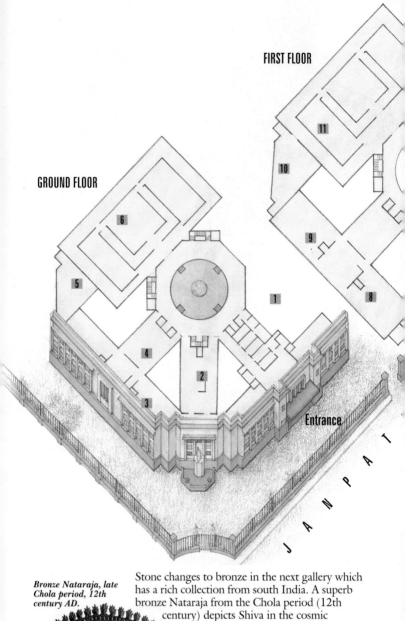

FIRST FLOOR

GROUND FLOOR

11

10

6

9

5

1

8

4

2

3

Entrance

J A N P A T

Bronze Nataraja, late Chola period, 12th century AD.

Stone changes to bronze in the next gallery which has a rich collection from south India. A superb bronze Nataraja from the Chola period (12th century) depicts Shiva in the cosmic dance pose. Do not miss the rare one of Kamdeva, the Hindu god of love, with his consort.

Also on the ground floor is a newly opened gallery of precious jewellery. The beaten gold armlets with their subtle designs from 2500 BC are amazingly contemporary. The Mughal jewellery, heavily decorated with huge emeralds, diamonds and pearls, are startling in contrast. This gallery has on display a poison ring decorated with precious stones, massive bejewelled belts, buckles from the Mughal era and solid gold ornaments from south India.

The first floor houses a varied collection of Indian
miniature paintings from different schools, Mughal,
Rajasthani, Pahari. An important series of paintings
is the Ragamala miniatures which are illustrations
of Indian musical notes and depict the mood of a
particular raga using images of women and nature.
There are beautiful palm leaf illustrations from
Bengal and Gujarat on display in the manuscript
section on this floor. The collection includes
Tulsidasa's *Ramcharitmanas* from the 17th century
in Devnagiri script.

The first floor also has on display a few excellent
Tanjore paintings on glass from south India and
some interesting paintings from the Company
School which was patronised by the British East
India Company. The Maritime Heritage Gallery set
up by the Indian Navy is also on this floor.

On the same floor is the Central Asian Antiquities
gallery with material collected during Sir Aurel
Stein's expeditions into Chinese Turkestan during
1901-1916. The dimly lit gallery has Buddhist
temple banners, clay figurines and Tibetan *tangkhas*,
large paintings on silk.

Do not miss the two rare engraved copper plates as
you enter the gallery which displays arms and
armour, the best gallery on the second floor. The
fabulous weapons on display seem more like works
of art than means of warfare. Some are elaborately
decorated, often with touches of gold, silver or
precious stones as befitting the status of a warrior.

Wooden images of Bhutas, or protective spirits, from coastal Karnataka.

Crafts Museum

Pragati Maidan, Bhairon Road.
☎ 3371817.
Open 10 am to 5 pm.

The museum shop sells beautiful handcrafted objects.

Opposite Purana Qila, off the busy Mathura Road, is one of the most interesting museums in India. Designed by Charles Correa, there is more to see in this museum than its impressive collection of folk and tribal arts, crafts and textiles. There is a village complex where you can study the architecture of village houses.

The museum galleries are located on the right as you enter the complex and on display are a fascinating variety of art and craft objects. Begin at the Tribal and Rural Craft Gallery which displays wooden figures of *bhutas,* carved in coastal Karnataka to honour dead ancestors. There are rare tribal bronzes from Madhya Pradesh and Orissa. An intriguing piece is a tiny bronze of a man being executed with an axe. Some of the tiny bronze figures of porcupines, crabs and tortoises from Orissa were part of a child bride's dowry. There are woodcarvings, pieces of head gear and masks and puppets from Nagaland.

The courtyard is dominated by a ceremonial chariot while the gallery on the left has a fine collection of lamps and incense burners used in worship. The smaller courtyard on the right has a domed wooden pigeon house with arches and lattice work panels.

Rudraksha bead necklace with gold pendant, 19th century Tamil Nadu.

Early 20th century painted hand fan from south India.

The Gallery of Courtly Crafts has festive bullock carts and a fabulous 19th century caparison for elephants embroidered with gold and silver threads. The interior of a Kathiawar mansion from 19th century Gujarat has been recreated in one corner. In the *haveli*'s cool interior, light filters through an open window on the roof. Intricately designed jewellery is on display in this gallery.

Move on to the textiles gallery, a mini museum by itself. The fine *chikan* work of Lucknow, embroidered *rumals* from Chamba, applique work from all over India, and from Andhra Pradesh, *kalamkari* pieces involving a special technique of printing with vegetable dyes using a *kalam* (reed). Also on display are old pieces of *phulkari* work from Punjab and *kantha* from West Bengal. You can admire exquisite saris from every corner of India in silks, cottons and brocades.

There is a reference section with about 15,000 objects which can be used by scholars, designers and craftspersons.

Gold leaf printed fabric from Rajasthan.

National Rail Museum

Shanti Path,
Chanakyapuri.
(6881816.
Open 9.30 am to 5.30 pm.
Entry Rs.5 (adult)
Rs.3 (child).

Set amidst a sprawling park, this museum is a must not just for train buffs but for everyone. A compact but informative indoor museum displays a range of interesting objects, but the main attractions are the old steam engines parked outside.

The line-up of old coaches includes the handsome Prince of Wales Saloon built in 1875 for the visit to India of the Prince of Wales, later King Edward VII for the Royal Durbar of 1876. Not to be outdone is the Maharaja of Mysore's saloon built in 1899 with its brocade covered chairs and an elegant rosewood bed. Another royal coach is the Maharaja of Baroda's saloon built in 1886. To enter the royal saloons you have to buy a ticket for Rs.50, but one can peer in through the windows for a good look.

In stark contrast are the simple carriages for ordinary people, goods and cattle. The Nilgiri coach built in 1914 for a hill journey is a spacious carriage with open windows which once had canvas flaps to keep the sun out.

A star attraction is the Fairy Queen, born in 1855 and considered to be one of the best preserved steam locomotive engines of her age. Amongst the other old steam engines is the beautiful EM 922 locomotive built in 1907 at the Glasgow North British Locomotive Works. This engine had the privilege of hauling VIP and royalty trains, changing its name each time to flatter the dignitary it carried, thus switching titles from Lord Clyde, to Roosevelt, to the Queen Empress herself.

Splendid interiors of a royal coach.

Children can take a ride on the toy train. It goes around the museum yard at a surprisingly high speed and does not allow close inspection of the various engines and carriages. On your way out do not miss the handsome Fire Engine displayed on the left, built in 1914 by John Morris and Sons, UK, for the Nizam of Hyderabad.

Tibet House

The small museum in Tibet House is a treasure house of Tibetan arts and crafts. There are rare *tangkhas* from 15th century Tibetan monasteries, an excellent collection of bronze Buddha figurines and antique jewellery. A fascinating item is an engraved silver and leather saddle with silver stirrups and a matching helmet. An elderly lama chanting from his prayer book usually guards this tiny museum.

National Museum of Natural History

The museum has a large collection of stuffed animals and birds. There are regular film shows and illustrated lectures on wildlife and conservation for children.

Shankar's International Dolls Museum

Nehru House.
Bahadur Shah Zafar
Marg. (3316970-4.
Open 10 am to 5 pm.

Children find this museum a dream house. It has a collection of over 6,000 dolls not only from India but from all over the world. There are some antique dolls on display like a 250 year old Swiss doll or the dolls from the British Royal collection.

1 Institutional Area,
Lodi Road.
(4611515.
Open 9.30 am to
5.30 pm.
Closed Saturdays
and Sundays.

Federation House,
Tansen Marg.
(3314849.
Open 10 am to 5 pm.

Red Fort Archaeological Museum

Red Fort.
☎ 3267961 / 3273703.
Open 10 am to 5 pm.
Closed Fridays.

Entry Rs.2 (also allows
entrance to Indian War
Memorial Museum and
Swatantrata Sanghralaya
Museum).

Housed in Mumtaz Mahal inside Red Fort, a part
of the museum is dedicated to Bahadur Shah Zafar.
On display are a few of the emperor's personal
belongings including his silk robes embroidered
with pearls and a silver *hookah*. The museum has
some beautiful pieces of 19th century embroidered
textiles and some unusual decorative blue tiles from
the 13th century.

Indian War Memorial Museum

This dimly lit museum just above the Naubat
Khana (Royal Drum House) has a small collection
of weapons, most of them from the First World
War. There are also a few swords and firearms from
the Mughal period.

Swatantra Sanghralaya Museum

Devoted to India's freedom struggle, this museum
has life-size plaster casts of famous freedom
fighters. Worth seeing is a well preserved copy of
the Delhi Gazetteer of 1846-47.

Field Museum

Purana Qila, Mathura
Road. ☎ 4615387.
Open 10 am to 5 pm.
Closed Fridays.

The museum has a few articles which were found
during archaeological excavations at the site,
considered to be the oldest in Delhi. There are
pieces of Painted Grey Ware pottery which has been
dated to around 1000 BC and terracotta figures
from the Mauryan period (300 BC), which include
beautiful animal forms. There are also some coins of
Mohammed bin Tughlaq. Other interesting objects
include some 16th century Chinese porcelain and
glass wine bottles from the Mughal period.
However, poor lighting does not allow you to
admire the objects properly.

Gandhi National Museum

Across the road from Raj Ghat is Gandhi National Museum which has on display a few personal belongings of a man who hardly possessed anything. A stone bowl and a brass plate, the clothes Gandhiji wore on the day he was assassinated, a pair of wooden sandals, his bamboo walking stick, a few reed pens he carved himself and a diary in his own handwriting are the few interesting items on display. There is a library and an information centre in the same complex.

Opposite Raj Ghat,
Ring Road.
(3310168.
Open 9.30 am to
5.30 pm.

Gandhi Smriti

Birla House is the place where Mahatma Gandhi was assassinated on 30 January 1948, on his way for his customary evening prayers. The museum has a large collection of photographs on his life and a few of his personal belongings. Gandhiji's life has been illustrated in an unusual way at this museum by using a series of small dolls' houses and terracotta dolls portraying the major events in his life. The spartan room where he lived during his periodic visits to Delhi is preserved as it was during his lifetime. Gandhiji's last footsteps from this room to the garden have been marked out.

Birla House,
5 Tees January Marg.
(3011480 / 3012843.
Open daily 10 am to
5.30 pm.

The hearse which carried Gandhiji's body to Raj Ghat in Gandhi National Museum.

Teen Murti House.
(3017173.
Open 10 am to 5 pm.

Nehru Memorial Museum

This elegant colonial building, once the official residence of the British commander-in-chief of the Indian army is a memorial to Jawaharlal Nehru, India's first prime minister, who lived here for sixteen years. His life is depicted using rare photographs from his family album. The building is as interesting as the contents of the museum. The teak-panelled rooms with high ceilings, spacious verandahs and a well laid out garden speak of the opulence of imperial Delhi.

Nehru Planetarium
Teen Murti House.
(3014504.
Entry Rs.8.

English shows
11.30 am, 3 pm.
Hindi shows
1.30 pm, 4 pm.

Nehru Memorial Library within Teen Murti House is an excellent library and research centre for Modern Indian History. Temporary membership is available on request.

Indira Gandhi Memorial Museum

1 Safdarjang Road. (3010094.
Open 9.30 am to 5 pm.

The bungalow in which Mrs. Indira Gandhi lived as prime minister of India has been converted into a memorial. Some of the well-furnished rooms and a few personal belongings can be seen through large picture windows. It has a collection of photographs covering the nationalist movement and the lives of the Nehru-Gandhi family. In the garden, under a protective glass frame, is the spot where she was assassinated in 1984. In spite of its limited display, the museum is very popular with Indian tourists.

Sanskriti Museum of Indian Terracotta, Sanskriti Museum of Everyday Art

Anandgram, Mehrauli-Gurgaon Road,
Opposite Ayanagar.
☎ 6801796.
Open 10 am to 5 pm.

Set amidst beautifully landscaped gardens on the outskirts of Delhi, Sanskriti Museum of Everyday Art displays objects like jars, combs, mirrors, boxes, toys and kitchen utensils which are functional yet exquisitely crafted. The core collection of these objects of everyday life of traditional India was put together by O.P. Jain.

Next door is the Museum of Indian Terracotta with a large display of mythological figures, playful animals, relief panels, decorative tiles and lovely, polished clay pots. Sanskriti Kendra is also a centre for interaction between artists and scholars.

Entry is free unless otherwise indicated.
Weekly closing is Monday unless otherwise indicated.
Closed on Public Holidays.

Other Museums

Air Force Museum
Near Indira Gandhi International Airport (Terminal 1). ☎ 3035684. Open 10 am to 5 pm. Closed Mondays and Tuesdays.

Bal Bhawan National Children's Museum & Aquarium
1 Kotla Road. ☎ 3234701. Open 9 am to 5 pm. Closed Sundays and Mondays.

Musical Instruments Gallery
Sangeet Natak Akademi, Rabindra Bhawan, Copernicus Marg. Open 9.30 am to 6 pm. Closed Saturdays and Sundays.

National Philatelic Museum
Dak Bhawan, Patel Chowk, Sansad Marg. ☎ 3710154. Open 10.30 am to 4.30 pm. Passes available from Head Post Office.

National Science Centre
Bhairon Road. ☎ 3371893/3371945. Open 10 am to 5.30 pm.

Srinivas Mallah Theatre Crafts Museum
5 Deen Dayal Upadhyay Marg. Open 10 am to 5 pm. Closed Sundays and Mondays.

Two Women
Amrita Shergil
(1913-1941).

Flowerface
Abanidranath Tagore
(1871-1951).

Lady in Moonlight
Raja Ravi Verma
(1848-1906).

Art Galleries

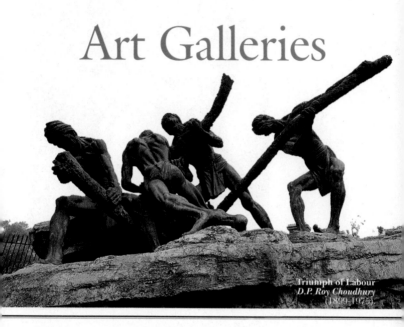

Triumph of Labour
D.P. Roy Choudhury
(1899-1975)

Delhi has overtaken Mumbai and Calcutta in
recent years to become the most vibrant and
creative art centre in India. The city has more
than twenty five active galleries and many new
ones open up during the peak winter season.
Many of India's leading artists live and work
here.

National Gallery of Modern Art

The gallery is housed in a magnificent building
which once belonged to the Maharaja of Jaipur. Its
vast rooms with high ceilings are a perfect setting
for viewing the works of art on display. Some of the
best sculptors in India have their works displayed in
the gardens flanking the huge gates.

Jaipur House,
India Gate. (3382835.
Open 10 am to 5 pm.
Closed Mondays.

NGMA has preserved works of modern Indian
artists dating from 1850. Do not miss the water
colours by Gaganendranath Tagore and Nandalal
Bose and the paintings of Raja Ravi Varma, Amrita
Shergil and Jamini Roy. NGMA has a collection of
about 15,000 paintings, sculptures and graphics
which are exhibited from time to time. Its
international collection has works by Henry Moore,
Jacob Epstein, Sonia Delaunay, Kozo Mio, among
others. The gallery has retrospective shows of
Indian and foreign artists.

NGMA organises group visits for school children,
conducted tours, seminars, film shows
and study classes on art appreciation,
history and conservation. It has a
reference library which is well-catalogued
but not so well-maintained. It has a sales
counter which stocks reproductions,
catalogues, picture postcards and posters.

Ram Kumar (b.1924).

Lalit Kala Akademi

Rabindra Bhawan, Firoz Shah Road. (3381361. Open 11 am to 6 pm. Closed Sundays.

This large spacious gallery is spread over three floors and artists from all over India show their work here. There are often several exhibitions being held at LKA at the same time. LKA does not charge the stipulated 33 per cent commission for works sold which most galleries officially deduct. It is a non-profit organisation that patronises emerging talent. The government-run Lalit Kala Akademi had its first national exhibition of art in 1958. LKA holds the prestigious Triennale India in which 30 to 40 countries participate, and a national exhibition of photography and art. There is always something interesting happening here, especially during the winter months.

Garhi Studio

Kala Kutir, East of Kailash. (6432225. Open 11 am to 5 pm. Closed Sundays.

Garhi Studio is run by Lalit Kala Akademi. It could be an exciting place to visit if you are interested in the live processes of art. The gallery often has wonderful shows. If you are lucky, you can actually pick up a painting fresh off the easel or some inexpensive prints. The graphic studio has an old etching press which is worth seeing. Well known artists from India and abroad often hold workshops and illustrated lectures here.

Vasundhara Tiwari (b.1955).

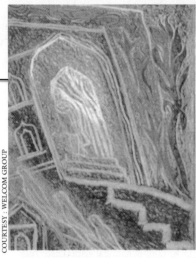

Bulbul Sharma (b.1952).

Triveni Kala Sangam

There are four galleries in this cultural complex, including the basement gallery run by Art Heritage. Shridharani Gallery, the largest gallery here, holds regular shows by both established as well as young artists. Triveni Gallery has smaller format works on display. The complex has a Sculpture Court for exhibitions and a bookshop with unconventional books, journals and cassettes. The bare and rudimentary Coffee Shop at Triveni is very popular with artists, theatre persons and students.

Tansen Marg. (3718833.
Open from 11 am to 7 pm.
Closed Sundays.

Art Heritage

This gallery was founded in 1977 by Roshen Alkazi, a highly respected name in the art world. It holds a series of exhibitions throughout the year of some of the best known artists in India. Eminent painters like Bikash Bhattacharjee, K.G. Subramanyan, Akbar Padamsee, have their works exhibited here. Art Heritage organises interactive workshops with students and art lovers.

Triveni Kala Sangam,
Tansen Marg. (3719470.
Open 11 am to 7 pm.
Closed Sundays.

Paresh Maity (b.1965).

Art Today

A 1 Hamilton House,
Connaught Place.
℃ 3320689.
Open 11 am to 7 pm.
Closed Sundays.

Its collection includes top names and its
exhibitions are often commercially high profile.
Works by Krishen Khanna, Satish Gujral,
Rameshwar Broota, have been part of its many
exhibitions. It does not restrict itself to big names
but also holds shows of beginners, like a group
show by Baroda University art students. It
produces well designed catalogues and posters. The
gallery is open all year round.

Dhoomimal Art Gallery

8 A Connaught Place.
℃ 3328839.
Open 10 am to 7 pm.
Closed Sundays.

One of the older commercial galleries which runs
regular shows. The entire spectrum of artists over
the years have had their works displayed here. It
has a regular clientele and permanent collection.

Eicher Gallery

14 Commercial Complex,
Greater Kailash II.
℃ 6445521 Ext 406.
Open 10 am to 7 pm.

A young, non-commercial gallery that has faith in
marginal art forms. Landmark exhibitions include a
series of shows by and about women, with an
ironic collection, *Icons of Femininity in Indian
Calendar Art (1955-95)*. The pioneer of Indian
studio pottery, Gurcharan Singh's retrospective was
held here. To mark India's 50 years of
independence, a thought-provoking exhibition on
Khadi was held. Apart from paintings, the gallery
has given sustained impetus to textile art, ceramics
and mixed media.
Illustrated talks,
workshops and film
shows have been held,
as well as an art
appreciation course.

Anjolie Ela Menon
(b.1940).

Gallerie Ganesha

Started in 1989, this gallery focuses on promoting young talent. Two well-known artists on the Indian contemporary art scene, Paresh Maity and Neeraj Goswami, have been promoted successfully by this gallery. Their large collection consists of paintings, graphics and sculptures.

E 557
Greater Kailash II.
✆ 6447306.
Open 10 am to 7 pm.
Closed Sundays.

Gallery Espace

It has carved a niche for itself because of its specialised, unconventional focus. J.Swaminathan, Manjit Bawa and Ganesh Haloi have also been exhibited here. In this gallery, a Krishna Reddy show of prints can be spontaneously accompanied by a two-hour discussion of the artist with art students. It produces informative catalogues.

16 Community Centre,
New Friends Colony.
✆ 6830499.
Open 10 am to 6 pm.
Closed Sundays.

LTG Gallery

Copernicus Marg. ✆ 3384111.
Open 11 am to 7 pm. Closed Sundays.

LTG Gallery comes up with some meaningful exhibitions. Its group shows by ceramic artists, theme shows on Nelson Mandela, Mahatma Gandhi and Kashmiri immigrants have made an impact. Its collection includes work by Jamini Roy, Krishen Khanna, F.N.Souza, among others. The gallery often provides encouragement to not so big names and comes up with surprises.

Saroj Gogi Pal
(b.1945).

Satish Gujral (b.1925).

The Village Gallery

14 Hauz Khas Village.
☎ 6853860.
Open 10.30 am
to 6.30 pm.
Closed Sundays.

This gallery has done 'innovative' shows in graphic design, drawings and sketches by Satyajit Ray, monoprints by women inmates of Tihar Jail and Haku Shah's homage to Gandhiji with straw, rags and cotton wool. The gallery also holds printmaking workshops with NGOs, designers and artists.

Vadhera Art Gallery

40 Defence Colony.
☎ 4615368.
Open 10 am to 7 pm.
Closed Sundays.

This gallery opened about ten years back with a group show by artists from the Delhi College of Art. It is a quiet gallery with a big glass window. You will notice that the heavy traffic outside appears to move almost soundlessly when seen through the glass. The permanent collection here includes works by M.F. Husain, Ram Kumar, Manu Parekh, Paramjit Singh, Anjolie Ela Menon. There is a documentation centre which is open to researchers.

Narendra Pal Singh (b.1963).

Other Galleries

Academy of Fine Arts and Literature
4 Siri Fort Institutional Area. ☏ 6438070.

AIFACS Gallery
Rafi Marg. ☏ 3711315.

Art Indus
Santushti Complex, Opp. Samrat Hotel ☏ 6883738.

Art Konsult
6 A Hauz Khas Village. ☏ 6827264.

Art Motif
A 1/178 Safdarjang Enclave.
☏ 6165433.

Aurobindo Gallery
Aurobindo Market, Aurobindo Marg.
☏ 6862593.

Delhi Art Gallery
29 Hauz Khas Village. ☏ 6967619.

Gallery 55
55 Sundar Nagar.
☏ 4623701.

Gallery 42
D 42 Defence
Colony.
☏ 4621289.

Gallery Twenty Five
25 Anand Lok, Khel Gaon Marg.
☏ 6410454.

India International Centre
40 Lodi Estate, Max Mueller Marg.
☏ 4619431.

Jharokha Art Gallery
24 Hauz Khas Village. ☏ 6864638.

MEC Art Gallery
70B Khan Market. ☏ 4635266.

Foreign cultural centres that regularly hold art exhibitions

British Council Division
17 Kasturba Gandhi Marg. ☏ 3711401. Open 10 am to 7 pm. Closed Sundays.

Gallerie Romain Rolland
Alliance Francaise, D 13 South Extension II. ☏ 6258128. Open 2 pm to 6.30 pm. Closed Sundays.

Max Mueller Bhawan
3 Kasturba Gandhi Marg. ☏ 3329506. Open 10 am to 7 pm. Closed Sundays.

Santhal Family
Ram Kinkar Baij
(1910-1980).

246

Annual Cultural Events

January
SAHMAT Festival
(Safdar Hashmi Memorial Trust)
Mandi House

International Film Festival
(Directorate of Film Festivals)
Siri Fort Auditorium

February
Kalka Bindadin Mahotsava
(Kathak Kendra) Kamani Auditorium

Dhrupad Festival
(Dhrupad Society)
IIC/Kamani Auditorium

Bharatendu Natya Utsav
(Sahitya Kala Parishad) Shri Ram Centre

March
Music Festival
(Rajiv Gandhi Foundation)
Siri Fort Auditorium

Sangeet Sammelan
(ITC Ltd) Siri Fort Auditorium

March-April
Shankarlal Sangeet Sammelan
(Shri Ram Bharatiya Kala Kendra)
Kamani Auditorium

May-June
Summer Theatre Festival
(National School of Drama)
Kamani Auditorium

June-July
National Film Festival
(Directorate of Film Festivals)
Siri Fort Auditorium

August
Krishna Katha
(Shri Ram Bharatiya Kala Kendra)
Kamani Auditorium

August-September
Vishnu Digambar Samaroh
(Gandharva Mahavidyalaya)
Kamani Auditorium

Chhatrotsava
(Kathak Kendra)
Shri Ram Centre

September-October
SPIC-MACAY Programmes
Schools/Colleges

October
Naina Devi Memorial
Festival
(Raag Rang Music Circle)
Kamani Auditorium

Qutb Festival
(Delhi Tourism) Qutb Complex

Ram Lila
(Shri Ram Bharatiya Kala Kendra)
Kamani Auditorium

November
Folk Dance and Music Festival
(Indian Trade Promotion
Organisation)
Shakuntalam in Pragati Maidan

December
Kathak Utsav
(Kathak Kendra) Shri Ram Centre

*A folk dancer pirouettes
with oil lamps.*

247

Music, Dance, Theatre AND Cinema

Navtej Singh Johar in a dance-theatre piece.

Delhi has always been a great centre for the performing arts. As the capital of India for centuries, a flourishing courtly culture attracted the itinerant artist to seek the patronage of kings. In the field of classical Hindustani music, Delhi even boasts of its own *gharana* (literally, family tradition) of music. Over time, the patronage and support of emperors have been replaced with the sponsorship of state agencies and corporate houses. Patronage has its advantages. For the casual visitor, the good news is that many concerts are free.

However, as far as theatre and cinema are concerned, it used to be fashionable to say that Delhi is a desert. That is no longer true. Both theatre and cinema are becoming increasingly popular. Music festivals, dance recitals, art exhibitions, theatre and cinema are no longer confined to a few connoisseurs – thousands are involved.

Ustad Bismillah Khan playing the shehnai.

Pandit Ravi Shankar.

Music

Indian music boasts of centuries-old oral traditions. On Thursday evenings wander into the *dargah* of Sheikh Nizamuddin, the 13th century Sufi saint, to hear *qawwals* sing the lyrics of his celebrated disciple, Amir Khusro. Buried in the same complex, Amir Khusro is said to have fused Persian music with the existing tradition of *dhrupad* singing, evolving *khayal*, the popular form of classical Hindustani music. Khusro is also credited with crafting the sitar and tabla, two instruments made famous world over by Ravi Shankar and Zakir Hussain.

Qawwals at the Nizamuddin Dargah.

Also buried there is the late Mughal emperor, Mohammed Shah Rangila, whose concern for music overrode his interest in his empire. He is said to have been busy listening to *khayals* when the Persian king, Nadir Shah, attacked and looted Delhi in 1739. Rangila himself survived and continued to patronise musicians.

The British had an inadequate understanding of Indian music and predictably Delhi suffered an artistic decline after the British took over the reigns of government. It was only after India became independent that patronage picked up once again.

The advent of monsoons is always a time for celebration in India. August-September are more or less the unofficial months when the cultural calendar of the capital begins to reinvigorate itself after the long sweltering summer. The music lover can easily pack the cold winter evenings with various concerts of Indian classical music which are hosted all over the city.

Girija Devi at a classical music concert.

SPIC-MACAY, a voluntary youth movement, organises interactive lectures and demonstrations in schools and colleges by eminent artistes. For the uninitiated, these are a fine introduction to classical music and dance. A detailed programme is advertised in all the newspapers and there is no entry fee.

Delhi has a small but dedicated audience for **classical western music**. Delhi Music Society, which also runs the Delhi School of Music in Chanakyapuri (6115331, organises regular concerts at different venues.

Eminent Hindustani classical vocalist, Pandit Jasraj.

For **jazz and rock** enthusiasts, there are musicians who perform in a small number of hotels and restaurants. The Jazz India (Delhi Chapter) hosts international stars once in a couple of years. A relaxed and less expensive way of enjoying popular western music is organised by the Friends of Music at the Farmhouse Restaurant, near Qutb Minar (6960045.

Popular Hindi music, primarily Hindi film songs, is best imbibed second hand, while travelling in a bus or over the public address system if there is a community festival. Also popular are 'film nites' where playback singers and matinee idols from Bollywood entertain the audience with music and dance. These events are well advertised, though the prices of tickets are usually steep.

Kuchipudi dancers, Radha and Raja Reddy.

Dance

Internationally renowned dancers, Yamini Krishnamurty (Bharatanatyam), Raja and Radha Reddy (Kuchipudi), Uma Sharma and Birju Maharaj (Kathak), Sonal Mansingh (Odissi) and Singhajit Singh (Manipuri) have their schools in Delhi, though programmes centred around dance are not regular. Kathak Kendra in Bahawalpur House is the only institution with a regular calendar of events in which accomplished dancers participate.

Astad Deboo in a contemporary dance rendition.

Renowned Kathak dancer,
Uma Sharma.

Troupes of dancers from India's different states perform at a folk dance festival at Talkatora Indoor Stadium held every year immediately after Republic Day, 26 January. The entry fee is nominal.

Two beautifully choreographed ballets by the Shri Ram Bharatiya Kala Kendra, the Krishna Katha and Ram Lila, based on a mixture of classical and modern styles have a run of about two weeks in August and October at the Kamani Auditorium.

Mandi House Area

Outside the National School of Drama.

Theatre

Om Puri at a SAHMAT Festival.

Delhi does not have the kind of deep-rooted tradition of theatre which exists in Calcutta or Mumbai, but there are several successful production companies here, and many amateur groups who very often come up with original performances.

National School of Drama (NSD), founded in 1975, is India's premier institution for theatre. It has a repertory company which frequently presents plays by Indian and western playwrights. The annual Summer Theatre Festival organised by the NSD repertory brings together the best in the profession.

An integral part of Delhi's theatre scene is the doyen of alternative theatre, Habib Tanvir, whose rustic wit and experimental finesse is now legendary. His successful plays and musicals are often staged.

The cultural centre of Delhi is called, rather inaccurately, Mandi House. The palace of the Raja of Mandi no longer exists. The site is occupied by the imposing headquarters of Doordarshan, the state-owned television company. To theatre and music lovers, however, the whole area with its array of auditoria around an extremely busy traffic roundabout is known as Mandi House.

Open air auditorium at Triveni Kala Sangam.

A Hindi film hording.

Cinema

There are over seventy cinema halls scattered all over Delhi and most of them screen commercial Hindi films. Some of the older ones like the Regal have seen better times, but are still attractive with their quaint interiors. The 'boxes' in Regal, for instance, are an unique experience in privacy.

The Basant Lok complex in Vasant Vihar with Priya cinema, Modern Bazaar, Nirula's and McDonald's fast food joints, is very popular with young people. The newly renovated Satyam cinema in Ranjeet Nagar near West Patel Nagar and the Anupam PVR multiplex in Saket also screen the latest English films.

Thanks to the cultural centres attached to some foreign mission in Delhi, you can see films by the best names in international cinema. Entry is through free passes that are available in advance.

Every alternate year, the International Film Festival of India is held in January. There is also the annual National Film Festival, in June-July, where Indian films which have won national awards are screened. Local newspapers carry details.

Cultural Centres

Academy of Fine Arts and Literature
4/6 Siri Fort Institutional Area. (6438070.

AIFACS
Rafi Marg. (3711315.

Alliance Francaise
D-13 South Extn II.
(6258128.

American Centre/USIS
24 Kasturba Gandhi Marg.
(3316841 / 3314251.

British Council Division
17 Kasturba Gandhi Marg.
(3711401 / 3711402.

Delhi Music Society
8 Nyaya Marg, Chanakyapuri.
(6115331.

French Cultural Centre
2 Aurangzeb Road.
(3014682.

Gandharva Mahavidyalaya
212 Deen Dayal Upadhyaya Marg.
(3233791.

Hungarian Cultural Centre
1A Janpath. (3011152.

India International Centre
40 Lodi Estate, Max Mueller Marg. (4619431.

India Habitat Centre
Lodi Road. (4691921.

Indian Council for Cultural Relations
Azad Bhawan, I.P. Estate.
(3312274.

Indira Gandhi National Centre for the Arts
Central Vista Mess, Janpath.
(3384901 / 3389535.

Israel Culture Centre
3 Aurangzeb Road.
(3013238.

Italian Cultural Centre
50E Chandragupta Marg, Chanakyapuri.
(6871901.

Japan Cultural Centre
32 Firoz Shah Road.
(3712124.

Kathak Kendra
Bahawalpur House.
(3385065.

Lalit Kala Akademi
Rabindra Bhawan, Firoz Shah Road.
(3387243.

Max Mueller Bhawan
3 Kasturba Gandhi Marg.
(3329506.

National School of Drama
Bahawalpur House, Bhagwandas Road.
(3389402.

Portuguese Cultural Centre
13 Sunder Nagar.
(4602695.

Rajiv Gandhi Foundation
Jawahar Bhawan, Dr. Rajendra Prasad Road.
(3755118.

Sahitya Kala Parishad
18A Satsang Vihar Marg, Special Institutional Area.
(6867637 / 6964124.

Sangeet Natak Akademi
Rabindra Bhawan, Firoz Shah Road.
(3387246 / 3387247.

Sanskriti Kendra
Anandgram, Mehrauli-Gurgaon Road, Opposite Ayanagar.
(6801796.

Shri Ram Bharatiya Kala Kendra
1 Copernicus Marg.
(3386429 / 3383568.

Auditoria

Air Force Auditorium
Subroto Park, Dhaula Kuan.
(3292834 /3292386.

Ambedkar Auditorium
1 Ashok Road. (3389182.

Falaknuma & Hamsadhwani Theatre
Pragati Maidan. (3371849.

FICCI Auditorium
Federation House, Tansen Marg. (3316121.

Gandhi Memorial Hall
2 Bahadur Shah Zafar Marg.
(3311049.

Ghalib Auditorium
Mata Sundari Lane, near Bal Bhawan.

Tagore Hall
Azad Bhawan, Indraprastha Estate.
(3319309.

India International Centre
40 Lodi Estate, Max Mueller Marg. (4619431.

Jawaharlal Nehru Auditorium
AIIMS, Ansari Nagar.
(6864851.

Kamani Auditorium
Copernicus Marg.
(3388084.

LTG Auditorium
Copernicus Marg.
(3389713.

Mavlankar Hall
Vitthalbhai Patel House, Rafi Marg. (3719780.

Cinema Halls

Alankar
Lajpat Nagar. ☏ 6831460.

Alpana
Model Town. ☏ 7413104.

Amba
Shakti Nagar. ☏ 2916000.

Anupam PVR
Saket. ☏ 6865999.

Batra
Mukherjee Nagar.
☏ 7654202.

Chanakya
Chanakyapuri.
☏ 4674009 / 4670423.

Chanderlok
Alaknanda. ☏ 6444885.

Delite
Asaf Ali Road. ☏ 3272903.

Eros
Jangpura Extn. ☏ 4694642.

Filmistan
Sadar Bazaar. ☏ 7773821.

Golcha
Daryaganj. ☏ 3265192.

Grandlay
Friends Colony. ☏ 6310782.

Imperial
Paharganj. ☏ 528253.

Jagat
Jama Masjid. ☏ 3268781.

Jubilee
Chandni Chowk.
☏ 2965475.

Kumar
Chandni Chowk.
☏ 2961761.

Liberty
Karol Bagh. ☏ 5722998.

Minerva
Kashmere Gate.
☏ 2914245.

Moti
Chandni Chowk.
☏ 2960383.

Novelty
S.P. Mukherjee Marg.
☏ 2513152.

Odeon
Connaught Place.
☏ 3322167.

Paras
Nehru Place. ☏ 6432842.

Plaza
Connaught Place.
☏ 3320753.

Priya
Vasant Vihar. ☏ 6140048.

Rachna
Rajendra Place.
☏ 5713586.

Regal
Connaught Place.
☏ 3362245.

Ritz
Kashmere Gate.
☏ 2961761.

Rivoli
Connaught Place.
☏ 3362227.

Sangam
R.K. Puram. ☏ 6172442.

Sapna
East of Kailash. ☏ 6431787.

Satyam
Ranjeet Nagar. ☏ 5797387.

Sheila
Paharganj. ☏ 7772100.

Stadium
Mathura Road.
☏ 3383307.

Parsi Anjuman Hall
Bahadur Shah Zafar Marg.
☏ 3318615.

Rabindra Rangshala
Upper Ridge Road.

Shakuntalam Theatre
Pragati Maidan.
☏ 3371849.

Shri Ram Bharatiya Kala Kendra
1 Copernicus Marg.
☏ 3386429 / 3383568.

Shri Ram Centre
Safdar Hashmi Marg.
☏ 3714307.

Siri Fort Auditorium
Asiad Village Complex.
☏ 6493370.

Studio Theatre
Bahawalpur House,
Bhagwandas Road.
☏ 3389402.

Triveni Kala Sangam
205 Tansen Marg.
☏ 3718833.

Vigyan Bhawan Auditorium
Maulana Azad Road.
☏ 3022231.

Teen Murti Auditorium
Teen Murti Bhawan.
☏ 3015026.

Akshara Theatre
11,12B Baba Kharak Singh Marg.
☏ 3732083.

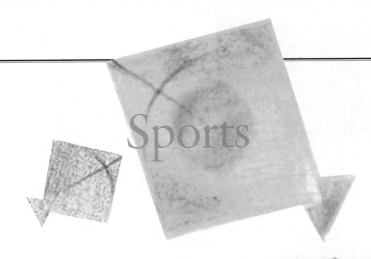

Sports

For the sports lover, Delhi is well equipped with stadia, gymnasiums and opportunities for indoor and outdoor sports. Each season brings its own sporting activities. In the hot summer months, there is swimming and boating along the ramparts of Purana Qila in the late evenings, riding at dawn, even all-night tennis on the floodlit courts of Delhi Lawn Tennis Association. The season after summer is for kite flying and the dark monsoon clouds are splashed with brightly coloured diamonds as kite flyers try to outdo each other. The bracing air of a Delhi winter is ideal for all kinds of sports, both for the spectator and the active participant. You can play golf, basketball, tennis, go rock climbing – and above all there is cricket.

The moat surrounding Purana Qila offers a picturesque setting for paddle boating.

Cricket

Delhi is passionate about cricket. People from different backgrounds, languages, cultures, come together around this game. Cricket is played everywhere. The public gardens, the narrow lanes between rows of houses, all becoming makeshift cricket pitches.

Excitement over cricket reaches fever pitch if a professional match is being played in the city. Long queues at ticket booths form days ahead, high prices are paid and big favours are granted to acquire tickets. The stadium at Firoz Shah Kotla hosts most professional cricket matches.

For major cricket events, contact :

Delhi District Cricket Association
Firoz Shah Kotla Stadium, Bahadur Shah Zafar Marg.
(3319323 / 3313143.

Sports Authority of India, Jawaharlal Nehru Stadium Lodi Estate.
(4649781 / 4629400.

Tennis

Delhi Lawn Tennis Association Africa Avenue. (6176140 / 6193955.

Cosmic Sports Centre Benito Juarez Marg, Anand Niketan. (6892293.

Delhi Gymkhana Club 2 Safdarjang Road. (3015531.

Siri Fort and Saket Sports Complexes run by Delhi Development Authority, and most stadia, have courts available by the hour at moderate rates.

Golf

Delhi offers great opportunities for golfers, with its several golf courses in and around the city. Most offer golf sets on hire.

Delhi Golf Club Zakir Hussain Marg. (4362768 / 4362235. Green fees are Rs.300 for weekdays and Rs.500 for weekends. Foreign nationals have to pay in foreign currency - US $35 on weekdays and US $40 on weekends. Weekend bookings are essential.

This 27 hole golf course is the best in the city. It has had the privilege of conducting more PGA tournaments than any other club in India.

Army Golf Club Dhaula Kuan. (3291972. Green fees are Rs.250 on weekdays and Rs.300 on weekends. For foreign nationals green fees are US $25 on weekdays and US $30 on weekends.

A very friendly and challenging 18 hole course which has been hosting sponsored PGA tournaments.

Air Force Golf Club Safdarjang Road. (3012372. Green fees are Rs.300 on weekdays and Rs.450 on weekends.

A dainty 9 hole course in the heart of Delhi with excellent facilities. Foreign nationals are not allowed.

NOIDA Golf Course Sector 38, NOIDA. (91572753. Green fees are Rs.150 on weekdays and Rs.300 on weekends. For foreign nationals green fees are US $30 for weekdays and US $40 for weekends.

Away from the city's noise and pollution, this lush green 18 hole course is also very popular with golfers from south Delhi and foreigners.

Aravali Golf Club NIT, Faridabad. (91214810. Green fees are Rs.50 on weekdays and Rs.100 on weekends and holidays. For foreigners green fees are US $10 for weekdays and US $25 for weekends and holidays.

This 9 hole golf course is laid out with a lot of greenery. This is the only course which has a motel run by Haryana Tourism.

Sterling Golf & Sports Country Club D40, Sector 40, NOIDA. (91577881-3. Green fees are Rs.400 on weekdays and Rs.500 on weekends.

This is a new 18 hole golf course, designed by Greg Norman, 45 km from Connaught Place.

The Resort Country Club Panchgaon-Tauru Road, Gurgaon, Haryana. (91325280. City office (6221300 / 6460900. Green fees are Rs.200 on weekdays and Rs.250 on weekends.

This is a 9 hole golf course on the Jaipur highway.

Meadows Golf and Country Club Fazilpur Jharsa Village, Gurgaon-Sohna Road, Haryana. (0124-671260. City office (6147148. Green fees for non-members are Rs.400 for weekdays and Rs.500 for weekends.

A pretty 18 hole course on the main Sohna Road, about 30 km from the Dhaula Kuan roundabout.

DDA Siri Fort Sports Complex. (6497482 / 6496657. Casual membership for the Driving Range is Rs.25 per day and Rs.25 for a basket of 50 balls.

Great stands of old trees, ancient monuments and scattered wildlife make the Delhi Golf Club course one of the most beautiful in the world.

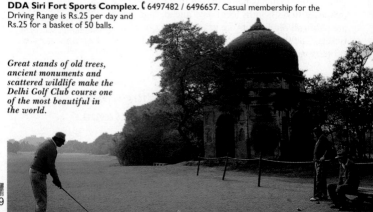

Swimming

Most 5-star hotels offer membership to their health club and swimming pools. Prices range from Rs.200 to Rs.400 per day.

DDA Sports Complex Siri Fort. (6497482. Casual membership Rs.50 per day.

DDA Sports Complex Saket. (6965742. Casual membership Rs.50 per day.

Bowling

Qutb Hotel Shaheed Jeet Singh Marg. (6862711. Tariff Rs.150 per game.

Leisure Bowl Bawa Potteries Complex, Aruna Asaf Ali Road. (3351730. Tariff Rs.125 per game.

First Bowl, 32nd Milestone Delhi-Jaipur Highway. (91322528 / 91325834. Tariff Rs.100 per game.

There are two new bowling centres on Mathura Road, Faridabad, just beyond the Badarpur border.

Little Paradise 12/7 Mathura Road (91275156.
Destination Point 12/2 Mathura Road. (91274602.

Polo

Polo, a strenuous and sweaty sport for both man and beast, miraculously becomes an elegant and glamorous event for the spectator. Nothing could be more pleasant than watching a few *chukkars* in the pale wintry sunshine of the polo season in Delhi.

The Polo Club c/o 61st Cavalry, Cariappa Marg, Delhi Cantonment. (5699444 / 5699777. **Season** October-November; February-March (Ring for important matches).

Arena Polo requires fewer players and a much smaller area than traditional polo. Played outdoors, indoors or under floodlight, the game becomes dramatic as all the action is at close range.

Delhi Equestrian and Polo Association c/o Scindia Potteries Compound, Ring Road, Sarojini Nagar. (6878853. Fax 6881140.

Riding

The Children's Riding Club Safdarjang Road (Behind Safdarjang's Tomb).
☎ 3012265. Timings for non-members 8 am to 9 am and members from 2.30 pm to 7 pm.
Tariff Rs.150 for 50 minutes.

Delhi Riding Club Safdarjang Road (Behind Safdarjang's Tomb). ☎ 3011891.
Timings 6.30 am to 9.30 am and 2.45 pm to 5.45 pm. Tariff Rs.210 per hour.

DDA Sports Complex Saket. ☎ 6965742 / 6967581. Timings 6 am to 9 am and 4 pm to
6 pm. Closed Mondays. Tariff Rs.150 for 50 minutes.

Racing

The Delhi race course is not as grand as the Bombay
or Calcutta race courses. However, several important
races take place here, including the North Indian
Derby and the President of India Gold Cup.

Delhi Race Club (1940) Ltd. Near Ashoka Hotel. ☎ 3012943 / 3019909 / 3019286. Season
mid July-April. Race day in Delhi is Monday.

*Statue of the
legendary hockey
player, Dhyan Chand,
in National Stadium.*

Sports Complexes

Sports complexes scattered around Delhi
offer a wide range of sports facilities.
Facilities for tennis, badminton, squash,
swimming, billiards, cricket, riding,
yoga, aerobics and gymnastics are
available. Most of them also offer
excellent coaching facilities.

DDA Sports Complex Siri Fort. ☎ 6497482 /
6496657. Closed Mondays.

DDA Sports Complex Saket. ☎ 6965742 /
6967581. Closed Mondays.

National Stadium Opp. India Gate.
☎ 3389740. Closed Sundays.

Jawaharlal Nehru Stadium Lodi Estate.
☎ 4629400 / 4649786. Closed Saturdays and
Sundays.

Other Stadia

Firoz Shah Kotla Cricket Stadium
Bahadur Shah Zafar Marg. ☎ 3319323.

Dr. Ambedkar Stadium
Bahadur Shah Zafar Marg. ☎ 3361604.

Shivaji Stadium
Jain Mandir Road. ☎ 3365720.

Indira Gandhi Indoor Stadium
Indraprastha Estate. ☎ 3379711.

Talkatora Indoor Stadium
Willingdon Crescent. ☎ 3018178.

*Jawaharlal Nehru
Stadium.*

*Indira Gandhi Indoor
Stadium.*

Rock Climbing

Lado Sarai, in the vicinity of the historic Qutb Minar, offers an ideal setting for aspiring rock climbers. Requisite gear is supplied and a trained coach lends a helping hand. The variety of plant, bird and insect life makes it a pleasant experience.

Lado Sarai DDA Park Mehrauli Road. Timings 9 am to 1 pm. Tariff Rs.40 for a course of 4 hours. Season October-March.

For bookings contact **DTTDC** N 36, Connaught Place (Middle Circle) ☏ 3365358.

Indian Mountaineering Foundation offers **artificial wall climbing**. The Foundation houses the Himalayan Museum which has exhibits, photographs and panoramas unfolding the history and development of mountaineering in the Himalayas.

Indian Mountaineering Foundation Benito Juarez Marg, Anand Niketan. ☏ 4671211 / 6883412.

Yoga and Fitness

Yoga is a traditional Indian technique for relaxation and stress release through which one is both filled with peace and a sense of well being. There are many centres in Delhi where one can learn yoga.

Sri Aurobindo Ashram Sri Aurobindo Marg. ☏ 667863 / 669225.

Central Research Institute for Yoga 68 Ashok Road. ☏ 3721472 / 3718301.

Servants of the People Society Nature Cure and Yoga Health Centre, Lajpat Bhawan, Lajpat Nagar IV.

Sivananda Yog Vedanta Nataraja Centre 52 Community Centre, East of Kailash. ☏ 6480869 / 6453962.

Most 5-star hotels in Delhi offer membership to their **fitness and health clubs** to non-residents for a fee. Check with individual hotels for tariff and timings.

The following offer temporary membership :

Itkhas Fitness Centre 8 Community Centre, New Friends Colony. ☏ 6844380 /6844381.

Scorpio Strength and Fitness Centre 55A Siddharth Chambers (near Azad Apts), Hauz Khas. ☏ 6962000.

Total Fitness Centre Sector 6, R.K. Puram. ☏ 6192687.

Slimshape Health Club B21 Nizamuddin East. ☏ 4619361.

Flying

Delhi Gliding Club Safdarjang Airport. (4636052. Closed Wednesdays.

Delhi Flying Club Safdarjang Airport. (4618271/4699596. Closed Wednesdays.

White Water Rafting & Trekking

Himalayan River Runners
F5 Hauz Khas Enclave.
(6852602. Fax 6865604.

Aqua Terra Adventures
309 Oriental House,
Gulmohur Enclave
Commercial Complex.
(6518625 / 6864771.

Ibex Expeditions
G 66 East of Kailash,
(6912641 / 6917829.

Wanderlust Travels
M 51-52 Palika Bhawan,
Opp. Hyatt Regency Hotel.
(6881206 / 6111889.

If you have two or three days to spare, white water rafting and trekking offer a different sports adventure a few hours from Delhi.

Rafting is done on a section of the Ganga, 23 km north of Rishikesh (5 hours north of Delhi), which includes some of the great rapids. Between the thrills of the rapids are calm float sections which allow one to enjoy the lovely scenery of the wooded mountains. Kayaking and hiking trips are also possible. Given here are some groups which offer professionally-run rafting trips for one, two or three days. The rafting season is from mid September to end April.

PHOTO BY **SANJEEV SAITH**

Children's
DELHI

Some indigeneous games have been refined over the years. *Kabaddi* and *kho kho* which are uniquely Indian team games requiring no sports equipment are now included in national sports tournaments. These games are as popular in distant villages as on Delhi streets and parks.

A common sight on a sunny winter afternoon is children involved in bat and ball games like *gulli-danda* and cricket, or *pitthu*, a team game played with small stones. Games played with gusto, reiterating the special ability of children to transform hostile streets and dingy alleys into makeshift playgrounds. The sky is their limit. Literally. In August kites dot the sky as rooftops reverberate with joyous shrieks of children, and adults too, as they down their opponent's kite.

Playing pitthu in the lanes of Delhi.

Delhi can be an exciting place for children. There are parks and museums, a planetarium and an amusement park, places which combine learning with pleasure.

National Zoological Park

Mathura Road. (4618070.
Open 8.30 am to 5.30 pm (April to October) 9.30 am to 4.30 pm (October to March). Entry Rs.4 (adult) Rs.2 (child). Closed Fridays.

Appu Ghar Amusement Park

Pragati Maidan, Mathura Road.
(3371838 / 3371856.
Open 1 pm to 9 pm (April to October) 12 noon to 8 pm (October to March). Entry Rs.10 (adult) Rs.5 (child). Extra charges for every ride or game.

Fun and Food Village

Delhi-Gurgaon Road, Kapashera. (5565500.
Open 9 am to 7 pm. Entry Rs.100 (adult) Rs.70 (child). Open all days.

National Science Centre

Bhairon Road. (3371893 / 3371945.
Open 10 am to 5.30 pm. Entry Rs.5. Student Rs.2. Children
below five are admitted free. Closed Mondays.

Nehru Planetarium

Teen Murti House. (3014504.
English shows 11.30 am, 3 pm. Hindi shows 1.30 pm, 4 pm.
Entry Rs.8. Closed Mondays.

Bal Bhawan

Kotla Road. (3234701.
Open 10 am to 5 pm. Entry free. Closed Sundays and Mondays.

A creative centre for children with regular
workshops on theatre, music, painting and clay
modelling. National Children's Museum and
Science Park are within the Bal Bhawan complex.

Shankar's International Dolls Museum

Nehru House, Bahadur Shah Zafar Marg. (3316970.
Open 10 am to 5 pm. Closed Mondays.

Children's Libraries

Children's Book Trust (CBT), B. C. Roy
Memorial Library, Nehru House, Bahadur Shah
Zafar Marg. (3316970.
Annual membership fee Rs.225. Open 9.30 am to 5 pm. Open all days.

National Book Trust (NBT) A5 Green Park,
Aurobindo Marg, publishes and retails reasonably
priced children's books in English and other Indian
languages. It also has a mobile library.

Pragati Maidan

Pragati Maidan, India's premier exhibition complex, is located in the very heart of New Delhi, next to Purana Qila. Spread over an area of 149 acres, Pragati Maidan is one of the finest exhibition grounds in Asia.

India Trade Promotion Organisiation (ITPO) manages Pragati Maidan and promotes trade related fairs. The exhibition halls and conference rooms are adequately backed up by administrative offices, warehouses and a comprehensive security and public address system. It has large open spaces and adequate parking facilities. The roads within Pragati Maidan measure up to 10 km and are named after Indian rivers. ITPO offers free shuttle service for visitors from Gates 1, 2 and 3 when there are major exhibitions.

The masterplan for Pragati Maidan was proposed by Raj Rewal, a Delhi-based architect, while other eminent architects, including Charles Correa, J.A. Stein and Satish Grover, were involved in designing individual buildings. The complex witnessed innovative ideas take shape in steel and concrete. Some of the interesting buildings within the complex are the National Science Centre *(see: **Children's Delhi**)*, the Hall of Nations and the unique Crafts Museum *(see: **Museums**, p.231)*.

The complex is kept alive throughout the year with cultural activities that cater to both the common man and the connoisseur. There are two popular auditoria, Shakuntalam and Falaknuma, and several restaurants. Appu Ghar, an amusement park, the first of its kind in Delhi, is within the complex *(see: **Children's Delhi**, p.265)*.

1	Hall of Technology (#18)
2	Hall of States (#14)
3	Defence Pavilion
4	Hall of Special Displays (#8-11)
5	Phoolwari Restaurant
6	Shakuntalam Theatre
	Falaknuma Theatre
7	Conference Centre (#7)
8	Administration Gate
9	Vatika Restaurant
10	Hall of Nations (#6)
11	Hall of Industries (#2-5)
12	Handloom Pavilion

Gate 4

Appu Ghar

Mathura Road

Gate 3

Gate 2

Gate 1

Crafts Museum

National Science Centre

B h a i r o n   R o a d

Car Park

Pragati Maidan has 54,685 square metres of covered space in 15 halls, besides 10,000 square metres of open display area for trade related exhibitions. Modernised and upgraded from time to time, Pragati Maidan offers the kind of ambience that is conducive to exhibiting a wide range of products - from gigantic machinery and equipment to jewellery and a range of precision engineering products.

Major Exhibitions at Pragati Maidan

EXHIBITION : Item : MONTH : Organiser

PETROTECH : Petroleum related eqpt./services : JAN (1999 Biannual) : Confederation of Indian Industry. (4626225. Fax 4626271.

DELHI INTERNATIONAL MOTOR SHOW : Automobiles & components : JAN (1999 Biannual) : ITE (I) Pvt. Ltd. (6319413. Fax 6319416

AUTO EXPO : Automobiles and components : JAN : (2000 Biannual) : Confederation of Indian Industry. ACMA (5501669 Fax 5593189. AIAM (4648555. Fax 4648222.

TEX-STYLES INDIA : Fabrics, yarns, threads : JAN : India Trade Promotion Organisation. (3314857. Fax 3318142

IMTEX : Machine tools : FEB/MAR : (2001 Triennial) Confederation of Indian Industry.

INDIAN HANDICRAFTS & GIFTS FAIR : Handicrafts & gift items : FEB/OCT : Export Promotion Council for Handicrafts. (6140861. Fax 6143772.

WISITEX : Industrial process control & medical instruments : FEB (2000 Biannual) : Wisitex Foundation. (6917808. Fax 6910170.

WORLD BOOK FAIR : Books & journals : FEB (2000 Biannual) : National Book Trust of India. (664020. Fax 6851795.

INDIAN ENGINEERING TRADE FAIR : Engg. goods, technology transfer, R & D : FEB : (1999 Biannual) : Confederation of Indian Industry.

PLAST INDIA : Plastic & plastic mfg. eqpt. : MAR : Plast India Foundation, Mumbai. Fax 022-8375907.

ENVIRONMENT INDIA : Pollution control & building eqpt. : APR : Exhibitions India. (4622710. Fax 4633506.

INDIA INTERNATIONAL TRAVEL & TOURISM SHOW : Travel & tourism related goods : APR (2000 Biannual) : ITE (I) Pvt. Ltd.

CONSUMEX : Consumer goods : MAY : India Trade Promotion Organisation.

INDIA INTERNATIONAL GARMENTS FAIR : High fashion garments : JUL : Apparel Export Promotion Council. (6188505. Fax 6188584.

INTERNATIONAL SHOE FAIR : Shoes & Shoe-uppers : JUL : India Trade Promotion Organisation.

SHOE COMP : Shoe components & accessories : JUL : India Trade Promotion Organisation.

AHARA : Food products & processing technology : AUG : India Trade Promotion Organisation.

DELHI BOOK FAIR : Books & periodicals : AUG : India Trade Promotion Organisation.

POWER GEN ASIA : Electric power generation : SEPT (2000 Biannual) : Interads Ltd. (6285482. Fax 6228928.

METALLURGY INTERNATIONAL : Forging & alloy castings : OCT (2000 Biannual) : Tafcon Group. (4633881. Fax 4635215.

INTERNATIONAL JEWELLERY & WATCH EXHIBITION : Jewellery : OCT : ITE (I) Pvt. Ltd.

INTERNATIONAL EXHIBITION ON MINING MACHINERY & EQUIPMENT : Mining machinery & eqpt. : OCT : Confederation of Indian Industry.

INDIA INTERNATIONAL TRADE FAIR : All aspects of industry, agriculture and trade : NOV : India Trade Promotion Organisation.

SPORTS EXPO : Fitness eqpt. & adventure tourism : DEC : Tafcon Group.

NATIONAL CHILDREN'S FAIR : Sports & hobbies : DEC : India Trade Promotion Organisation.

IT INDIA/COMDEX : All areas of information technology : DEC : Business India Exhibitions. (6859402. Fax 6859401.

INSIDE OUTSIDE MEGA SHOW : Furniture, furnishings, construction products : DEC : Business India Exhibitions.

COMMSINDIA : Telecom eqpt. : DEC : Exhibitions India.

For exact dates contact

India Trade Promotion Organisation

(3314857 / 3371437. Fax 3318142.

All fax and phone numbers are of Delhi, unless specified.

All exhibitions are annual unless specified.

Delhi Tourism

ADVENTURE ACTIVITIES

From time immemorial Delhi has attracted people with a penchant for adventure providing as it did opportunity as well as patronage. It is this spirit of adventure for which Delhi Tourism now provides avenues.

Trekking : Delhi Tourism's infrastructural network and trained outdoor staff help you to choose from the endless trekking options India offers- ranging from some of the world's highest mountains, greatest deserts, rivers, lakes, sea beaches and rain forests.

Rock Climbing : Equipment and training is provided to aspiring rock climbers in and around Delhi from October to March.

Parasailing : For the truly adventurous, parasailing is available at Kanwar Shikha near Sohna in Haryana, about 60 kms from Delhi. Soar like an eagle under the watchful eyes of professional instructors.

Water Sports : A multi-sports and leisure complex has been created by Delhi Tourism at Bhalswa Lake, situated at Delhi's northeastern edge. This offers facilities for boating in pedal boats, kayaks, canoes and speed boats. Keen anglers can also indulge in fishing. Hovercraft and water scooters have been introduced for the first time in Delhi at this lake. Pedal boats at reasonable rates are available at the Hari Nagar, India Gate, Purana Qila, Prasad Nagar and Naini lakes. Special training programmes in kayaking and canoeing are organised at Prasad Nagar Lake and Naini Lake.

Adventure Club : Open to all Indian nationals above the age of ten years, this club promotes adventure activities. The club provides special packages in all adventure activities - parasailing, mountain expeditions, trekking , rock climbing, adventure camps and water sports, including river rafting in the Ganga. Delhi Tourism has also established a water sports club. Latest information on adventure activities can be obtained from: Delhi Tourism and Transportation Development Corp., Adventure Tourism Division, Coffee Home 1, Baba Kharag Singh Marg, New Delhi- 110001. Tel: 3363607, 3365358. Fax: 3313637 .

DILLI HAAT

Situated in the heart of Delhi, the unique Dilli Haat is an upgraded version of the traditional weekly market, offering a delightful amalgam of craft, food and cultural activities. However, while the village haat is a mobile, flexible arrangement, at Dilli Haat, a permanent haat, it is the craftsmen who are mobile and ever-changing thereby offering a kaleidoscopic view of the richness and diversity of Indian handicrafts and artifacts.

Spread over a spacious six acre area, imaginative landscaping, creative planning, and the traditional village architectural style have combined to produce the perfect ambience for a haat or market place. A plaza paved with stone and brickwork skilfully interspersed with grass, flowering shrubs and towering eucalyptus trees, plus a play corner for children, have conjured up an oasis in which visitors can browse at their leisure.

The food plaza enables visitors to savour the inimitable flavours of gastronomic delights from the various regions of India. The different stalls offer a wide choice of ethnic food which is clean, hygienically prepared and reasonably priced. It often is a venue for regional food festivals.

A wide variety of skilfully crafted handicrafts, intrinsic to each part of the country are available in this exotic bazaar. These range from intricate rosewood and sandalwood carvings, embellished camel-hide footwear, to sophisticated fabric and drapery. Gems, beads, brassware, metal crafts, silk and woollens ..... the range is limitless.

The handicraft stalls are allotted on a rotational basis to craftsmen from all corners of the vast and varied land of India, usually for fifteen days. Thus ensuring that different handicrafts are available to visitors at each visit, and also enabling them to buy authentic wares at prices that have not been inflated by high maintenance costs. Shows promoting handicrafts and handlooms are held at the exhibition hall in the complex.

The Dilli Haat offers you the Indian experience in a microcosm. A destination in itself. And your window to a land filled with myriad colours and vibrant contrasts.

Dilli Haat, Sri Aurobindo Marg, Opp. INA Market,
New Delhi-110023.
Tel: 4629365, 6119055.
Fax: 4610500.

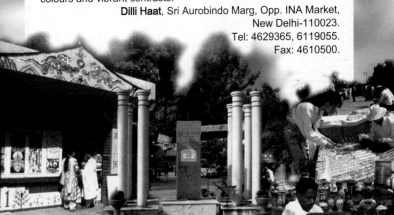

Delhi Tourism

FESTIVALS

The seat of empire for centuries, royal patronage ensured that Delhi remained the cultural epicentre of the country, attracting the best of painters, musicians and dancers. Delhi Tourism puts on display this rich and diverse cultural heritage by holding a series of festivals during the year.

The scattered citadels of erstwhile dynasties which co-exist with high rise residential localities and crowded commercial complexes, form the picturesque backdrop for the haunting melodies and graceful dances rendered by leading artistes during the festivals organised by Delhi Tourism, amongst which some of the popular ones are the **Roshanara** and **Shalimar Bagh Festivals**. These festivals mirror the multiplicity of cultures and reflect the fusion of regional diversities which constitutes modern day Delhi, where the ancient and the modern blend most harmoniously into a whole.

Traditionally, Delhi Tourism holds the **Qutub Festival** of classical music and dance around Sharad Purnima in the month of October at the Qutub Minar complex. The Qutub and its surrounding monuments, bathed in the silvery radiance of the full moon, create a spine-tingling ambience which heightens enjoyment of the evocative melodies and graceful dances performed by outstanding classical musicians and leading exponents of dance.

Delhi is one of the greenest capitals in the world, with a long tradition of laying out of gardens, which dot the city. It is this tradition that Delhi Tourism keeps alive by holding the **Garden Tourism Festival** at the end of February which is generally spread over three days and generates much enthusiasm amongst the gardening fraternity. This is not only a visual feast since Delhi is ablaze with flowers at this time, but also a useful meeting ground for gardening enthusiasts, as well as fun and frolic for children of all ages.

To celebrate the advent of the king of fruits, Delhi Tourism holds the **Mango Festival** in the month of July. Mentioned in the Vedas and Upanishads, the mango is considered auspicious and a symbol of life and joy forever. The largest producer of mangoes, India grows more than eleven hundred varieties of mangoes in different parts of the country. The Mango Festival is the place to discover the magic of mangoes in all their immense variety.

In addition, Dilli Haat offers tantalising glimpses of the vast storehouse of Indian culture by holding regional festivals at its open air theatre. These are held from time to time throughout the year. These festivals reflect the immense diversity, the colour and the vibrancy of this ancient land, ranging as they do from the Pongal and the Onam festivals from South India; Ganesh Chaturthi from Maharashtra; Basant Panchami from North India and Bengal; Teej, the swing festival with

Delhi Tourism

which Rajasthani women in particular, welcome the monsoon; Baisakhi, celebrated in various forms all over India, including Assam where it is known as Rangoli Bihu; and Diwali, the auspicious festival of lights. Many more regional festivals from all over India are held at the popular Dilli Haat and are advertised periodically. Latest information on these festivals can be obtained at: **Dilli Haat**, Sri Aurobindo Marg, Opp. INA Market, New Delhi-110023. Tel: 4629365, 6119055. Fax: 4610500.

MUSICAL FOUNTAIN

Delhi Tourism's musical fountain at Ajmal Khan Park is spread over an area of five acres and provides a refreshing getaway from the bustle of the city.

The scintillating lights synchronised with music, and the cascading water turn this complex into a quiet haven, particularly during the heat of summer.

SON ET LUMIERE: IMMORTAL DELHI

For those desirous of delving into Delhi's glorious and tumultuous past, Delhi Tourism puts on a spectacular sound and light show at the Purana Qila which makes the 5,000 years old history of the city come alive. Amidst the tranquility of the splendidly panoramic and historic environs of the Purana Qila, select episodes from the annals of Delhi's historic and legendary past are vividly brought to life. Special effects combine with the unique ambience to make this show a hauntingly unforgettable experience. For details about the show contact : 4629365, 4603178.

Timings of the show	Hindi	English
Sept. to Oct.	7.00 - 8.00 PM	8.30 - 9.30 PM
Nov. to Jan.	6.00 - 7.00 PM	7.30 - 8.30 PM
Feb. to April	7.00 - 8.00 PM	8.30 - 9.30 PM
May to Aug.	7.30 - 8.30 PM	9.00 - 10.00 PM

Tickets available at :* DTTDC Office, N-36, Connaught Place.
Tel: 3315322
* Connaught Place Coffee Home.
Tel: 3363607
* At the site. Tel: 4603178

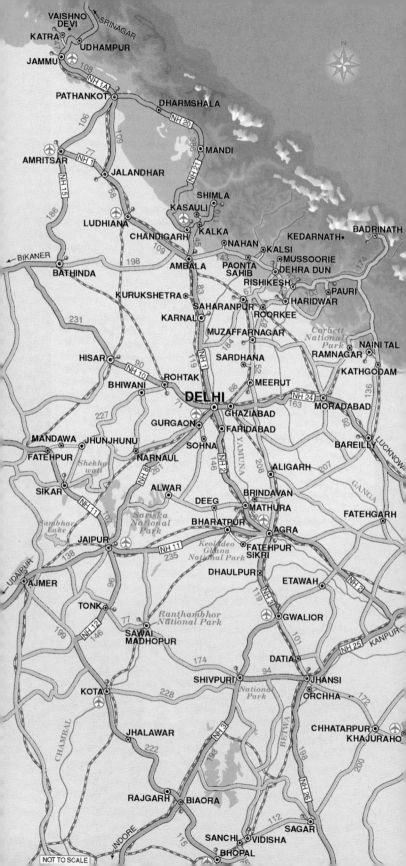

Short Excursions

Mathura

One of the seven sacred cities of Hinduism, the ancient town of Mathura, on the banks of the Yamuna, lies 146 km southeast of Delhi *en route* to Agra. It is the birthplace of Lord Krishna and the miracles associated with his life continue to give the surrounding villages a magical air of rural devotion, especially during the festivals of Holi, Janamashthami and Dussehra.

To the west before reaching Mathura is Barsana, a village on a rocky hillock, where Krishna's consort Radha was born. Snaking through country lanes towards Yamuna you come to Brindavan, where the medieval saint from Bengal, Chaitanya Mahaprabhu, established his Vaishnavite cult of devotion for Radha-Krishna, which is practiced to this day, with the addition of foreign devotees.

A late 18th century map of Brajbhumi (from Jaipur City Palace Museum).

The *ghats* on the banks of Yamuna, perpetually thronged with pilgrims from all over India, have witnessed the building and razing of Buddhist, Hindu and Muslim structures over the centuries. Mathura Museum run by Archaeological Survey of India has a superb collection of ancient masterpieces which makes Mathura's name famous in the world of art as well as religion. Visit Kesava Deo Temple and Vishram Ghat.

On the way to Brindavan is Gita Mandir, and the ambitious ISKCON spiritual campus is in Brindavan. Accommodation in the Mathura environs is designed for the devotional. For material comforts Agra is a more inviting choice.

Krishnajanmabhumi Mandir, Mathura.

276

Much of the beauty of the Taj lies in its feminine wile of switching dress according to the time of day. Its range of moods is impressive, hence the need to see it at different hours of the day.

The tombs of Shahjahan and Mumtaz Mahal.

Agra Fort, begun in 1565 by Emperor Akbar, offers a superb angle on the Taj.

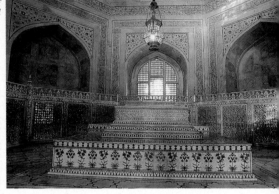

Agra

One of the world's most sought-after tourist destinations (56 km from Mathura, 200 km from Delhi), it is vital for the visitor to approach Agra with eyes open to its treasures but firmly shut to its less salubrious manifestations. Go by train, either the Shatabdi or Taj Express (both leave early morning), and earmark a good hotel near Taj Mahal. The Taj is closed on Mondays. Entry fee is Rs.15 during the day but a glimpse of the Taj at sunrise (6 to 8 am) or sunset (5 to 7 pm) will cost Rs.100. Entry is free on Fridays.

If you have to go by road to Agra, choose a Sunday when there are fewer trucks. Agra does not lack accommodation to suit every pocket.

Emperor Akbar's massive red sandstone mausoleum is 10 km northwest of Agra at Sikandra.

Across the river is the superlative mausoleum of Itmad-ud-Daula, a connoisseur's scale model of the Taj.

Fatehpur Sikri

Every inch an imperial capital, Fatehpur Sikri (38 km west of Agra) is built proudly on a ridge that yielded enduring stone. This dream city of Akbar that became a ghost town within two decades of its investiture, speaks of that rare moment in architecture when a ruler has the means and energy to fulfill his vision of grandeur. The strength and quality of Fatehpur Sikri's remarkable unified layout has been able to withstand the arid hands of time and scorching weather.

Akbar conceived Fatehpur Sikri in 1571 as a thanks-offering to the Sufi saint, Sheikh Salim Chishti, who predicted male successors to the Mughal line. Massive in parts and tenderly evocative in places, the layout reflects Akbar's attempt to reconcile his Islamic heritage of Central Asia with the cultural seductions of Hinduism's urge to openmindedness. Less likely than the call to business in a warring age, was the suggestion that Fatehpur Sikri failed because of its water supply. (Travel the road westwards to Bharatpur and you pass a huge reservoir).

The main entrance to Fatehpur Sikri's Jama Masjid is through the 54-metre-high Buland Darwaza. Young daredevils jump into the deep well outside the Darwaza, in order to earn some money from tourists.

The childless still visit the marble-clad dargah of Sheikh Salim Chishti with the hope that their dreams will be fulfilled.

Bharatpur

Keoladeo Ghana National Park in Bharatpur provides marvellous exposure to more than 350 species of birds. Bharatpur is the only wintering ground in India of the endangered Siberian Crane. Despite the droves of tourists, the birds continue to steal the show. The setting is so lovely that it induces a hush even amongst those for whom no picnic is complete without a transistor. The finest way to explore the sanctuary is on a cycle, which can be hired from the entrance gate, or on a cycle rickshaw. The local rickshawalas are experts on birds and are often the best guides.

Bharatpur is about 120 km from Delhi and 17 km from Fatehpur Sikri. It is linked to Agra and Jaipur by train. Reasonable accommodation is easily available in Bharatpur.

Deeg

Small but stunningly caparisoned with massive fortifications and beautifully maintained gardens with hundreds of fountains, Deeg is well worth a detour.

Deeg is 36 km north of Bharatpur and 90 km from Agra. A market town, it boasts the distinguished Gopal Bhawan of Maharaja Suraj Mal (1750), an architectural treat with the added attraction of still-furnished royal apartments. Ask at the local *desi theka* (country liquor vendor) for a bottle of Kesar Kasturi. Though this retail outlet is very downmarket, the drink makes an excellent tonic unique to this region.

Having driven from Delhi via Mathura on the main road, the tourist can return through the Aravalli Hills via Alwar (Deeg is 38 km west of Mathura and Alwar lies another 90 km west). Many small fortified villages can be discovered as compensation for wandering off the main road, a few of which have been converted into motels. However, be careful about driving late at night, unless you are very sure of the locality.

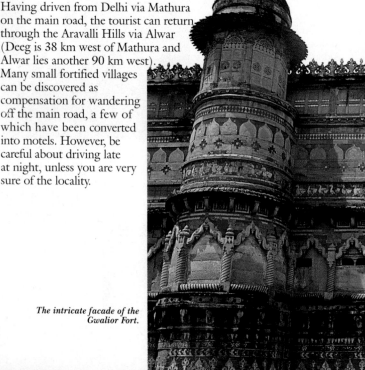

The intricate facade of the Gwalior Fort.

Gwalior

The landscape at Gwalior (320 km from Delhi, 120 km from Agra) is irresistibly royal, the fortifications a gift of nature. The palaces of the Scindias are magnificent and contain exotic trifles mixed with priceless antiques. Visit Man Singh and Jai Vilas Palaces and the Archaeological Museum. The Scindias managed to maintain loyalty both to Indian inspiration (Chhatrapati Shivaji, the scourge of Aurangzeb) and to the paramountcy of the British Raj. The state became famous in an age of conservative Maharajas who resisted the coming of the railways, by setting up a comprehensive network of narrow gauge lines.

The Maharaja not only had a line laid up to his palace gate but the railway engineers who built his fabulous engines also designed a silver line for his dining table that served the replete Maharaja with brandy and cigars. The Usha Kiran Palace Hotel transports the visitor to the mood of the 1930s.

The colourful annual mela in Gwalior.

Shivpuri

The picturesque Madhav National Park in Shivpuri is set on a salubrious plateau, 114 km south of Gwalior. The spectacular royal hunting lodge of the Scindias is situated within the park. Stay in the Madhya Pradesh Government Tourist Lodge, amongst the finest of its kind. One can travel 94 km east to Jhansi, or about 200 km west to Ranthambhor, through delightful forested tracts. But passage over the Chambal river is by a leaky tin tub that claims to be a municipal ferry.

Jhansi

Jhansi, 415 km southeast of Delhi, 215 km southeast of Agra, makes an excellent base for nearby Orchha and Datia, and connects with India's finest temple encounter, Khajuraho, another 200 km east into the interior. Shatabdi Express to Bhopal gets you to Jhansi from Delhi in a little over four hours.

Datia

This tiny former state, 74 km south of Gwalior and 27 km north of Jhansi, has the seven-storied palace of Raja Bir Singh Deo (called Gobind Mandir) which is brilliant in its strength and harmony. But be careful you do not get lost in its eerie echoing labyrinth. The cluster of Jain shrines at Songir, 60 km south of Gwalior on the road to Datia, bristle brilliantly on a ridge approached by crossing the main railway line.

The river Betwa.

Orchha

One of the last unspoilt jewels of Bundelkhand culture, Orchha, lies 20 km south of Jhansi. This atmospheric, abandoned city with dreaming spires reflected in the blue Betwa river, is Raja Bir Singh Deo's creation. You can stay in a palace hotel run by Madhya Pradesh Government and breathe in the beautifully relaxed pace of Madhya Bharat. Nothing quite like Orchha for a getaway far from tourist touts.

Bhopal

Although a hefty 700 km south of Delhi, Bhopal, the attractive capital of Madhya Pradesh, is worth visiting. Bhopal also makes a good base for three fabulous ancient sites in Madhya Pradesh - **Sanchi**, **Vidisha** and **Bhimbetka**.

Sanchi, the excellently preserved Buddhist site, 46 km northeast of Bhopal, was built around 3rd century BC.

Vidisha, 9 km north of Sanchi, has a column erected by Heliodorus, a Greek devotee of Lord Vishnu, dated between 1st and 2nd century BC. A few kilometres from Vidisha are the caves of Udaygiri containing superb reliefs of the Gupta period. The prehistoric cave paintings at Bhimbetka, 45 km south, are remarkably well preserved because of the nature of pigments used. The oldest paintings are believed to be 12,000 years old.

For accommodation, Bhopal is a good bet for the discriminating tourist. Jehan Numa Palace Hotel evokes the past, and Hotel Lake View Ashok, the present. With hired transport and a sober driver, the visitor can fit in all three sites over a long weekend.

Khajuraho

See Khajuraho and you have glimpsed the essence of India. The Taj is a mausoleum to love, the Kandariya Mahadev temple a living ode. It is the architectural inspiration rather than the erotic details that bewitch the visitor to this hideaway village. Few temples in the world exude the spiritual serenity that infuses this scattered array of buildings. The temples of Khajuraho have uplifting lines that move the viewer as a range of mountains does, the design being borrowed from the perspective of receding ranges leading to the climax of Mount Kailash.

Khajuraho enjoys the infrastructure of comfortable hotels. If the five hour road journey from Jhansi to Khajuraho seems an avoidable extra, recall that but for its inaccessibility, Khajuraho would not have survived the centuries with iconoclasts, graffitists and moralists seeking to downplay one of the richest examples of wholeness in the world of art, the natural interplay of flesh and spirit.

Khajuraho is a useful base for exploring the Bundelkhand region. **Panna**, 40 km away, has diamond mines and some bizarre palaces. Panna National Park with its fine waterfalls is worth a visit, while the famous forts of Ajaigarh and Kalinjar are not too far away.

Khajuraho Festival of Dances held in February-March every year.

A Stone's Throw Away

Dhauj with its imposing red cliffs and reservoir is the nearest of Delhi's weekend getaways, around 40 km south, off the road from Faridabad to Sohna. It nestles hidden in the lee of the Aravalli ranges providing opportunities for rock climbing and bird watching.

The craggy outcrops of the Aravallis and the wide expanse of the **Damdama Lake** offer an ideal setting for boating and rock climbing. A Haryana Tourism motel caters to the leisure-bent. It is 8 km east of **Sohna**, which with its hot springs, is another popular destination for picnickers from Delhi.

Only 55 km southwest of Delhi, beyond Gurgaon, the lake at **Sultanpur** has a rich variety of migratory birds in winter. Accomodation in huts and rooms is available. The area is also rich in railway history. Nearby is the very first metre gauge passenger line laid in the world (to Farrukhabad).

Alwar

This quaint and dramatic capital of a former Rajput state is 160 km from Delhi. The palaces live up to exotic expectations, as does the City Palace Museum. Alwar offers a reasonable range of accommodation and lies along the railway route to Jaipur (150 km). Share royal lifestyle at the discount end, at the Palace Hotel in **Siliser**, some 20 km away. **Sariska National Park** is 35 km southwest of Alwar and 200 km from Delhi. Unfortunately, the once viewable tiger has become rather rare. Evening at a hide-out overlooking a water hole, is the best time to view the wildlife. Hotel Sariska Palace offers accommodation within the Park.

Jantar Mantar.

Jaipur

Connected to Delhi by a good but crowded road and excellent railway, Jaipur (250 km), with its broad streets and grid plan invites easy inspection. Maharaja Jai Singh's observatory, Jantar Mantar dates to 1728 and Hawa Mahal, the five-storey palace with a facade of extensive lattice work in stone, to 1799. Inside the elaborate city palace is located the fabulous Maharaja Sawai Man Singh Museum. For a great view of Jaipur go to the fort of Nahagarh overlooking the town.

The grandeur of the palaces and the wealth of the museums can overwhelm the indiscriminate victim of guided tours. While shopping in the bazaars beware of manufacturers of instant antiques, but do spend some time in the jewellery shops. Jaipur is a major centre for precious and semi-precious stones.

The range of accommodation available is excellent. Rambagh Palace Hotel retains discreet references to past opulence and the sybaritic lifestyle.

Amber Fort, situated 11 km outside Jaipur, exudes the flamboyance of Rajput warrior traditions. It is stunningly positioned on a hilltop which overlooks a lake. The Fort is a 15 minute walk from the road, though it is *de rigeur* to ascend on elephant back.

The fabulously decorated Samode Palace, 42 km north-west of Jaipur, has now been turned into a hotel.

The intricate architecture inside Amber Fort, the original capital of the Jaipur rulers.

Ranthambhor National Park

Ranthambhor National Park is the superbly scenic sanctuary near the Chambal gorge, ideal cover for the tiger. It is 160 km southeast of Jaipur via Sawai Madhopur. Poaching has diminished the number of tigers, in spite of the efforts of honest environmentalists. There are good lodges at the park gate, with jeep hire arrangements. The best time to visit is from November to May.

Shekhawati

The Shekhawati region in the semi-arid triangle between Delhi, Jaipur and Bikaner has spectacular art treasures adorning the walls of its *havelis* (mansions). The mansions in the small market towns of Shekhawati are deserted and crumbling, inhabited by chowkidars or squatters. Their owners have moved to big cities but these mansions with their painted walls are not to be missed.

The *havelis* belong to Marwaris, India's most successful merchant community. Every available inch of space, inside and out, is covered with vibrant paintings, astonishing not just for the quantity but for the quality.

Jhunjhunu is the nearest of the Shekhawati painted towns from Delhi (about 220 km via Narnaul). It makes a good base for study tours of the cluster of smaller towns that boast of painted *havelis*, **Fatehpur**, **Mandawa**, **Ramgarh** and **Sikar**.

Hotel Shiv Shekhawati at Jhunjhunu has a range of comfortable accommodation including resort facilities.

The painters of Shekhawati have shown great skill in mixing court styles with folk idiom.

The walled city of Mandawa, 27 km west of Jhunjhunu, is built around the Maharaja's palace which has been turned into a hotel where the royal family are well-informed hosts. The *havelis* are tall, narrow buildings where the artist was commissioned to fill every available space with bright blues, deep reds and yellows to give a primary impact that announces to one's neighbours that your family has arrived in the pecking order of Marwari *seths*. The local textiles are superb in colour and design, and wear well.

Fatehpur, 8 km west of Mandawa, also boasts a medieval *baoli* (step well). Fatehpur has a Rajasthan State Tourism bungalow which is well-run and reasonably priced. It makes a good base to see Ramgarh, 15 km to the north, perhaps the ultimate Shekhawati painted town.

Ajmer

About 450 km southwest of Delhi by the Shatabdi distance shrinker, this town is famous for the *dargah* of Khwaja Moinuddin Chishti, a Sufi saint who settled here in 1192. Also worth visiting is the mosque, Adhai Din ka Jhonpra, built from a despoiled Jain college. Accommodation at Pushkar, only 11 km away, is fairly simple, while at Ajmer it is passable. The brilliantly beautiful Pushkar Lake, is sacred to Hindus and is irresistible to young western tourists. Pushkar also has one of the only Brahma temples in the country.

On the banks of Pushkar Lake.

A huge camel fair is held in Pushkar on Kartika Purnima.

Bikaner

This true desert town flaunts the mood of feudal Rajasthan and everything about it is appealing. It is an overnight journey by train from Delhi (460 km).

Going by the palace size and fittings, the Bikaner motto seems to have been 'anything other dynasties can do, we can do better' and the buildings are not just impressive but overwhelming in their pomp and style.

It was Maharaja Ganga Singh (1887-1943) who dragged Bikaner from its medieval status to an invigorating modern style. His rambling Lalgarh Palace is now a hotel.

The museums of Bikaner are the last word in exotic memorabilia and inspired upmarket junk (including a soup-strainer for the walrus-mustachioed Maharaja, Prussian helmets with villainous looking spikes and shot down enemy aircraft in a shot-up

Intricate jaali work inside Junagadh Fort.

condition). Do not fail to see the bed that says it all about these desert princes, forever on guard against treachery.

Outside the well laid-out town is the palace of Gajner (32 km), once famous for its gargantuan bags of sand grouse and now a hotel. Another famous excursion is to the Karni Mata Mandir at Deshnok (32 km southwest) where rats are allowed religious right of way. Otherwise Bikaner is essentially camel territory and a visit to the Camel Breeding Farm (10 km) is a must. The Bikaner royal family cenotaphs at Devi Kund (8 km) merit a visit.

The desert landscape around Bikaner.

Chandigarh

Chandigarh hosts the governments of both Punjab and Haryana. It lies 250 km northeast of Delhi and is extremely well connected by trains and buses. With the lived-in experience of its model layout sobering the original hype of its designer, Le Corbusier, Chandigarh as a city is still striving to find its soul. The government buildings in Sector I almost bully the landscape. The Rose Garden, the Museum and Art Gallery are worth a visit. The latter has a fine collection of Indian miniature paintings.

Kasauli is an unspoilt hill station only 60 km northeast of Chandigarh in Himachal Pradesh. From the railhead at Kalka, it is just 35 km. Kasauli has maintained both its tree cover and its period charm.

Sukhna Lake relieves the monotony of Le Corbusier's grid while Nek Chand's rock garden is a work of sheer landscaping genius. For the rock garden alone, Chandigarh is worth a visit. Accommodation in the city is limited.

Vaishno Devi

One of the most popular temples in north India, Vaishno Devi, situated at a height of 1700 metres, is 61 km north of Jammu. The cave shrine of the three Hindu goddesses, Mahakali, Mahalaxmi and Mahasaraswati, possesses a rural mystique enlivened by media exposure. As at all popular pilgrim places, queues are inevitable unless you time your *darshan* right. Jammu is 585 km from Delhi, Katra 645 km, and the shrine another 13 km climb from Katra. The weekly Rajdhani to Jammu is the most convenient train to take. Accommodation is available in *dharmashalas* and in the J&K Tourism bungalow in Katra. The food is strictly vegetarian.

Dehradun

No longer a place of sylvan beauty for the retired, Dehradun, like other UP towns, is badly in need of a bypass. Coming from Delhi (230 km) you can turn west at Clement Town and drive to the Indian Military Academy (IMA), then through the Cantonment to Rajpur Road, missing the potholes and fumes of innumerable three-wheelers. The institutions for which Dehradun has always been famous, IMA, Doon School and the Forest Research Institute, the latter with a fine museum and a rich collection of forest species, lie on this route.

Mussoorie

Once the 'Queen of the Hills', the 36 km climb from the Doon Valley now introduces the visitor to Mussoorie's modern claim to fame, the largest number of hotels in any hill resort in India, 350 at the last count. But it is still cool and salubrious if you know where to find the shady walks. Landour Cantonment, for example, remains untouched by the building boom. Mussoorie is an excellent base for treks into the interior of Garhwal, Nag Tibba at 3,000 metres, through dense unspoilt jungle can be done in a weekend.

The Mussoorie season only lasts six weeks in May and June and for the rest of the year there is the prospect of more reasonable room rates and the likelihood of more reliable drinking water. Mussoorie's so-called suburban expansion west to Kempty Falls, and east along the great snow view ridge to Dhanolti and Sarkhanda Devi, attracts visitors who come to get away from Delhi's traffic jams though Mussoorie's Mall is worse in the tourist season!

Taxis and buses ply regularly between Mussoorie and Dehradun. You can drive to Rishikesh along the ridge (via Chamba and Narendranagar) but it takes half the time via Dehradun.

Rishikesh

The Ganga, free of the Himalayan valley, broadens out at Rishikesh. Loudspeakers on both banks blare out spiritual sustenance from the numerous ashrams lining this athletic river. A footbridge enables the visitor to cross to the opposite bank. Walk up to Lakshman Jhula and return over the much narrower gorge section. This would give an idea why the Ganga is believed to be the releaser from sin. Though Haridwar is known as the 'gate' of the abode of Shiva to the plains, it is the swelling of the uncaged river at Rishikesh that arouses the feeling of deliverance.

Rishikesh is the starting point of pilgrimages by car or bus, to the Char Dham of Uttarakhand. Twenty-five km upstream near Vyasi is Shivpuri, a centre for white water rafting which offers short and memorable trips for all ages, the perfect tonic for jaded urban appetites *(see: Sports, p.263)*.

Haridwar

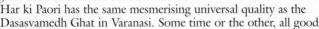

The bazaar at Haridwar is beautifully devotional while the *ghats* tend to be more businesslike. Har ki Paori has the same mesmerising universal quality as the Dasasvamedh Ghat in Varanasi. Some time or the other, all good Hindus must make the rounds of Haridwar and the air is full of the spirit of thankfulness.

High-rise ashrams between Rishikesh and Haridwar offer the ultimate 'best of both worlds', packaged ancient wisdom with all mod cons. Shatabdi Express from Delhi has now made Haridwar a convenient day outing.

The clock tower at Har ki Paori.

The best time to be on the waterfront at Haridwar is during evening aarti when Ganga Mata is worshipped. Devotees float leaf boats with earthenware lamps. There is something profoundly moving about the ceremony.

Pauri

Thanks to an overnight train to Kotdwar (300 km from Delhi), it is possible to enjoy Pauri over a long weekend. At Satpuli, a road diverts to the angler's paradise at Vyasi (where the Nayar river meets the Ganga) and a diversion to the west takes you to Lansdowne, a hill station famous as the regimental centre of the Garhwal Rifles. Higher still, Pauri is perched in front of the snow peaks of the Great Himalaya, Chaukhamba, Nilkanth, Trishul and others in a marvellous close-up panorama of the inner Himalayas. Accommodation is available in the Garhwal Mandal Vikas Nigam bungalow in Pauri and in the PWD bungalow at Lansdowne. Pauri is 110 km from Kotdwar, 100 km from Rishikesh; Lansdowne is 42 km from Kotdwar, 110 km from Pauri.

Najibabad, 20 km from Kotdwar on the road to Bijnor, has the vast and rambling Patthargarh, a mud fort, which was the original home of the famous Robin Hood bandit, Sultana.

Sardhana

Fifteen kilometres north of Meerut is the startlingly magnificent basilica built by the diminutive Begum Samru who led her own forces to battle. She was spouse to two foreign soldiers of fortune and turned to religion after retirement. This Roman Catholic structure, built in 1819, has some fine furniture and monuments and is an incredible architectural achievement to emerge from an age of freebooting anarchy. The marble gateway was said to be imported from Italy no doubt at the instance of the Begum's French husband.

Corbett National Park

The oldest of north India's game sanctuaries, Corbett is situated on the generous flow of the Ramganga, a river that divides Garhwal from Kumaun. The main entrance to the park lies north of Ramnagar some 300 km from Delhi. The facilities are wide enough to satisfy every taste. The mix of sal forest, blue river and receding hills make it a perfect getaway, in spite of the number of tourists. The main accommodation is at Dhikala, some 50 km from Ramnagar, but private resorts outside the sanctuary at Ramnagar and Kalagarh offer tempting facilities. Tiger Tops Corbett Lodge on the river Kosi near Ramnagar is top of the range. The best time to visit is between November and May.

Corbett offers not-to-be-missed tours into the interior of Kumaun. The drive to Ranikhet (85 km) follows a breathtakingly beautiful panorama of the snow-capped mountains along a ridge road. An overnight train to Kathgodam now makes the Kumaun hills accessible from Delhi for a weekend.

An interesting excursion is a trek to Ramnagar from Nainital by the high ridge route via Binayak (2 days).

Boats on the serene Nainital Lake.

South Extension, 1998. Impressions of a Mughal miniature artist, Firozuddin.

Traveller's
Needs

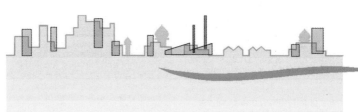

Where to Stay

Where to Eat

Where to Shop

Where to Stay

Delhi has a wide range of accommodation – from deluxe five star hotels that are as good as the best in the world and come expensive, to middle-range hotels and guest houses that are often well-appointed and offer good service and comfortable stay, to down-market tourist lodges in crowded localities which are really inexpensive but offer minimal amenities.

Many of the city's best hotels have tie-ups with international hotel chains like Sheraton, Hyatt and Hilton. The two well-known Indian hotel chains – the Taj and the Oberoi groups – offer services that are more than a match for international hotel chains. Although expensive (Rs 6000 and more for a standard double room), the top-end hotels are reliable and offer impeccable service. What makes them special is the Indian brand of hospitality offered.

The deluxe five star hotels offer facilities comparable to those available in this category worldwide. These include swimming pools, tennis courts, health clubs, shopping arcades, gardens, 24-hour coffee shops and well-equipped business centres. Most of these hotels have a number of speciality restaurants which are among the best in the city. Tourists, of course, feel pampered in these plush hotels, and business travellers too find them extremely comfortable. The business centres provide round-the-clock service, which include efficient secretarial service and facility to send and receive faxes at any time. Single and double rooms have desks with telephone, and in some cases, fax machines. Separate lounges, complimentary breakfast and happy hours at the bar all add to the feel-good factor.

Most of these hotels have arrangements with golf clubs and it is possible to tee-off at short notice. The shopping arcades sell anything from curios to ornate jewellery, and have florists, barber shops and beauty salons. Some of them have excellent health clubs with all the latest equipments. These as well as some middle-level hotels have conference facilities and offer the service of interpreters. As a matter of fact, right through the winter months international conferences are held in Delhi, many of them in the top-end hotels.

Air and train bookings can be made from hotels, either by in-house travel agencies or resourceful hotel staff. Cars are available for hire – from swanky limousines to the locally-made Ambassadors. Tour and travel agencies also arrange local sight-seeing tours with multi-lingual guides.

The government-run Ashok group has two five star hotels, Ashok and Kanishka, and a number of middle-range hotels which offer reasonable accommodation at central locations. Of them, the Ashok Yatri Niwas, a budget hotel, is quite popular with young tourists.

There are a number of middle-level hotels and guest houses in the Connaught Place area, central and south Delhi. Hotels such as The Connaught and Nirula's, located in the city centre, offer good rooms and efficient service. While the Nirula's has a wide range of restaurants, others like The Connaught have a number of restaurants within walking distance. There are also several guest houses in the same range, among them, the Maharani and Jukaso Inn, in Sunder Nagar. This range of accommodation may lack the ambience of five star hotels, but this is often compensated by personalised service and a hassle-free attitude.

Noise levels in Delhi are, by and large, pretty high and sound-proofing in middle-level or budget hotels is not exactly great. So, if you are staying in a crowded area, it would be a good idea to ask for a room away from the road.

The budget hotels and down-market tourist lodges, are mostly located in Connaught Place, Paharganj and in the old city area of Shahjahanabad. These offer inexpensive rooms (some within Rs 500 for a night) or dormitory accommodation at a lesser rate. What is lacking in amenities here is perhaps compensated for young foreign tourists – who often patronise the lodges in Paharganj and Connaught Place – with a sense of adventure. Promises made at the front desk in such hotels often prove to be inaccurate. So it would be a good idea to personally check out the room to find out whether it really has hot and cold running water, the condition of the toilet, room service and general cleanliness.

Most Delhi hotels are not well-equipped to provide adequate facilities for the disabled. Only top-end five star hotels have facilities like wheelchairs, ramp at the hotel entrance, special lifts at ground level and expert help. These conform to international standards of care for the disabled. Many of them offer a discount in tariff for their disabled guests. Most middle-level and budget hotels do not have these facilities and it is advisable to check details before making a reservation.

For the convenience of the first-time traveller to Delhi, here is an attempt to classify hotels based on tariffs and location. We hope this will assist the reader to choose his place of stay as well as the location of his choice. We have been unbiased and have not made any recommendations, however all the hotels in our list offer value for money.

The area around **Connaught Place,** the city centre, is a good place to stay. For tourists pushing a tight schedule, the location is particularly useful as many places of interest are nearby. Connaught Place is also Delhi's prime shopping centre – it has a wide range of shops, from those on footpaths to fashionable department stores. The state emporia are also in this area.

Paharganj is a congested area in the heart of the city, next to New Delhi Railway Station. It has a large number of cheap lodges which are rather popular with young budget tourists. The bustle of the area, the chaos on the roads and the high noise level probably adds to the romance of the orient, but if you are fussy, do stay away from hotels and lodges here, for the accommodation is rudimentary and service not necessarily reliable. Tourists choosing this area for their stay should not expect more than a clean room, and still, it is advisable to check personally that the hotel is indeed providing one.

The area **South of India Gate** is an oasis of tranquillity with landscaped gardens and manicured lawns. Unfortunately, there are not many hotels in this area, barring a few top-end hotels and a couple of guest houses in Sundar Nagar. Of the top-end hotels, The Oberoi and Taj are good, while The Claridges, a little less expensive, and has an old-world charm.

Hotels located in **South Delhi** – in areas such as Lajpat Nagar and Nehru Place – are ideal for those who have business in that part of the city. They are close to a number of historical sites in south Delhi.

North Delhi in which we have included the area beyond Delhi Gate, has several small hotels and one five star hotel, one of the oldest in the city in area beyond Kashmere Gate – Oberoi Maidens. The area between Delhi Gate and Kashmere Gate, Shahjahanabad, is crowded with winding lanes and bylanes which tempt exploration.Small businessmen find it useful to stay in this area because of most wholesale markets are located here.

gurudwaras run by Hindu and Sikhs religious trusts. Retiring rooms are available at Delhi Main and New Delhi Railway Station for upper class train passengers. There are also dormitory facilities, camping sites and youth hostels for students and travellers.

YMCA Tourist Hostel, Jai Singh Road, Connaught Place. (3746031. Fax 3746032

Youth Hostel, 5 Nyaya Marg, Chanakyapuri. (6119841

YWCA Blue Triangle Family Hostel, Ashok Road, Connaught Place. (3734807

YWCA International Guest House, 10 Sansad Marg, Connaught Place. (3361561

Vishwa Yuvak Kendra (International Youth Hostel) Circular Road, Chanakyapuri. (3013631

Camping Sites

Tourists Camp, Jawaharlal Nehru Marg. (3272898

Qudsia Gardens Tourist Camp, Kashmere Gate (2523121

Railway

Retiring Rooms, New Delhi Railway Station and Delhi Main Railway Station

Rail Yatri Niwas, Ajmere Gate. (3233484

(Basic accommodation is available for a maximum of three days against proof of train journey.)

Indira Gandhi International Airport (IGIA)

Terminal I (5665126
Terminal II (5652011

(Airconditioned rooms and dormitories are available for a maximum of 24 hours for transit passengers with confirmed departure tickets).

Hotels around **Chanakyapuri** and **Vasant Vihar** are in the top and middle-level categories. The area is close to the airport and diplomatic missions. Visitors with related work in the city or with quick business might find it useful to be located in this area.

It is advisable to **book** your accommodation in advance as availability in the busy tourist season is difficult. You may book directly by letter or fax, or indirectly with the help of your travel agent.

The **checking-out** hour is usually 12 noon, although some hotels do it according to 24 hours of stay. So, do ask in advance. It is also advisable to verify bills and retain receipts.

Hotels offer **discounts** during off-season. But you must bargain for it, because even in the hot summer months when few tourists come to Delhi it is common for hotels to first offer the printed official tariff. All hotels, especially the smaller ones, give discounts for tourist groups and children.

Taxes Levied Do remember that over and above the room rent, government levies a hotel entertainment tax on airconditioned hotels and an additional luxury tax in case of deluxe and five star hotels. An expenditure tax and a food and beverage is also applicable in case of five star hotels. If you are not an Indian passport holder, it would be advisable to find out whether the hotel you wish to stay in, accepts payment only in foreign exchange or at the dollar rate which would mean an additional amount over the rupee rate.

Apart from hotels, there are other options that one may consider when selecting a place to stay – guest houses, railway and airport retiring rooms, dharamshalas and

Connaught Place, Paharganj

Ashok Yatri Niwas, Ashok Road
(3344511. Fax 3368153 (547 rooms);
From airport 18.5 km ▪

Cama Guest House 3037 Paharganj
(7770245. Fax 7528633 (34 rooms);
From CP 2.5 km; From
airport 22 km ▪

Central Court N Block, Connaught
Circus Telefax 3317582 (36 rooms);
From airport 20.5 km ▪

Fifty Five H55 Connaught Place
(3321244. Fax 3320769 (15 rooms);
From airport 19.5 km ▪

Hans Plaza Barakhamba Road
(3316868. Fax 3314830 (67 rooms);
From airport 20 km ▪▪▪▪

Imperial Janpath
(3341234. Fax 3342255 (285 rooms);
From airport 19.5 km ▪▪▪▪

Janpath Janpath
(3340070. Fax 3347083 (213 rooms);
From airport 19.5 km ▪▪

Jukaso Inn Down Town L Block,
Connaught Place 3324451.
Fax 3324448 (40 rooms); From
airport 20 km ▪

Kabeer 3/4 Arakashan Road, Ram
Nagar (7521300. Fax 7523656
(38 rooms); From CP 2.5 km; From
airport 21.5 km ▪

Kanishka Janpath (3344422.
Fax 3368242 (317 rooms); From
airport 19 km ▪▪▪

Le Meridien Windsor Place
(3710101. Fax 3714545 (355 rooms);
From airport 19 km ▪▪▪▪▪

Madras Hotel P Block
Connaught Circus (3363652.
(20 rooms); From airport 19.5 km. ▪

Marina Connaught Circus
(3324658. (46 rooms); From
airport 19 km ▪▪▪

Metropolis Hotel
Near Rajguru Road, Paharganj
(3558052 Fax 7525600 (13 rooms);
From CP 3 km; From airport 22 km ▪

New Delhi Hilton Barakhamba
Avenue (3320101. Fax 3325335
(445 rooms); From airport 21 km ▪▪▪▪▪

Nirula's L Block, Connaught Place
(3322419. Fax 3324669 (29 rooms);
From airport 20 km ▪▪

Ranjit Maharaja Ranjit Singh Road
(3231256. Fax 323366 (187 rooms);
From airport 21 km ▪▪

The Connaught Shaheed Bhagat
Singh Marg (3364225. Fax 3340757
(76 rooms); From airport 19.5 km ▪▪▪

The Park Sansad Marg
(3733737. Fax 3732025 (26
rooms); From airport 19.5 km ▪▪▪▪

Tourist 7361 Ram Nagar
(7510334. Fax 3559418 (65 rooms);
From CP 2.5 km; From
airport 21.5 km ▪

Vishal Hotel Main Bazaar Road,
Paharganj (527629. (31 rooms);
From CP 3 km; From
airport 22 km ▪

Vivek 1534-50 Main Bazaar
Paharganj (521948. Fax 7537103
(50 rooms); From CP 2 km;
From airport 21 km ▪

YMCA Tourist Hostel Jai Singh
Road (3746031. Fax 3746032
(127 rooms); From airport 18.5 km ▪

York K10 Connaught Circus
(3323769. Fax 3352419
(27 rooms); From airport 19.5 km ▪▪

YWCA Guest House Jai Singh
Road (3746668. (122) rooms;
From airport 19 km ▪

South of India Gate
Khan Market, Pandara Road

Ambassador Hotel Sujan Singh
Park (4632600. Fax 4638219
(85 rooms); From CP 5.5 km;
From airport 21 km ▪▪▪

Jukaso Inn 50 Sunder Nagar
(4690308. Fax 4694402
(50 rooms); From CP 5 km;
From airport 23 km ▪▪

Lodhi Hotel Lala Lajpat Rai Marg
(3329465. Fax 3324669
(205 rooms); From CP 7 km;
From airport 21 km ▪▪

Maharani Guest House 3 Sunder
Nagar (4693129. Fax 4624562
(24 rooms); From CP 4.2 km;
From airport 23.5 km ▪

Oberoi Dr. Zakir Hussain Marg
(4363030. Fax 4360484
(290 rooms); From CP 5.5 km;
From airport 21.5 km ▪▪▪▪▪

Rajdoot Hotel Mathura Road
(4319585. Fax 4317442
(55 rooms); From CP 7 km;
From airport 23 km ▪

The Claridges Aurangzeb Road
(3010211. Fax 3010625
(162 rooms); From CP 4 km;
From airport 20 km ▪▪▪▪

Taj Mahal Hotel Mansingh Road
(3016162. Fax 3017299
(300 rooms); From CP 4 km;
From airport 21 km ▪▪▪▪

Price Range in Rupees
Below 1500 ▪   1500-2500 ▪▪   2500-4000 ▪▪▪   4000-6000 ▪▪▪▪   6000+ ▪▪▪▪▪

North Delhi
Daryaganj, Shahjahanabad, Civil Lines

Agra Hotel 16 Daryaganj
(3278042/44. (30 rooms); From CP
4 km; From airport 23 km ▪

Broadway Hotel Asaf Ali Road
(3273821. Fax 3280887 (32 rooms);
From CP 3 km; From
airport 22 km ▪

Flora Dayanand Road, Daryaganj
(3273634. Fax 3280887 (24 rooms);
From CP 3.5 km; From
airport 22.5 km ▪

Kastle Guest House 16 Daryaganj
(3272694 (19 rooms); From CP
4 km; From airport 23 km ▪

New Frontier S.P. Mukherji Marg
(2527332 (25 rooms); From CP
3.7 km; From airport 22.7 km ▪

Oberoi Maidens 7 Shyam Nath Marg
(2914841. Fax 2929800
(53 rooms); From CP 9 km;
From airport 28 km ▪▪▪

Punjab Hotel Fatehpuri (2525045
(73 rooms); From CP 4.5 km;
From airport 23.5 km ▪

Regal Near Old Delhi RS, Fatehpuri
(2526232 (37 rooms); From CP
4 km; From airport 23 km ▪

South West Delhi
Vasant Vihar Chanakyapuri

Ashok 50B Chanakyapuri
(6110101. Fax 6873216
(563 rooms); From CP 7 km;
From airport 15.5 km ▪▪▪▪▪

Centaur Indira Gandhi International
Airport (5652223. Fax 5652256
(376 rooms); From CP 16.6 km;
From airport 2.7 km ▪▪▪▪

Diplomat 9 Sardar Patel Marg
(3010204. Fax 3018605 (25 rooms);
From CP 4.7 km; From
airport 14.5 km ▪▪▪▪

Hyatt Regency Bhikaji Cama Place
(6181234. Fax 6186833
(518 rooms); From CP 9.2 km;
From airport 13.5 km ▪▪▪▪▪

Maurya Sheraton Sardar Patel Marg
(6112233. Fax 6113333
(500 rooms); From CP 6.2 km;
From airport 12.7 km ▪▪▪▪▪

Qutab Hotel Shaheed Jeet Singh
Marg (6521010. Fax 6968287
(92 rooms); From CP 12 km;
From airport 15.5 km ▪▪▪

Samrat Chanakyapuri (6110606.
Fax 4679056 (250 rooms); From
CP 7 km; From airport 15.5 km ▪▪▪

Taj Palace Sardar Patel Marg
(6110202. Fax 6110808
(420 rooms); From CP 6.5 km;
From airport 12.2 km ▪▪▪▪▪

Vasant Continental Vasant Vihar
(6148800. Fax 6148900
(123 rooms); From CP 12 km;
From airport 13.2 km ▪▪▪▪

Vishwa Yuvak Kendra Circular
Road, Chanakyapuri (3013631.
Fax 3016604 (35 rooms); From CP
4.5 km; From airport 16 km ▪

South Delhi
South Extn, Hauz Khas, Defence Colony, Friends Colony, Greater Kailash

Anchor Inn A12 Kailash Colony
(6417765. (14 rooms); From CP
10 km; From airport 22 km ▪

Best Western Surya New Friends
Colony (6835070. Fax 6837758
(236 rooms); From CP 11 km;
From airport 23.5 km ▪▪▪▪▪

International Inn 9A Ring Road
Lajpat Nagar (6437391/6437392.
(17 rooms); From CP 8 km;
From airport 18.5 km ▪

Jor Bagh 27 27 Jor Bagh
(4698475. Fax 4698475 (18 rooms);
From CP 6 km; From
airport 18.5 km ▪

Kailash Inn 10 Sunder Nagar
(4617401. Fax 91578941
(16 rooms); From CP 4.3 km;
From airport 23.3 km ▪

Madhuban Holiday Inn B11 Greater
Kailash I (6431923. (29 rooms);
From CP 10 km; From
airport 21 km ▪

Orchid G4 South Extn I
(4643529. Fax 4626924 (18
rooms); From CP 9.5 km; From
airport 17.7 km ▪▪

Park Royal Nehru Place
(6223344. Fax 6224288
(215 rooms); From CP 11.5 km;
From airport 21 km ▪▪▪▪▪

Sartaj A3 Green Park (6857644.
Fax 6864240 (41 rooms); From CP
9 km; From airport 17 km ▪

Silver Oak B46 Soami Nagar
(6436367/6423320 (21 rooms);
From CP 11.5 km; From
airport .18 km ▪

Vikram Lajpat Nagar (6436451.
Fax 6435657 (72 rooms); From CP
9 km; From airport 18.5 km ▪▪

Karol Bagh

Gautam Delux 2105 D.B. Gupta Road, Karol Bagh (5729163. Fax 6411242 (48 rooms); From CP 3.5 km; From airport 19.5 km ■

Oasis D8 Pitampura (7246869. Fax 7434665 (10 rooms); From CP 15 km; From airport 28 km ■

Siddharth Rajendra Place (5762501. Fax 5781016 (98 rooms); From CP 5 km; From airport 19.5 km ■■■■

Sobti 2397-98 Hardrian Singh Market, Karol Bagh (5729035. Fax 5756999 (27 rooms); From CP 3 km; From airport 19.5 km ■

South Indian Ajmal Khan Road (5723651 (25 rooms); From CP 3 km; From airport 18.5 km ■

Wood Inn Kirti Nagar (5438500/ 5439136 (15 rooms); From CP 9.5 km; From airport 20 km ■

Just out of Delhi

If you wish to get away from the noise and bustle of the city and yet remain within couple of hours drive from Connaught Place, these may be the options you are looking for.

32nd Milestone (20 rooms) Delhi-Jaipur, Chandernagar Gurgaon ((91) 322528. Fax (91)322272

Ashok Country Resort (80 rooms) Rajokri Road, Kapashera (5564590. Fax 5563054

Rajhans (75 rooms) Surajkund ((91) 252055 Fax (91) 252842

Resort Country Club (20 rooms) Pachgaon Tauru Road, Dist. Gurgaon Road, Haryana ((91) 325280

Sita Holiday Resorts Ltd. (80 rooms) Manesar, Gurgaon ((91) 331295.

Vatika (12 rooms) Garden Retreat, Sohna-Gurgaon, Haryana ((0124) 662548 Delhi (6442921. Fax 6476641

The Heritage Village Naharpur Opp. National Highway No 8 ((91) 331291-95. Fax (91) 331272

Heritage Hotels

Given below is a list of Heritage Hotels outside Delhi. These are old forts and *havelis* that have been converted into hotels with all the modern facilities. Most of the hotels mentioned in this list involve 4-6 hours drive from the city.

Ajit Bhawan Palace Opp. Circuit House, Jodhpur ((0291) 37,410. Fax (0291) 37774

Bhadrawati Palace Vill. & Post Bhandarej, Dist. Dausa. ((01427) 8351 Fax (0141) 382810 (Jaipur)

Bissau Palace Outside Chandpole Gate, Jaipur ((0141) 304391. Fax (0141) 304628

Castle Mandawa Mandawa Dist. Jhunjhunu, Shekhawati ((01592) 23124/23480. Fax (01592) 23171

Dera Dundlod Kila P.O. Dundlod, Dist. Jhunjhunu ((015945) 2519. Fax (0141) 211276 (Jaipur)

Dundlod Castle P.O. Dundlod, Dist. Jhunjhunu ((015945) 441Fax (0141) 211118 (Jaipur)

Fateh Prakash Palace City Palace, Udaipur ((0294) 28239/41. Fax (0294) 528001

Golden Castle Pachar P.O. Pachar, Dist. Sikar. ((01576) 64611 Fax (0141) 382810 (Jaipur)

Karni Bhawan Defence Lab Road, Jodhpur ((0291) 32220/39380. Fax (0291) 33495

Lallgarh Palace Ganga Avenue Road, Bikaner ((0151) 5226103. Fax (0151) 522253

Mukundgarh Fort Mukundgarh ((01594) 52396/97/98. Fax 6885344(Delhi)

Narain Niwas Palace Kanota Bagh, Narain Singh Road, Jaipur ((0141) 563448/561291. Fax (0141) 563448

Narain Niwas Palace Malka Prol, Jaisalmer ((02992) 52408. Fax (02992) 52101

Neemrana Fort Palace P.O. Neerana Dist. Alwar ((01494) 6007. Fax (01494) 5004 Fax 4621112 (Delhi)

Pushkar Palace Pushkar Lake, Dist. Ajmer ((0145) 72001. Fax (0145) 72226

Raj Mahal Palace Sardar Patel Marg, C Scheme, Jaipur ((0141) 381676. Fax (0141) 381625

Ramgarh Lodge P. O. Jamuva, Ramgarh Dist. Jaipur ((014262) 217 Fax (0141) 381098

Rohet Garh P.O. Rohet, Dist. Pali. ((02931) 66231 Fax (0291) 49368 (Jodhpur)

Samode Haveli Gangapole, Jaipur ((0141) 630943. Fax (0141) 630943

Samode Palace Samode Dist. Jaipur ((01423) 4113. Fax (01423) 4123

Sariska Palace Sariska Dist. Alwar ((014652) 4247. Fax 677703 (Delhi)

Sawai Madhopur Lodge Ranthambore National Park, Sawai Madhopur ((07462) 20541. Fax (07462) 20718

Usha Kiran Palace Jayendragang Lashkar, Gwalior ((0751) 323213

Woodville Palace Raj Bhawan Road, Shimla ((0177) 72763/77513

Price Range in Rupees
Below 1500 ■   1500-2500 ■■   2500-4000 ■■■   4000-6000 ■■■■   6000+ ■■■■■

Where to Eat

CHOR BIZARRE

Delhi could be very exciting for those interested in food. It offers good food from all over the world and all parts of India. So, you will not be homesick for your kind of food. If you are not an Indian and adventurous about food, it may be worth sampling Indian food, both the food typical of north India and other parts of the country. The restaurants in the city are varied – not only in their ambience, or the lack of it, but also in their rates.

In an earlier chapter, *Food*, we have written about the traditional cuisines of Delhi, especially about the many smaller eateries strewn all over the city.

> ***Booking :*** It is advisable to book a table in a restaurant, especially during the festive season to avoid a tedious wait or even disappointment.
>
> ***Taxes :*** Certain additional taxes are levied over and above the listed price on the menu. It may be worthwhile to check at the restaurant.

Here we give you a list of the better-known restaurants in the city. The list has been made area-wise so as to make it convenient for you to find an eatery close to where you are staying or working. There is something to suit every pocket and palate. Also, each restaurant comes with a description of its speciality cuisine. A sumptuous meal for two could cost anything from Rs 200 to over Rs 2000 (and that's not including wine)! Read on and make your choices.

NAME, TYPE OF FOOD (SPECIALITY), ADDRESS, PHONE, FACILITIES, PRICE RANGE

Connaught Place, Paharganj

Amber Indian
N Block, Connaught Circus Opp.
Scindia House (3312092
☐ ☐ ⴵ •••

Appetite European
Vishal Hotel Main Bazaar Road
Paharganj (527629 •

Baluchi Indian
New Delhi Hilton Barakhamba
Avenue (3320101 ☐ ☐ ⴵ ❖

Berco's Chinese
E Block, Connaught Place
(3318134 ☐ ☐ ••

Blue Elephant Oriental (Thai)
New Delhi Hilton Barakhamba
Avenue (3320101 ☐ ☐ ⴵ ❖

Price Range in Rupees (meal for two)
Below 300 •   300-600 ••   600-900 •••   900+ ❖

Cafe 100 European
B Block Connaught Place
(3350051 ••

Cellar Multi cuisine
13 Regal Building Connaught Place
(3361444 ☐ 🗁 ☥ ••

Chinese Room Oriental
Nirula's, L Block, Connaught Place
(3322419 ☐ 🗁 ☥ ••

Clay & Coal Indian (Mughlai)
Hans Plaza, Barakhamba Road
(3316868 ☐ 🗁 ☥ •••

Club Med European
Gopaldas Bhawan, Near Fire
Station, Connaught Place ☐ ☥ ••

Coconut Grove Indian (South
Indian) Ashok Yatri Niwas, Ashok
Road (3344511 ☐ 🗁 ☥ ••

Degchi Multi cuisine
13 Regal Building, Connaught Place
(3361444 ☐ 🗁 ☥ ••

Dilli Darbar Indian (Mughlai)
L Block Connaught Place
(3311527 ☐ 🗁 ☥ ••

Dilkhusha Indian (Mughlai)
Kanishka, 19 Ashok Road
(3344422 ☐ 🗁 ☥ ••

El-Arab Middle Eastern
Regal Building, Connaught Place
(3361444 ☐ 🗁 ••

Embassy Multi cuisine
11D Connaught Place (3320480
☐ 🗁 ☥ ••

Fa Yain Oriental (Chinese)
A 25/2, Middle Circle (3324603
☐ 🗁 ••

Food Plaza Multi cuisine
Janpath Hotel (3340070
☐ 🗁 ••

Gaylord Multi cuisine
16 Regal Building, Connaught Place
(3360717 ☐ 🗁 ☥ ••

Gola Indian (Tandoori)
K 24 Connaught Place (3321660 ☐
🗁 ••

Golden Phoenix Chinese
Le Meridien, Windsor Place
(3710101 ☐ 🗁 ☥ ✣

Gurudev Indian (Punjabi)
Arakashan Road (731696 ✻ •

Kake da Hotel Indian (Punjabi)
Connaught Circus, Near Shanker
Market ☐ •

Kanchi Indian (South Indian)
Centre Point Hotel, 13 KG Marg,
Connaught Place (3329124
☐ 🗁 •

Kovil Indian (South Indian)
E Block, Connaught Place
(3710585 ☐ 🗁 •

Kwality Multi cuisine (Punjabi)
Regal Building, Connaught Place
(3732352 ☐ 🗁 ☥ •••

La Belvedere European
Le Meridien, Windsor Place
(3710101 ☐ 🗁 ☥ ✣

Le Pierre European (French)
Le Meridien, Windsor Place
(3710101 ☐ 🗁 ☥ ✣

Las Meninas European (Spanish)
The Park, Sansad Marg
(3733737 ☐ 🗁 ☥ ✣

Lords Café European
Vishal Hotel, Main Bazaar Road,
Paharganj (527629 •

Madhuban Multi cuisine
Maharaja Hotel & Restaurant, 8194,
Arakashan Road ☐ •

Mandarin Room Oriental
Janpath Hotel
(3340070 ☐ 🗁 ☥ •••

Mandarin Oriental
Kanishka Hotel, 19 Ashoka Road
(3344422 ☐ 🗁 ☥ •••

Mehfil Restaurant
Indian (Mughlai)
198/11 Chelmsford Road •

Metropolis Hotel & Restaurant
European
Near Rajguru Road, Paharganj ☐ ••

Minar Indian (Mughlai)
L Block Connaught Place
(3323259 ☐ 🗁 ••

Noble House Oriental (Chinese)
New Delhi Hilton, Barakhamba
Avenue (3320101 ☐ 🗁 ☥ ✣

Pakwan Multi cuisine
Arakashan Road (7515906 •

Parikrama Multi cuisine
Antriksh Bhawan, K.G. Marg
(3721616 ☐ 🗁 ☥ ••

Pindi ka Famous Chholey Bhature
Indian (Punjabi)
3570 Ram Main Road (3546656 ✻ •

Pot Pourri European (Salad Bar)
Nirula's Hotel, L Block Connaught
Place (3322419 ☐ 🗁 ☥ ••

Princess Cafe Multi cuisine
UCO Bank Bldg, Sansad Marg
(3710502 ☐ ✻ •

Rodeo Multi cuisine (Mexican)
A Block, Connaught Place
(3713780 ☐ 🗁 ☥ ••

Safari Multi cuisine
M Block Connaught Circus
(3315013 ☐ 🗁 ☥ ••

Shangrila Oriental (Chinese)
Central Court, N Block
Connaught Circus
(3317582 ☐ 🗁 ☥ ••

airconditioning ☐   credit card 🗁   bar ☥   only vegetarian ✻ 300

Sidhartha Restaurant Indian (South Indian) 3428 D.B.Gupta Road Paharganj ✳ ◆

Sona Rupa Indian (South Indian) 46 Janpath ☎ 3326807 ☐ ☶ ✳ ◆

Standard Indian (Mughlai) Regal Building, Connaught Place ☐ ☞ ◆◆

Taste of China Oriental N18 Connaught Place, Opp. Scindia House ☎ 3310957 ☐ ☞ ☶ ◆◆◆

Tavern European Imperial Hotel, Janpath ☎ 3341234 ☐ ☞ ☶ ◆◆◆

The Host Multi cuisine F Block Connaught Place ☎ 3316576 ☐ ☞ ☶ ◆◆◆

The Rendezvous Multi cuisine New Delhi Hilton, Barakhamba Avenue ☎ 3320101 ☐ ☞ ☶ ✿

Vega Indian P 16/90 Connaught Circus ☎ 3344328 ☐ ☞ ✳ ◆◆

Volga Multi cuisine B Block, Connaught Place ☎ 3321473 ☐ ☞ ☶ ◆◆◆

York Multi cuisine K10 Connaught Circus ☎ 3323769 ☐ ☞ ☶ ◆◆◆

Zen Oriental (Chinese / Japanese) B Block Connaught Place ☎ 3724455 ☐ ☞ ☶ ◆◆

North Delhi
Daryaganj, Shahjahanabad, Civil Lines

Balgopal Indian 111 Ansari Road ☎ 3267844 ☐ ☞ ✳ ◆

Bhaja Govindam Indian Asaf Ali Road, Near Delite Cinema ☎ 3546656 ✳ ◆

Brijwasi Indian (Punjabi) Kucha Ghasi Ram, Chandni Chowk ☎ 2521376 ✳ ◆

Chor Bizarre Indian (Kashmiri) Broadway Hotel, Asaf Ali Road ☎ 3273821 ☐ ☞ ☶ ◆◆

Curzon Room European Oberoi Maidens, 7 Shyam Nath Marg ☎ 2914841 ☐ ☞ ☶ ◆◆◆

Flora Indian (Mughlai) Matia Mahal, Jama Masjid ☐ ◆

Garden Terrace Multi cuisine Oberoi Maidens, 7 Shyam Nath Marg ☎ 2914841 ☐ ☞ ☶ ◆◆◆

Green Restaurant Indian (Punjabi) Church Mission Marg ☎ 2510554 ◆

Kake Di Hatti (Deepak Restaurant) Indian (Punjabi) Church Mission Marg ☎ 2511717 ◆

Karim Indian (Mughlai) Gali Kababiyan, Matia Mahal, Near Jama Masjid ☎ 3269880 ◆

Khyber Restaurant Indian (Mughlai) 1514 Kashmere Gate ☎ 2965259 ☐ ◆

Kumar's Restaurant Indian (Punjabi) 4 Ansari Road, Daryaganj ☎ 3270615 ☐ ✳ ◆

Makhanlal Tika Ram Restaurant Indian (Punjabi) 1258 Bara Bazar, Kashmere Gate ☎ 2516660 ◆

Moti Mahal Indian (Mughlai) 3704 Netaji Subhash Marg ☎ 3273661 ☐ ☞ ☶ ◆◆

New Jawahar Restaurant Indian (Mughlai) Matia Mahal, Jama Masjid ◆

Rajasthan Restaurant Indian Church Mission Marg ☎ 239381 ✳ ◆

Shakahari Indian Hauz Qazi, off Ajmere Gate Road ✳ ◆

Standard Restaurant Indian 3505 Chawri Bazar ☎ 3283079 ✳ ◆

Suhaag Multi cuisine 5050 Netaji Subhash Marg ☎ 3279192 ☐ ☞ ◆◆

Sukhsagar Indian 638 Khari Baoli ☎ 2922726 ✳ ◆

Vikrant Restaurant Indian Mall Road, Kingsway Camp ◆

South of India Gate
Khan Market, Pandara Road

Baan Thai Oriental (Thai) The Oberoi, Dr. Zakir Hussain Marg ☎ 4363030 ☐ ☞ ☶ ✿

Captain's Cabin European Taj Mahal Hotel, Mansingh Road ☎ 3016162 ☐ ☞ ☶ ✿

China Fare Oriental (Chinese) 27A Khan Market ☎ 4618602 ☐ ☞ ◆◆

Corbetts Indian (Tandoori) The Claridges, Aurangzeb Road ☎ 3010211 ☐ ☞ ☶ ◆◆◆

Dasaprakash Indian (South Indian) Ambassador Hotel, Sujan Singh Park ☎ 4632600 ☐ ☞ ✳ ◆◆

Dhaba Indian (Punjabi)
The Claridges, 12 Aurangzeb Road
(3010211 ☐ ⌂ ⓨ •••

Gulati Indian (Mughlai / Punjabi)
Pandara Road (3782949 ☐ ⌂ •

Haveli Indian (Mughlai)
Taj Mahal Hotel, Mansingh Road
(3016162 ☐ ⌂ ⓨ ✣

Have More Indian (Mughlai /
Punjabi) Pandara Road Market
(3387070 ☐ ⌂ •

House of Ming Oriental (Chinese)
Taj Mahal Hotel, Mansingh Road
(3016162 ☐ ⌂ ⓨ ✣

Ichiban Oriental
Pandara Road Market
(3386689 ☐ ⌂ ••

Jade Garden Oriental (Chinese)
The Claridges, 12 Aurangzeb Road
(3010211 ☐ ⌂ ⓨ •••

Kandahar Indian (Tandoori)
The Oberoi, Dr. Zakir Hussain Marg
(4363030 ☐ ⌂ ⓨ ✣

Karim Indian (Mughlai)
168/2 Nizamuddin West
(4635458 ☐ ⌂ ••

La Rochelle European (French)
The Oberoi, Dr. Zakir Hussain Marg
(4363030 ☐ ⌂ ⓨ ✣

Larry's China Oriental (Chinese)
Ambassador Hotel, Sujan Singh
Park (4632600 ☐ ⌂ ⓨ •••

Longchamp European
Taj Mahal Hotel, Mansingh Road
(3016162 ☐ ⌂ ⓨ ✣

Mini Mughal Indian (Tandoori)
1/6 Jorbagh Market (4617979
☐ ⌂ ••

Pindi Indian (Mughlai / Punjabi)
Pandara Road Market
(3387932 ☐ ⌂ •

Taipan Oriental (Chinese)
The Oberoi, Dr. Zakir Hussain Marg
(4363030 ☐ ⌂ ⓨ ✣

South Delhi
South Extn, Hauz Khas, Defence Colony, Friends Colony, Greater Kailash

Academy Book Café European
4 Siri Fort Inst. Area, opp. Siri Fort
Auditorium ☐ ⌂ ••

Ajit Khalsa Dhaba Indian (Punjabi)
Andheria More (6801804 •

Akasaka Oriental
Defence Colony Market
(4691265 ☐ ⌂ ••

Al Kauser Indian (Mughlai)
No 1 DDA Market,
Anand Lok (6252402 ✳
(Open only for dinner)

Angeethi Indian (Tandoori)
Asian Games Village Complex
(6493945 ⌂ ••

Ankur Indian (Mughlai)
Asian Games Village,
Siri Fort Road
(6493628 ☐ ⌂ ⓨ ••

Bistro European
12 Hauz Khas Village (6853857
☐ ⌂ ⓨ •••

Brindavan Indian (South Indian)
M 45 Greater Kailash I (6421208
☐ ✳ ••

Cafe Ole Multi cuisine (Mexican)
E556 Greater Kailash II
(6232233 ☐ ⌂ •••

Chic-Fish Indian (Punjabi)
Malviya Nagar (6460404 ☐ •

Chopsticks Oriental (Chinese /Thai)
Asian Games Village Complex
(6493628 ☐ ⌂ ••

Chung Wah Oriental (Chinese)
M 34 Greater Kailash II (6227877
☐ ⌂ ••

Colonel's Kababz Indian
(Tandoori) Defence Colony Market
(4624384 •

Copper Chimney Indian Pamposh Enclave, Greater Kailash I (6413999 ⌂ ⌂ ••

Curry on the Roof Indian (South Indian) 24 Hauz Khas Village (6859495 ⌂ ⌂ ••

Daitchi Oriental (Chinese) E 19A South Extn Part II (6447511 ⌂ ••

Dawaat Multi cuisine Vikram Hotel, Lajpat Nagar (6436451 ⌂ ⌂ ☓ ••

Deez Biryani Corner Indian (Mughlai) 91 Defence Colony Flyover Market (4691687 ⌂ ••

Delhavi Indian (Mughlai) Park Royal, Nehru Place (6223344 ⌂ ⌂ ☓ •••

Dilli Darbar Multi cuisine M 35 Greater Kailash I (6418896 ⌂ ⌂ ☓ ••

Drums of Heaven Oriental (Chinese) S14 Green Park, Near Uphaar Cinema (661779 ⌂ ⌂ ☓ ••

Duke's Place European 22 Hauz Khas Village (6864909 ⌂ ⌂ ☓ ••

Ego European 4 Community Centre, New Friends Colony (6318185 ⌂ ⌂ ☓ •••

El Rancho Multi cuisine Friends Colony (6925233 ⌂ ⌂ ••

Empress of China Oriental Park Royal, Nehru Place (6223344 ⌂ ⌂ ☓ •••

Essex Farms Indian (Mughlai) 4 Aurobindo Marg, IIT Crossing (6963537 ⌂ ⌂ ••

Gourmet Affaire European Greater Kailash II, Near Savitri Cinema (6472690 ⌂ ⌂ ••

Idris Indian (Awadhi) Mehrauli, Gurgaon Road (6803086 (Open only for dinner) ⌂ ⌂ ••

Kabila Indian (Mughlai) 1st Floor, DDA Shopping Centre, Aurobindo Place, Hauz Khas (668494 ⌂ ⌂ ••

Kalpavadi's Ahaar Indian (South Indian) A 178/22 Sanatan Dharm School, Dayanand Colony, Lajpat Nagar IV (6474178 •

Karnataka Indian (South Indian) Aurobindo Marg (6862026 ⌂ ✳ •

Keraleeyam Indian (South Indian) 6 DDA Community Centre, Yusaf Sarai (6866267 ⌂ •

Lee's Garden Oriental Greater Kailash II (6442519 ⌂ ••

Lotus Pond Oriental K185 Sarai Jullena, New Friends Colony (6839526 ⌂ ⌂ ☓ ••

Moet's Multi cuisine 50 Defence Colony Market (4626814 ⌂ ⌂ ☓ ••

Moet's Sizzler European 27 Defence Colony Mkt (4626690 ⌂ ⌂ ••

Moti Mahal Indian (Mughlai) M Block, Greater Kailash I (6412467 ⌂ ⌂ ••

Naivedyam Indian (South Indian) 1 Hauz Khas Village (6960426 ⌂ ⌂ ✳ ••

New Delhi Metro Multi cuisine A 1 South Extn Part II (4623363/ 4699323 ⌂ ⌂ ••

Park Baluchi Indian (Mughlai / Tandoori) Inside Deer Park, Hauz Khas Village (6859369 ⌂ ⌂ ☓ ••

Peking Square Oriental 26 Defence Colony Market (4693388 ⌂ ⌂ ••

Prince's Garden Oriental (Chinese) South Extn Part II (6251860 ⌂ ⌂ ☓ ••

Rennaissance European Gourmet Gallery, South Extn II (6255652 ⌂ ⌂ ☓ ••

Sagar Indian (South Indian) Defence Colony Market (4698374 ⌂ ✳ •

Sagar Ratna Indian (South Indian) C2 Malviya Nagar (6442959 ⌂ ✳ •

Sampan Oriental Best Western Surya, New Friends Colony (6835070 ⌂ ⌂ ☓ •••

Scribbles Multi cuisine Gourmet Gallery, South Extn II (6224652 ⌂ ⌂ ☓ ••

Sikandra Indian Best Western Surya, New Friends Colony (6835070 ⌂ ⌂ ☓ ✧

Spice Oriental (Thai / Indonesian) Ambawatta Centre, Mehrauli (6854438 ⌂ ⌂ ☓ •••

Suko Thai Oriental (Thai) 24 Hauz Khas Village (6853846 ⌂ ⌂ ••

Tamarind Court Café European Qutb Colonnade, Mehrauli (6967537 ⌂ •••

The Farm House Indian Near Qutb Minar (6960045 ⌂ ⌂ ☓ ••

Price Range in Rupees (meal for two)
Below 300 •   300-600 ••   600-900 •••   900+ ✧

Turquoise Cottage of the Orient
Oriental (Thai)
81 Adchini Aurobindo Marg
(6853896 ⬚ 👝 ••

Vatika Multi cuisine
Madhubhan Holiday Inn, B71, GK I
(6435545/4633311 ⬚ 👝 ••

Viceroy European
Best Western Surya, New Friends
Colony (6835070 ⬚ 👝 ☖ ✣

Southwest Delhi
Vasant Vihar, Chanakyapuri

Andaaz Multi cuisine
Vasant Continental, Vasant Vihar
(6148800 ⬚ 👝 ☖ •••

Bali Hi Oriental (Chinese)
Maurya Sheraton, Diplomatic
Enclave (6112233 ⬚ 👝 ☖ ✣

Baradari Indian (Mughlai)
Samrat, Chanakyapuri (6110606
⬚ 👝 ☖ •••

Basil & Thyme European
Santushti Shopping Complex
(4674933 ⬚ 👝 ••
(Open only for lunch)

Bukhara Indian (Tandoori)
Maurya Sheraton, Diplomatic
Enclave (6112233 ⬚ 👝 ☖ ✣

Darbar Indian (Mughlai)
Ashok 50B, Chanakyapuri
(6110101 ⬚ 👝 ☖ ✣

Delhi ka Angan Indian
Hyatt Regency Bhikaji Cama Place
(6181234 ⬚ 👝 ☖ ✣

Dum Pukht Indian (Awadhi)
Maurya Sheraton, Diplomatic
Enclave (6112233
⬚ 👝 ☖ ✣

Frontier Indian (Tandoori)
Ashok 50B Chanakyapuri
(6110101 ⬚ 👝 ☖ ✣

Fujiya Oriental
12/48 Malcha Marg (6876059
⬚ 👝 ••

Handi Indian (Tandoori)
Taj Palace, Diplomatic Enclave
(6110202 ⬚ 👝 ☖ ✣

Jewel of the East Oriental
Ashok, 50B Chanakyapuri
(6110101 ⬚ 👝 ☖ ✣

La Piazza European (Italian)
Hyatt Regency, Bhikaji Cama Place
(6181234 ⬚ 👝 ☖ ✣

Mini Mahal Restaurant
Indian Vasant Vihar
(6144874 ⬚ 👝 ☖ ••

Orient Express European
Taj Palace, Diplomatic Enclave
(6110202 ⬚ 👝 ☖ ✣

Sahara Restaurant Indian   Vasant
Kunj (6895180 ⬚ 👝 ☖ ••

Shaolin Oriental
Centaur Hotel, Indira Gandhi
International Airport (5652223
⬚ 👝 ☖ •••

Sun City Multi cuisine
Bhikaji Cama Place
(6161177 👝 ✣ •

The Tea House of the August Moon
Oriental (Chinese) Taj Palace,
Diplomatic Enclave
(6110202 ⬚ 👝 ☖ ✣

TGI's Friday European
62 Basant Lok (6140761
⬚ 👝 ☖ •••

TK's Oriental (Japanese/Chinse)
Hyatt Regency, Bhikaji Cama Place
Ring Road (6181234
⬚ 👝 ☖ ✣

Tokyo Oriental (Japanese)
Ashok 50B, Chanakyapuri
(6110101 ⬚ 👝 ☖ ✣

West View European
Maurya Sheraton, Diplomatic
Enclave (6112233 ⬚ 👝 ☖ ✣

Karol Bagh

Khyber Indian
Siddharth Hotel, Rajendra Place
(5762501 ⬚ 👝 ☖ •••

Malika Restaurant & Bar
Multi cuisine
East Patel Nagar Market
(5788510 ⬚ 👝 ☖ ••

New Prem Dhaba Indian
Dariwalan, East Park Road
(524219 ⬚ •

Raffles Multi cuisine
6/7 Ajmal Khan Road
(5724824 ⬚ •

Sanjha-Chulla Indian (Punjabi) 2880
Hardhian Singh Road
(5723233 ✣ •

Seven-O-Seven Multi cuisine
104-107 Prabhat Kiran,
Rajendra Place (5741002 •

Sobti (Grace) Indian
2397-98 Hardhian Singh Road
(5729030 ⬚ 👝 ••

Suprabhat Indian (South Indian)
W.E.A. Karol Bagh, Arya Samaj
Road (5715116 •

Vaishali European
Siddharth Hotel, Rajendra Place
(5741002
⬚ 👝 ☖ •••

Further to our comprehensive listing of restaurants, we have attempted to capture the essence of a few restaurants of our choice.

The prices given below are for a meal for two persons and does not include beverages.

Indian

Bukhara Maurya Sheraton, Sardar Patel Marg (6112233

This is Delhi's best known restaurant for Northwest Frontier cuisine and features on the iteneraries of many celebrities passing through the capital. The decor featuring stone walls hung with original Bukhara carpets, copper pots, pans and ladles, suspended on rope, and solid wood tressle tables, ushered in a new concept in decor with the opening of the restaurant 20 years ago. Many Bukhara dishes have become household names, such as Dal Bukhara, and Murgh Malai Kebab. A meal for two is priced at around Rs 1800.

Chic-Fish Malviya Nagar (6460404

As the name suggests, this restaurant began with only chicken and fish made in the tandoori style. However, now a wide variety of kebabs and rotis are served with an assortment of pickles. A family restaurant, it only opens for dinner. The portions are large and there is plenty of variety, for vegetarians and non-vegetarians alike. The butter chicken is recommended. A meal for two comes to Rs 250.

Chor Bizarre Broadway Hotel, Asaf Ali Road (3273821

The decor of this restaurant is as zany as the name. Anything and everything from old wrought iron spiral staircases to ancient sewing machine bases, have been used to make the tables and chairs – and no two are the same! The cuisine is primarily Kashmiri and tandoori with a large variety to choose from. The restaurant is very popular with journalists from the nearby Bahadur Shah Zafar Marg. A meal for two at Chor Bizarre would cost around Rs 500.

Coconut Grove Ashok Yatri Niwas, Ashoka Road (3344511

Coconut Grove was one of the first restaurants to introduce non-vegetarian south Indian cooking to the Dilliwala. The cuisines of Andhra Pradesh and Kerala and the Chettinad region of Tamil Nadu are now highly popular. The decor of the restaurant is totally ethnic with bamboo matting, palms and terracotta tiles. A meal for two costs under Rs 450.

Colonel's Kababz Defence Colony Market (4624384

Owned by a retired army colonel, this restaurant began as a tiny takeaway catering to the upmarket Defence Colony. Over the years, the restaurant has grown in popularity and today its seekh kebabs and tikkas offer competition to those served at many five star restaurants. A meal for two is priced at around Rs 200.

Delhi ka Angan Hyatt Regency, Bhikaji Cama Place (6181234

Famous for its Punjabi and Mughlai cuisine, the restaurant has decor that is reminiscent of the old world charm of Delhi. Open at lunch and dinner, it is well known for its exceptionally good food. A meal for two at Delhi Ka Angan is priced at around Rs 1600.

Dhaba The Claridges, Aurangzeb Road (3010211

This is an interesting restaurant, where the roadside dhaba has been created within an enclosed space. A truck stands on one side of the restaurant. The wooden chairs and tables, with ropes and wooden planks have a rustic look. Punjabi specialities, served on copper platters are very popular. Open for lunch and dinner, this restaurant offers a splendid way to eat dhaba food in a star hotel. A meal for two is priced at around Rs 600.

NAIVEDYAM

KERALEEYAM

Dum Pukht Maurya Sheraton, Sardar Patel Marg (6112233

Dum Pukht cuisine is a recreation of the 200 year old cuisine of the Nawabs of Awadh. The food cooked over slow fire in large sealed pots has been refined to suit modern tastes. The waiters are dressed in flowing *chogas*, reminiscent of the Nawabi era. The most popular dish is the kakori kebab, which literally melts in the mouth, and the incomparable Dum Pukht biryani. A meal for two is priced at around Rs 1600.

Gulati Pandara Road Market (3782949

The Indian restaurants in Pandara Road Market, **Gulati**, **Pindi** (3387932 and **Have More** (3387070 serve excellent tandoori cuisine and robust Punjabi fare. Their popularity also stems from the fact that these are some of the last restaurants to close, catering to all those cinema-goers who prefer to eat after a late night show. Among the more popular items here are butter chicken and goat's brain curry! If the crowd outside Gulati is intimidating you could well try Pindi or Have More. A meal for two at any of these restaurants comes within Rs 300.

Karim Gali Kababiyan, Matia Mahal, near Jama Masjid (3269880

Probably the best eatery in Delhi for authentic Muslim cuisine. The burra kebab and mutton pasanda here are unparalleled. Nothing seems to have changed here in the last seventy years except for the clientele. Karim has an outlet in Nizammudin West near the Dargah which has all the accoutrements of a standard restaurant, carpets, tablecloths and liveried waiter, though for authenticity one would recommend the journey to Shahjahanabad.

A complete meal for two would cost Rs 300 here, while at the Nizamuddin outlet it would cost about a Rs 100 more.

Keraleeyam Yusuf Sarai, next to Indian Oil Bhawan (6866267

If you need a break from the routine south Indian vegetarian fare, Keraleeyam is the place for you. Fortify yourself with hot, delectable food from Kerala. If you don't wish to try the spicy Kozhikodan biryani, have a fluffy appam or a parotta, quite different from north Indian rotis and paranthas, with the main dish you order.

A meal for two will not cost more than Rs 200.

Naivedyam Hauz Khas Village (6960426

The large *nandi* bull guarding the entrance as in a south Indian temple sets the mood and the waiters, dressed in spotless white *veshtis*, welcome you with a bowl of hot rasam and appalam. The wholesome vegetarian meal from Karnataka will not cost more than Rs 300 for two.

Parikrama Antriksh Bhawan, Kasturba Gandhi Marg (3721616

The revolving restaurant offers a wide variety of cuisines ranging from the standard tandoori to fish and chips and club sandwiches. The restaurant is recommended for the view it offers of the busy Connaught Place area. Incidentally, one revolution takes 90 minutes, so feast your eyes. A meal for two would be around Rs 600.

Sagar Defence Colony Market (4698374

The crowds outside the south Indian Sagar restaurant, Defence Colony, around meal times, bears testimony to the popularity of its masala dosa or value-for-money vegetarian thali. It is, without doubt, one of Delhi's best south Indian restaurants. Sagar Ratna outlets in Malviya Nagar, Vasant Kunj and Noida are equally popular though Sagar Ratna in Lodhi Hotel offers most in terms of ambience and decor. A meal for two at a Sagar restaurant, complete with strong south Indian coffee, will be easily within Rs 150.

PAVILION

European

The Curzon Room Oberoi Maidens, Shyam Nath Marg
(2914841

One of the few continental restaurants in the area, for Raj period buffs a visit to the hotel and a meal at The Curzon Room, provide a nostalgic glimpse into India's colonial past, through both the food and the decor. However, in deference to demand, the menu includes Indian as well as continental dishes. A memorable meal for two is priced within Rs 800.

Duke's Place Hauz Khas Village
(6864909

Duke's Place has a live jazz band playing on Friday and Saturday evenings. The rest of the week, taped music works its own charm, and evenings continue to be lively with customers enjoying mocktails and an interesting continental fare which includes a variety of pasta dishes. A meal for two would work out to under Rs 500.

Ego 4 Community Centre, New Friends Colony (6318185

Ego offers good Italian cuisine often with personalised service by the lady owner. The menu changes often, and new dishes are introduced at short notice. A meal for two comes well within Rs 450. Remember to allow for one of the house speciality desserts.

La Piazza Hyatt Regency, Bhikaji Cama Place (6181234

La Piazza is the only restaurant in the capital with a wood-fired oven, essential for creating the special taste and aroma of an Italian pizza. The cheeses and many of the other ingredients are imported, and the chefs may be watched as they deftly create a special pizza to your specifications. A meal is priced within Rs 1200. Remember to allow for a glass of Italian wine to complete the experience.

GARDEN TERRACE

La Rochelle The Oberoi, Dr. Zakir Hussain Marg (4363030

A restaurant in the best French tradition, La Rochelle is among the capital's most formal restaurants. The menu features classical French cuisine and a fine selection of wines. The decor is understated and quietly elegant. Priced at Rs 2000 for a couple without wine.

Las Meninas The Park, Sansad Marg (3733737

In India's very first Spanish restaurant, elements from Spanish painter Velazquez' famous painting Las Meninas have been used imaginatively in creating an ambience that is warm and inviting. The staff uniforms, for instance, are based on the costumes of Spanish bullfighters. Genuine Mediterranean flavours, wines and cheeses are found here, served in generous portions. A meal for a couple would be upwards of Rs 1200 with beverages and liquor extra.

Le Pierre Le Meridien, Windsor Place (3710101

A French restaurant, Le Pierre, caters to those who enjoy all types of French cuisine - traditional as well as nouvelle. The restaurant recreates a gracious and charming lifestyle, designed in the best traditions of the French restaurants of Paris. A meal for two comes at Rs 2000.

TGI's FRIDAY

TAMARIND COURT

LAS MENINAS

Orient Express Taj Palace, Sardar Patel Marg (6110202

A railway carriage runs along one side of the restaurant and guests have the option of eating inside the carriage. The ambience of the original train has been creatively captured and elaborate and exclusive four-course dinners are served. This is one of the capital's oldest restaurants serving European cuisine, and Orient Express remains one of the best. Dinner for a couple is priced at around Rs 1800. Remember to allow for a bottle of champagne, to make the evening memorable.

Pot Pourri Nirula's, L Block Connaught Place (3322419

The salad bar at Pot Pourri is very popular both with Dilliwalas and young tourists, and the impressive array of vegetarian and non-vegetarian salads is real value for money at Rs 105. It also serves excellent breakfast with options ranging from south Indian *dosas*, bacon and eggs to pancakes. Open from 7.30 am to midnight, a standard meal for two, without drinks would be within Rs 400.

Renaissance Gourmet Gallery, South Extn II (6255652

Part of a complex consisting of five restaurants, Renaissance offers European fare. The bar does brisk business in beers, as shoppers wander in to quench their thirst and have a meal to recover lost energy. While soups and salads are popular for lunches, it is the restaurant's excellent roasts that find many takers in the evenings. A meal for two is priced at Rs 450.

Rodeo A Block Connaught Place (3713780

As the name suggests, this restaurant offers Mexican fare, but also includes Italian and other south European specialities. Located in the heart of the busiest shopping area in the capital, the service is quick and efficient.The decor takes after the theme, and the atmosphere is strong. A meal for two is priced within Rs 400.

West View Maurya Sheraton, Sardar Patel Marg (6112233

Antique pots and pans, old paintings by Dutch Masters, a wine cellar and dried herbs and garlic pods strung above a cooking range, create the warmth and comfort of an English country kitchen. There are no menus, and guests are invited to make a choice from the display of seafood, steaks, chicken and a number of vegetarian items. There is no limit to the quantity that a guest chooses to eat, and pricing remains the same with an extra charge for imported meats. The entire meal comes for about Rs 600 per head.

THE PALMS

Oriental

Baan Thai The Oberoi, Dr. Zakir Hussain Marg (4363030

Baan Thai offers quality Thai cuisine for which a number of ingredients are specially flown in every week. The menu offers a wide array of meat and seafood recipes, and also enough variety for vegetarians. A meal for two at Baan Thai comes upwards of Rs 1500.

Berco's Connaught Place (3318134

One of the older restaurants in Connaught Place, Berco's offers Chinese and Japanese cuisines, and the service is quick. The taste may have undergone Indianisation, but that has not had any effect on the popularity of the place, which tends to be rather crowded during the lunch hour but maintains a cool and pleasing atmosphere. A meal for two is priced at under Rs 400.

Chopsticks Asian Games Village Complex (6493628

Popular for Chinese and Thai delicacies, the restaurant has a bar and offers an aesthetically pleasing atmosphere. On holidays and at weekends there is a lavish Chinese buffet lunch, priced at Rs 250 per head.

An á la carte meal for two would work out to Rs 500.

House of Ming Taj Mahal, Mansingh Road (3016162

Arguably one of the best Chinese restaurants in Delhi, the House of Ming is a popular place for business lunches and dinners. The restaurant serves both the milder Cantonese as well as Schezwan style dishes which are liberally flavoured with red chillies. With its distinctive decor, table linen and crockery, the House of Ming recreates the designs that made the Ming porcelain famous world over. A meal for two would cost upwards of Rs 1300.

Suko Thai Hauz Khas Village (6853846

People visit the small rooftop restaurant Suko Thai for its excellent Thai cuisine but may stay longer to watch the impressive view of the medieval Hauz Khas complex. To ensure authenticity of the cuisine, ingredients which were earlier imported, have now been induced to grow locally, reducing overheads. The restaurant has soft furnishings, the walls sport Thai paintings, and potted palms fill the corners. A meal for two is priced at around Rs 350.

The Tea House of the August Moon Taj Palace, Sardar Patel Marg (6110202

Replete with a pagoda, a pond with lotuses and goldfish, the restaurant offers the visitor a picture-book image of China. Everyone prefers to sit on top of the pagoda, reached by crossing a bridge. The typically Chinese colours of black, red and gold have been judiciously used in the decor. A meal for two at the restaurant is priced at Rs 1200 for

THE GRILL

Tokyo Ashok, Chanakyapuri
(6110101

Tokyo pioneered Japanese cuisine in Delhi. An elegant restaurant, it has a regular clientele of old faithfuls. The menu is not very elaborate, and heavily weighed in favour of seafood. There are also a number of vegetarian items on the menu. Many of the ingredients are imported. A meal for two costs within Rs 1000.

TK's The Oriental Grill, Hyatt Regency, Bhikaji Cama Place
(6181234

This is the first restaurant in Delhi to capitalise on the oriental grill concept. The expert chefs can be watched creating your special grill right in front of you. The decor is simple but interesting with red brick walls and crockery that echoes the rustic look. Special sauces are offered and guests encouraged to try out new combinations. A meal for two at TK's is priced at around Rs 1000.

Fast Food and Takeaway

Like metro cities all over the world, Delhi has a large number of fast food outlets. Well-known international chains like **McDonald's**, **Wimpy's**, **Pizza Hut**, **Domino's Pizza** and **Kentucky Fried Chicken** offer international favourites. The Indian chain, **Nirula's**, which also serves excellent ice creams, has a loyal clientele for its pizzas and burgers, as do the other speciality takeaway-cum-fast food outlets like **Hot Breads**, **Slice of Italy**, among others.

Snak bars are dotted all over the city, and most neighbourhood markets have at least a couple of fast food outlets which serve vegetarian specialities. South Indian dosas, idlis and utthapams and north Indian favourites like samosas and chaats find many takers. The best known outlets in this category find people travelling from the other end of the city to snack out on their specialities.

Bread, Cakes and Mithai

All five star hotels in Delhi offer excellent confectionery – Hyatt is known for its bread, Maurya for walnut brownies, Ashok for black forest cake, Taj for chocolates and so on. There are also a large number of confectioners strewn across the city. Wengers in A16 Connaught Place is one of the oldest and remains one of the best. Nirula's Pastry Shop and Sugar and Spice serve good pastries and cookies in their several outlets, as do Claire's in Santushti Complex and the Chocolate Wheel in Jor Bagh Market.

Indian sweets are available all over the city, and among the most famous are Ghantewale in Chandni Chowk, Haldiram Bhujiawala on Mathura Road, Kaleva in Gole Market, Nathu's and Bengali Sweets in Bengali Market. Moreover, all neighbourhood markets have sweet shops, such as Krishna Sweets in Pandara Road Market and Annapoorna in Chittaranjan Park Market. The north Indian *laddoo*, *peda*, *kalakand*, and *balushahi* as well as *gulab jamun* and *rasgulla* in sugar syrup are among the most popular sweets (*see :* **Food**, *p.53-54*).

24-Hour Coffee Shops

Most hotel coffee shops serve a fairly varied menu, and some even offer elaborate lunch and dinner buffets to cater to the cosmopolitan mix that is constantly passing through the city. All the coffee shops listed serve European, Indian and oriental cuisine, and many also serve liquor. Prices at coffee shops are usually less than at the speciality restaurants, and some offer special group discounts. All major credit cards are accepted.

Blooms
Park Royal (6223344

Café
Hyatt Regency (6181234

Cana Cona
Vasant Continental (6148800

Caravan
Hans Plaza (3316868

Gardenia
Samrat (6110606

Garden Party
The Imperial (3341234

Isfahan
Taj Palace (6110202

La Brasserie
Le Meridien (3710101

La Plaza
The Meridien (3710101

Le Café
Best Western Surya (6835070

Lumbini
Siddharth Hotel (5762501

Machan
Taj Mahal (3016162

Open House
Janpath Hotel (3340070

Palm Court
Kanishka Hotel (3344422

Pickwick
The Claridges (3010211

Portico
The Park (3733737

Samovar
Ashok Hotel (6110101

The Coffee Shop
Ashok Hotel (6110101

The Palms
The Oberoi (4363030

The Pavilion
Maurya Sheraton (6112233

The Rendezvous
New Delhi Hilton (3320101

The Grill
Qutb Hotel (6521234

Tiffany Coffee Shop
The Connaught (3364225

Bars

Delhi does not have a culture of pubs and bars though there are quite a few excellent bars located at various hotels or attached to restaurants. Timings are usually between 11 am and midnight, and entry is prohibited to those below 21 years.

Liquor served at the bars vary according to the location. The bars at the higher priced hotels offer all varieties of foreign liquor, as well as some innovative cocktails. Snacks are also available, and it is quite possible to make a complete meal out of what is available on the menu. All major credit cards are accepted.

Aloha
Le Meridien (3710101

Burgundy
Best Western Surya (6835070

Captain's Cabin
Taj Mahal (3016162

Cavalry Bar
Oberoi Maidens (2914841

Pegasus Bar
Nirula's (3322419

Cinatra
Vasant Continental (6148600

The Club Bar
The Oberoi (4363030

The Garden Bar
Ashok Hotel (6110101

Henri's
Le Meridien (3710101

The Jazz Bar
Maurya Sheraton (6112233

La Terrace
Le Meridien (3710101

The Lounge Bar
New Delhi Hilton (6181234

The Lounge
Taj Palace (6110202 Extn 160

Someplace Else
The Park (3733737

Thugs
Broadway (3273821

Trishna
Siddharth Hotel (5762501

Village Pub
Asiad Village (6493995

Polo Lounge
Hyatt Regency (6181234

Discotheques

Delhi has a number of discotheques located at the better hotels which attract the active young-at-heart who can enjoy dancing to the latest hits till the wee hours of the morning. Most discos open between 10 pm and 4 am. Entrance is restricted to local members or hotel residents and their guests, who are allowed entry on payment of fee.

Entry is prohibited to those below 18 years. On special nights, ladies are allowed free entry. For more details on timings and special nights, the respective hotels can be contacted. An informal dress code operates at most discotheques, shorts are usually not acceptable.

All discotheques in Delhi have bars, and serve both foreign and Indian liquor as well as snacks. All major credit cards are accepted.

Annabelles
New Delhi Hilton (3320101

CJ's
Le Meridien (3710101

Ghungroo
Maurya Sheraton (6112233

Mirage
Best Western Surya (6835070

My Kind of Place
Taj Palace (6110202

Someplace Else
The Park (3733737

The Oasis
Hyatt Regency (6181234

Where to Shop

Delhi is a shoppers' paradise, a veritable cornucopia of silk, spices, dry fruits, handicrafts and much else that spill out of its many bazaars and markets (*see: **Bazaars***). There are markets in almost every locality though the larger ones are in Lajpat Nagar, South Extension, Ajmal Khan Road and Sarojini Nagar. There are also the occasional specialist shops that deal in a variety of exotica.

If you are in Delhi for just a couple of days, it would perhaps be best to head for Connaught Place, the city's best known market place. It would give you a chance to also take in the state emporia on Baba Kharak Singh Marg, the Central Cottage Industries Emporium on Janpath and Palika Bazaar, with its warren of small shops.

What makes Delhi a memorable shopping experience is the availability of products from all over the country. However, there are some items that are best bought in Delhi and worth looking out for.

Ready-to-wear Garments

Over the last twenty years ready-to-wear has become important in the city with flea markets, renowned brand names and high fashion designer salons vying with each other. The result is the easy availability of an enormous variety.

If you are in search of quality and reasonable prices in pure cotton casual wear, stop by **Fabindia** outlets at N14 Greater Kailash I (6212183 and 10 Nelson Mandela Marg, Vasant Kunj (6899775. **Anokhi** outlets in Khan Market (4603423 and Santushti Complex (6883076 are also worth a visit for their printed cotton garments.

There is a boutique bazaar under the Defence Colony flyover which has several shops. An impressive collection may also be found at the **Archana Complex** in Greater Kailash I and in the many shops across the street.

Also recommended:

Darzi 4A Shahpur Jat.
Kui Shop 5 Malcha Marg Market.
Kutir Aashirwad Complex, Green Park Market.
Lavanya E10 Greater Kailash II.
Vastrang 118 Shahpur Jat.

For fine embroidered *chikankari* garments go either to **SEWA** M1 Hauz Khas or **Lala Lal Behari Tandon** outlets in Palika Bazaar and Aurobindo Place.

If you have the time visit **Sarojini Nagar Market** which offers heaps of export surplus garments, shirts, skirts, blouses ... you name it, it is there. But patience and bargaining power is essential.

At the top of the line

Ritu's, the exclusive outlet of designer Ritu Kumar is at E4 Hauz Khas Market (6858597 and Archana Shopping Complex, Greater Kailash I (6426748. Here you would find traditional garments, sharara, salwar-kameez and saris as well as handcrafted leather accessories. Open 10.30 am to 7 pm. Closed Sundays.

Carma H5/11 Mehrauli Road (6865092, is one of the city's upmarket boutiques. Located in what was once a carriage house in the shadow of Qutb Minar, it stocks an exclusive range of outfits by well known Indian designers. Open 11 am to 6.30 pm. Closed Sundays.

J.J. Valaya's **Life** is on the road to Chhatarpur Temple (6802888. The prices may be steep but it is a good place to stop by if you are in search of something stylish. Open 11 am to 7 pm. Closed Mondays.

Anjuman A51/A Friends Colony East (6823953 has an enticing collection of western and traditional wear for women. Open 10 am to 7 pm. Closed Sundays.

Bizarre A11 South Extn I (6991395 has a trendy range of shirts, blouses and evening dresses in crepe, silk and cotton. Open 10.30 am to 7.30 pm. Closed Mondays.

Ensemble Santushti Complex (6882207 and Ambawatta Complex (6525422 has an elegant line of garments for both men and women by some of India's finest designers, Tarun Tahiliani, Vivek Narang, Asha Sarabhai among others.

Upmarket salons for men:

Janak 66 Greater Kailash I.
Ravi Bajaj C237 Defence Colony. (4641675. Also at M6 Greater Kailash I Market. (6418346.
Walter Johnson 1A Hauz Khas Village (6852101. Also at G7 South Extn II (4628070.

Saris are synonymous with India and in Delhi you can find saris from all over the country. If you want a wide range at reasonable prices begin at **Central Cottage Industries Emporium**.

Also recommended:

Kalamandir E31 South Extn II (6256181.
Nalli P7/90 Outer Circle, Connaught Place (3747154 and E12 South Extn I (4629926.
Padakam Santushti Complex for exquisite one-of-a-kind silk saris.
Ushnak Mal G9 South Extn I (4641700.
Utsav Krishi Vihar for beautiful cotton saris (6485420.
Vichitra G17 South Extn II. (4601104.

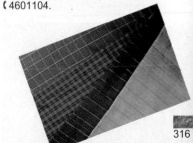

Gifts

Handicrafts have always been an integral part of Indian life. Potters, basket weavers and puppet-makers sit along pavements. Paper fans, wooden toys, terracotta gods and goddesses are thrust on you at traffic lights. Some are tacky and garish, some you want to keep forever. But if you want quality stuff go to **Central Cottage Industries Emporium** on Janpath, **Dilli Haat**, **Dastkar** 40A Shahpur Jat, **Crafts Museum** at Pragati Maidan, especially the small but well stocked museum shop.

Leather

There are about 100 shops in **Yashwant Place** in Chanakyapuri dealing only in leather. They have quality stuff, especially handbags and garments, reasonably priced and bargaining is permitted. **Palika Bazaar** has several shops specialising in luggage, shoes and jackets.

Good footwear, especially the big brand names .... Bata, Woodlands, etc., are available in all the major shopping complexes. For designer fare, go to South Extension or Connaught Place and for utilitarian, everyday wear, the line of shops in Ajmal Khan Road, Sarojini Nagar Market and Yusuf Sarai Market. For *kolhapuri chappals* and *juttis*, a good selection is available at the two small shops in the by-lane off South Extension I.

Also recommended for sandals for both women and men:

Bharat Leather Emporium E1 Connaught Place (3736170.
Da Milano 9A Connaught Place. (3325253.
Khazana Taj Palace Hotel (6110202 for handbags and luggage.
Hyde Park Boutique Lok Nayak Bhawan (behind Khan Market) for handbags.
The Kolhapuri Shop Shop No. 62 Janpath.
Queensway Footwear Shop No. 61 Janpath.
Tack Santushti Complex has a trendy range of jackets, handbags and office accessories.

Chinese shoemakers make shoes to order:

D Minsen & Co 17/2 Connaught Place.
John Bros 16/2 Connaught Place.
K K Lee 30B Khan Market.

Precious Jewellery

The Indian woman's love for gold ornaments is legendary. Nowhere else in the world is the yellow metal such an obsession. Delhi, like any other Indian metropolis, has numerous jewellery shops in various shopping complexes. For pure gold jewellery and those embellished with precious stones it is best to head for the well known establishments.

Delhi may not have a gold souk but Bank Street off Ajmal Khan Road comes close to one. All the well known jewellers have their branches here. South Extension and Sunder Nagar Market also have a cluster of shops, and in Shahjahanabad there are a row of shops which deal exclusively in gold jewellery in Dariba Kalan, the jewellers' street. Many of the big hotels have interesting jewellery shops. Highly recommended is the one at Hyatt Regency.

Also recommended:

Bharany Sunder Nagar Market for ethnic and tribal jewellery. They also keep enamelled *meenakari* jewellery and quality pieces from south India.
Gold Master F2 Connaught Place (3312878 specialises in contemporary designs.
Khanna Jewellers G3 South Extn I (4622377.

Lotus Eaters Santushti Complex (6882264 for exclusive silver and gold jewellery.
Mehrasons E1 South Extn II (4635555. Also at C11Connaught Place (3323950.
Monpri Santushti Complex (6887711 for gems and jewellery. They also take orders and authenticity is guaranteed.
Punjab Jewellers 161-162 Hardhyan Singh Marg, Karol Bagh (5728527.
The Studio 4 Sunder Nagar Market (4619360 and 14A Sunder Nagar Market (4623957.
Tanishq F42 South Extn I (4624586 and 7A Inner Circle, Connaught Place (3326594. Modern machine-made pieces are available here.
Tribhuvandas Bhimji Zaveri 2 Scindia House, Janpath (3313435.

The following shops are worth looking at for replicas of antique jewellery:

Art Karat S48 Panchshila Park (6416690; 57A Khizrabad Village, New Friends Colony (6922955.
Santram Mangatram 34 Aurobindo Place (6489688.

Delhi also has a market in semi-precious stones. It is worth visiting **Central Cottage Industries Emporium** Janpath (3321909 / 3321157 and **Yashwant Place** Chanakyapuri.

Silver Jewellery

Dariba Kalan, Delhi's ancient silver market in Shahjahanabad is worth a visit. You will find not just jewellery, but an amazing range of old silver artifacts, *hookah* bases, platters, water jugs and so on. Each piece is weighed and priced on the official bullion rates for the day but some amount of bargaining is permitted on the making charge.

Also recommended :

Jewel Mine 12A Palika Bazaar, Connaught Place (3320578.
Khazana Taj Mahal Hotel, 1 Mansingh Road (3016162.
Lotus Eaters Santushti Complex.
Silver Art 17 Palika Bazaar (3326577.
The Studio 4 Sunder Nagar Market (4619360.
Tibetan Market Janpath, has interesting pieces in stone, metal, bone and wood. Remember to bargain.
Tibet House Lodi Road (4602616 has an excellent collection reasonably priced typical Tibetan jewellery.
Utkalika B4 Baba Kharak Singh Marg (3364763 for filigreed silver jewellery.

Cosmetics

From ancient times the Indian woman has used natural ingredients ingeniously to enhance her beauty. Today, once more, the emphasis the world over is on natural products. Several Indian companies are marketing beauty products based on herbal and ayurvedic remedies and treatments.

The best known is **Shehnaz Hussain** who has outlets in 9 UB Bungalow Road, Kamala Nagar, Apsara Arcade, Pusa Road and 12B Khan Market. For special problems contact M55 Greater Kailash I (6463578.

Also recommended are **Biotique, Aroma Magic** and **Samara** range of products available at most quality stores.

Delhi is famous for *attar*, natural essence of herbs and flowers, used by Muslim aristocracy for centuries. Today it is used primarily in soaps and perfumes. Those interested must visit **Gulab Singh Johrimal**, 320 Dariba Kalan, off Chandni Chowk (3271345. Several shops in **Palika Bazaar** and **Roopak Store** 6/9 Ajmal Khan Road, Karol Bagh (5722569 have a fairly good selection.

Preoccupation with **health and fitness** is obviously in vogue today if the number of health clubs and gyms all over the city is anything to go by. Apart from exercise routines many of them specialise in therapeutic massages. Especially recommended are :

Shehnaz Hussain's Ayurvedic Panchkarma, Dhara and **Kerala Massage Centre** B40 Greater Kailash I (6464574. Here the traditional Kerala massage renowned for its therapeutic value is available. Open all days 9.30 am to 6.30 pm.

Kairali Ayurvedic Health Club 120 Andheria More, Mehrauli (6801552. They do massages using Ayurvedic medicines for relieving stress, obesity, arthritis, etc. Open all days 9.30 am to 6.30 pm.

Carpets and Shawls

Connoisseurs feel buying a carpet is almost like buying a precious stone. While size may be important, prices really depend on factors like the number of knots per square inch. For instance, the number of knots in a silk carpet varies from 256 to 1600 per sq. inch, while in a woollen carpet it seldom goes beyond 600 per sq. inch.

Cottage Industries Exposition M5 Hauz Khas (6862611 has a fine collection of Kashmiri and Afghan carpets. It also has a wide range of Mirzapur and Bhadoi carpets and chain stitch and crewel rugs from Kashmir. CIE has two branches : Barakhambha Road (3313833 and Aurobindo Place Market (6868550.

Also recommended :

Central Cottage Industries Emporium Jawahar Vyapar Bhawan, Janpath (3320439.
Gulam Mohidin & Sons C 17 Basement, East of Kailash (6848749.
Kathwari Rugs International Marble Arch, 9 Prithviraj Road (4626621.
Shyam Ahuja E3 Local Shopping Complex, Masjid Moth, Greater Kailash II (6440646 and Santushti Complex (4670112.
Zoon A7 Baba Kharak Singh Marg (3364723.

Dhurries are becoming increasingly popular - cotton *punja* dhurries from Haryana and Rajasthan, and pitloom dhurries from Panipat and Warrangal. Most household shops have interesting collections. It was Shyam Ahuja who took the lowly dhurrie to the international market. For real value for money you may visit **Fabindia**.

Like the carpetwalas who come down from Kashmir every winter there are also the shawlwalas who come with bundles of jamawars, pashminas and many other varieties. Some like **Maqbool Shawls** (6983941 and **S.S. Shawls** (6834436 will come by but if you are in a hurry, head for **Ahujasons** 6/44 Ajmal Khan Road (5720304.

Shawls from all parts of the country are available at the state emporia. There are the *tussar* silk shawls from Bihar and Assam; woollen shawls from Nagaland where patterns and colours represent a particular tribe; mirror work shawls made with camel hair from Gujarat and Rajasthan; fabulously embroidered Kashmiri jamawars and soft pashminas, and much more.

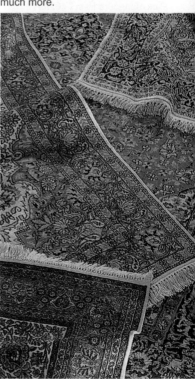

Antiques

Collectors will tell you that there are no authentic antiques available. In any case one is not allowed to take out of the country anything that is over a hundred years old. There are several shops that offer excellent reproductions and restored pieces.

Kumbakonam Arts 1/22 Burbal Park, Jangpura Extn (4629917 specialises in old furniture and objects d'art from south India.

Puratan A1 Gitanjali Enclave (6961757 has old furniture primarily from Gujarat as well as some good reproductions.

Raj Ambawatta Complex (6526891 has British-Portuguese-Dutch colonial and ethnic Indian pieces.

If you are not looking for anything in particular amble through Sunder Nagar market or the Tibetan Market on Janpath. Both have several shops dealing in 'antiques', brass lamps, wooden chests, miniatures, Buddhist *tangkhas* and other bric-a-brac. A little searching could yield rich results.

For the House

There are interesting household shops in every major shopping complex. One of the best is **The Shop** 10 Regal Building, Connaught Place. Quality stuff at reasonable prices.

Good Earth has exquisite hand-painted crockery, glassware, elegant silverware and stylish home furnishings. It has showrooms at Santushti Complex (600108; Qutab Colonnade (6858394; Ambawatta Complex (6856466.

Shyam Ahuja Greater Kailash II and Santushti Complex. Shyam Ahuja's range includes, apart from his trademark dhurries, furnishings, linen, etc.

If you are looking for the unusual and the wacky, the place to go is **IM Centre for Contemporary Arts** A15 Lajpat Nagar II. They also have an intriguing collection of modern sculpture and lamps in wrought iron. Open 9.30 am to 6.30 pm. Closed Sundays.

Also recommended :

Anokhi Santushti Complex for handprinted linen and Jaipuri quilts.

Coverline and **Natural Selection** Hauz Khas Village.

Fabindia Greater Kailash I and Vasant Kunj for household linen and furnishings.

Rohini Khosla India Style and **5th of April** Ambawatta Complex.

Sadhaka Santushti Complex (604458 for ceramic tiles, salad bowls, mirrors, a small but interesting selection of furnishing fabric and table linen.

Speciality Shops

TEA

You do not have to be an expert to buy quality tea because there are speciality shops with trained personnel who assist you in picking the right blends.

Aap ki Pasand 15 Netaji Subhash Marg, Daryaganj (3260373 has 21 varieties of tea, and a small sitting area where you can sample the tea before purchasing it. Closed Sundays.

Mittal Stores 12 Sunder Nagar Market (4610667 offers 15 varieties of tea in prices ranging from Rs.80/kg to Rs.2500/kg. Also at 8A Main Market, Lodi Colony. (4615709.

DRY FRUITS

The best place to buy dry fruits - almonds, cashew nuts, *chilgozas*, sultanas, *kishmish* - is the many shops in **Khari Baoli**, just beyond Fatehpuri Masjid in Shahjahanabad.

Also recommended :

Bharat Dry Fruit Mart Shop No.3, Janpath (3327140.
Kashmir Dry Fruit Mart 5 Shankar Market (3314942.
Mega Dry Fruit C11 Lajpat Nagar II (6845549.
Roopak Store 6/9 Ajmal Khan Road, Karol Bagh (5722569.

PAPER

Frontline 78/79 Scindia House has reams and reams of handmade paper in every conceivable shape, texture and hue. It also has a small selection of stationery and gift wrapping paper.

Books

The city has only a few good bookshops located mostly in south and central Delhi.

For general interest books:

Bahri & Sons (4694610,
Fakirchand & Sons (4618810 and **The Book Shop** (4697102, in Khan Market.
The Bookworm 29 B Connaught Place (3322260.
Children's Book Trust Nehru House, Bahadur Shah Zafar Marg (3316970.
Crossword Ebony D4 South Extn II (6217645.
Fact & Fiction Priya Complex, Vasant Vihar (6146843.
Midlands Aurobindo Place Market (6867121.
National Book Trust A5 Green Park (669962.
Oxford Book House Scindia House, Connaught Place (3315308.
Rupa & Co. Ansari Road, Daryaganj (3270260.
Teksons South Extn I (4617703.

For specialised interest:

Jain Book Agency for government publications, Law and Business books C9 Connaught Place (3321663.
Motilal Banarasi Dass Publishers 40-41 UA Bungalow Road, Jawahar Nagar (2911985.
Munisiram Manoharlal Publishers Rani Jhansi Road (7771668 for books on Indology, Indian Art and Culture.
Prabhu Book Service 30 Hauz Khas Village, 1st floor (661284 and **R.S Book and Prints** A40 South Extn II (6445059 for those interested in antiquarian books, old maps and prints.

If you enjoy browsing through old books, do visit the **book bazaar** that is held every Sunday morning on the pavement in Daryaganj.

Ambawatta Complex

For those in search of the elegant and the exclusive the place to go is Ambawatta Complex on the fringe of Mehrauli village. An interesting range of designer garments for both men and women is available at **Ensemble**. **Good Earth,** the ultimate household shop, has a particularly charming range of pottery, furnishings and linen. If you are there at lunchtime try the Thai and Indonesian fare at **Spice** (6526872.

Central Cottage Industries Emporium

At Central Cottage Industries Emporium (3320439 in Jawahar Vyapar Bhawan, Janpath, under one roof you will find a spectacular display of Indian handlooms and handicrafts. Spread over 8 levels covering a floor area of 36,000 sq. ft., it is a place that makes you want to linger awhile. Prices are fixed, quality is assured - shimmering silks, embroidered shawls, precious jewellery, carpets, painting and pottery, glassware you can keep or gift away. A useful destination to pick up a souvenir. Open 10 am to 7 pm. Closed Sundays.

Dilli Haat

Traditionally, haats are periodic markets though Dilli Haat is open every day of the week and craftspersons come from different parts of the country for a fortnight at a time. Authentic crafts are available at rates that have not been inflated by the middleman's commission. It is also the only place in town where regional food from all over India is available. Entry: Rs.5 (adults), Rs.2 (child). Open 11 am to 10 pm.

Hauz Khas Village

Delhi has many urban villages but none can quite compare with Hauz Khas. Here the old and the new, the modern and the traditional have come together in 'enforced' harmony. The village became a fashionable destination for Delhi's elite in the late 80s after a group of designers and entrepreneurs decided to open their studios and retail outlets here. Speciality restaurants and galleries followed and today there are about 100 shops dealing in carpets, old silver antiques, furniture and high fashion garments. Hauz Khas is recommended not just for its shops or restaurants, here you can also stroll around the ancient monuments and explore its winding lanes. Closed Sundays.

Khadi Gramodyog Bhawan

Khadi Gramodyog Bhawan (3360902 in Regal Building, Connaught Place, is run by Khadi Village Industries Commission. Here you can buy khadi cotton and silk yardage, readymade garments, handmade paper, incense sticks, pure honey and much else. The prices are down-to-earth and from Mahatma Gandhi's birth anniversary, 2 October, a 10% to 50% discount is available on various products for a 90 day period. Open 10 am to 6 pm. Closed Sundays.

Palika Bazaar

This underground market in the very heart of Connaught Place has about 400 small shops retailing a wide range of products. Prices are reasonable and bargaining is permitted. Because of its central location and proximity to the railway station, it has become a tourist attraction over the years. Open 10 am to 7 pm. Closed Sundays.

Qutab Colonnade

This upmarket shopping arcade next to Qutb Minar, housed in what was once the pleasure house of a wealthy merchant, has an amazing range of designer garments, pottery, old furniture, and much more. On warm summer evenings you can even have a drink or dinner at the outdoor cafe, **Tamarind Court**, or wander up to the terrace for a spectacular view of the flood-lit Qutb. Open 11 am to 6.30 pm. Closed Mondays.

Santushti Complex

Located opposite Samrat Hotel, Santushti Complex (6887179 / 6887180 has a handful of exclusive shops set in manicured lawns. Closed Sundays.

And if you happen to be in Santushti around lunchtime, the Cordon Bleu fare at **Basil & Thyme** is worth sampling.

State Emporia

Eighteen in all, the State Emporia on Baba Kharak Singh Marg are a showcase of handicrafts and handlooms of the states they represent. Here you are likely to get snowed in by the bric-a-brac but good buys are definitely possible. Prices are fixed and reasonable because in most cases it is subsidised by the state government concerned. Some particularly good bargains are the carpets and shawls in **Zoon**, the Kashmir emporium, the bronze icons and lamps at **Poompuhar**, the Tamil Nadu emporium and the silks at **Cauvery**, the Karnataka emporium. Open 10 am to 6.30 pm. Closed Sundays.

Central Market in Lajpat Nagar, **Ajmal Khan Road Market** in Karol Bagh and **Sarojini Nagar Market** are very popular with Dilliwalas for inexpensive readymades, attractive cotton yardage and embroidered garments.

South Extension is more upmarket, a must for seekers of quality garments, jewellery and footwear. Most international brands available in India have their outlets here, Benetton, Lacoste, Allen Solly, Louis Phillipe, among others.

Basant Lok Complex in Vasant Vihar is very popular with youngsters in Delhi. It has a movie hall, Priya, fast food joints and a scattering of quality stores.

This is a subjective and limited listing of shops and markets in Delhi. In an earlier chapter, Bazaars, we have written about the bazaars in the galis of Shahjahanabad.

Market Holidays

Sunday

Azad Market, Baba Kharak Singh Marg, Chandni Chowk, Chawri Bazaar, Connaught Place, Hauz Khas Village, Janpath, Khan Market, Khari Baoli, Meena Bazaar, Nai Sarak, Nehru Place, Paharganj, Palika Bazaar, Sadar Bazaar, Sabzi Mandi, Shanker Market, Yashwant Place.

Monday

Ajmal Khan Road, Defence Colony Market, INA Market, Karol Bagh, Lajpat Nagar Central Market, Nizamuddin, Sarojini Nagar Market, South Extension.

Tuesday

Aurobindo Place, Chittaranjan Park, Greater Kailash, Green Park, Hauz Khas, Munirka, New Friends Colony, R.K. Puram, Vasant Vihar, Masoodpur, Vasant Kunj, Yusuf Sarai.

Shopping Hours: 10 am to 7 pm.

When to come to Delhi

The best time to come to Delhi is between October and April. The flowers are in bloom and the sunshine is soft and lovely.

During the winter months of December and January, the day temperatures are around 18°C (64°F) and could go down to 4°C (39°F) at night. The streets are full of people and walking is a pleasure. This is the best time to explore the old forts and ruins or walk through the myriad lanes and bylanes of the old city which throb with life. It is exciting to face unmapped deadends and enter sudden zones of experience.

The summer months of May and June are hot, and the temperature can rise as high as 46°C (115°F). Tar melts on the streets and the walls burn with heat, while the overhanging dust clouds seem to trap the heat. Hot winds, or *loo* as they are locally called, blow through the streets of Delhi, carrying layers of fine dust. Staying indoor makes sense.

After the scorching heat, monsoons arrive in the first week of July and the rainy season stretches till mid-August. The rains in Delhi are not heavy as in some other cities of India like Mumbai or Calcutta. July, August and most of September are hot and humid, not the best time to visit Delhi. But you could always take trips out and soak in the lush greenery of the countryside, bathed in the first showers of the season.

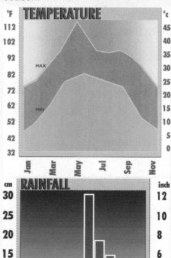

TEMPERATURE

RAINFALL

Time Zone

Indian Standard Time is 5½ hours ahead of Greenwich Mean Time, 10½ hours ahead of US Eastern Standard Time and 4½ hours behind Australian Eastern Standard Time.

Despite its vast geographical territory, India has just one time zone, and no daylight saving time in summer.

INDIAN DIPLOMATIC MISSIONS ABROAD

Australia 3-5 Moonah Place, Yarralumla, Canberra, ACT-2600.
((6) 273 3999.
Fax (6) 2733328.

25 Bligh Street, Level 27, Sydney, New South Wales 2000.
((2) 92239500.
Fax (2) 92239246.

Austria Karntnerring 2, A 1010 Vienna.
((1) 5058666.
Fax (1) 5059219.

Bangladesh House No.120, Road No.2, Dhanmondi Residential Area, Dhaka. ((2) 503606. Fax (2) 863662.

Bungalow 2, B2 Road No.1 Kulsi, Chittagong.
((31) 619965.

567/B Greater Road, Laxmipur, Rajshahi.
((80)7214841.

Belgium 217 Chaussee de Vleurgat 1050, Brussels.
((2) 640 9140.
Fax (2) 648 9638.

Bhutan India House Estate,Thimpu.
((9752) 22162.
Fax (9752) 23195.

Cambodia Villa No 777, Boulevard Monivong, Phnom Penh.
((23) 720912.
Fax (23) 364489.

Canada 10 Springfield Road, Ottawa. Ontario KIM 1 C9.
((613) 744 3751.
Fax (613) 7440913.

Suite No. 500, 2 Bloor Street West, Toronto. Ontario M4W 3E2.
((416) 9604831.
Fax (416) 9609812.

325 Howe Street, 2nd floor, Vancouver. BC V6C 1Z7.
((604) 6628811.
Fax (604) 6822471.

China 1Ri Tan Dong Lu, Beijing 100600.
((10) 5321903.
Fax (10) 5324684.

1008 Shanghai International Trade Centre, 220 Yan Anan (West) Road, Shanghai 200335.
((21) 2758885.
Fax (21) 2758881.

Denmark Vangehusvej 15, 2100 Copenhegan.
((45) 3118288.
Fax (45) 31299201.

Egypt 5 Aziz Abaza Street, Zamalek, PO Box No 718, Cairo 11511. ((2) 3413051.
Fax (2) 3414038.

Finland Satamakatu, 2A8 Helsinki 16.
((0) 608927.
Fax (0) 6221208.

France 15 Rue Alford Dehodencq, 75016 Paris. ((1) 40507070.
Fax (1) 40500996.

INDIAN DIPLOMATIC MISSIONS ABROAD

Germany Adenauerallee 262-264, 53113 Bonn.
((228) 54050.
Fax (228) 540 5153.

Majakowskiring 55, 13156 Berlin.
((30) 4853002.
Fax (30) 4853003.

Mittelweg 49, 60318 Frankfurt / AM Main.
((69) 1530050.
Fax (69) 554125.

Raboisen 6, 20095 Hamburg.
((40) 338036.
Fax (40) 323757.

Indonesia S1Jalan HR Rasuna Said, Kuningan Jakarta Selatan, 12950.
((21) 5204150.
Fax (21) 5204160.

Iran 46 Mir Emad, Corner of 9th Street, Dr Bheshti Avenue, P.O. Box 15875-4118 Tehran.
((21) 8755102.
Fax (21) 8755973.

Ireland 6 Leeson Park, Dublin 6.
((1) 4970843.
Fax (1) 4978074.

Israel 4 Kaufman Steet, Sharbat House, Tel Aviv 68012. ((3) 5101431.
Fax (3) 510 1434.

Italy Via XX Settembre 5, 00187 Rome.
((6) 4884642.
Fax (6) 4819539.

Via Larg 16, (5th & 6th Floor) 20122 Milan.
((2) 8057691.
Fax (2) 72002226.

Japan 2-2-11 Kudan Minami, Chiyoda Ku, Tokyo 102.
((3) 326 22391.
Fax (3) 32344866.

Osaka-Kobe Semba I.S.Bldg, 10th Floor, 9-26 Kyutaromachi, 1 Chome, Chuo-ku, Osaka 541.
((6) 2617299.
Fax (6) 2617799.

Kuwait Diplomatic Enclave, Arabian Gulf Street, P.O. Box 1540 Safat, 13015-Safat.
((965) 2530600.
Fax (965) 2525811.

Malaysia No. 2 Jalan Taman Duta, off Jalan Duta, P.O. Box 10059, G.P.O. 50704 Kuala Lumpur.
((603) 2533504.
Fax (603) 2533507.

Maldives Athireeg, Aage, Ameeru Ahmed, Magu, Henvieru, Male.
((960) 323014.
Fax (960) 324778.

Mauritius Life Insurance Corporation of India Bldg, 6th Floor, President John Kennedy Street, P.O. Box 162, Port Louis.
((230) 2083775.
Fax (230) 2086859.

Nepal Lain Chaur, P.O. Box 292, Kathmandu.
((71) 411940.
Fax (71) 413132.

The Netherlands Buitenrustweg 2, 2517 KD, The Hague.
((70) 3469771.
Fax (70) 3617072.

New Zealand 180 Molesworth Street, P.O. Box 4045, Wellington.
((4) 4736390.
Fax (4) 4990665.

WHAT TO WEAR

Delhi does not have a fixed dress code. Dress-wise, most of Delhi is just as modern as any other metro in the world. The dress code might be more conservative in certain parts of the city like parts of the old city, Mehrauli and west Delhi. Local dresses such as *salwar kameez* with *dupatta* is a wonderfully relaxed and easy-to-wear dress for women. For men it is the *kurta* and *pajama*, with sandals or leather *kolhapuri chappals*. The sari is the most popular attire for women, while young women and girls are seen in western clothes.

It would be sensible to wear comfortable clothes which do not attract unnecessary attention. A windcheater or a light jacket over a cardigan or a sweater should suffice in winter. Loose cotton clothes that are cool and protect the hands and legs from the heat and the dust are the best summer wear. It is advisable to wear a scarf or a hat to protect the head from the blazing heat of an Indian summer.

Cotton clothes are reasonably inexpensive in India and are available in a wide range. It would be a good idea to buy them here. There are many readymade garment shops in Delhi where you can pick up well-designed clothes in different textures and styles *(see: **Where to Shop**)*.

NOTES

WHEN TO COME
WHAT TO WEAR
BEFORE COMING
VISA
INDIAN DIPLOMATIC MISSIONS ABROAD

Before coming to Delhi

There are a few things you need to take care of before travelling to India.

VISA

There are three kinds of visas for tourists.

1. The 15-day single / double entry transit visa. This visa is valid for 30 days from the date of its issue.

2. The 3-month multiple-entry visa. This visa is valid for 90 days from the date of first entry into India, which must be within 30 days from the date of its issue.

3. The 6-month multiple-entry visa. This visa is valid for 180 days from the date of its issue, not from the date of entry into India.

Delhi is not a very safe city for unaccompanied women. Women arriving alone at night are advised to take pre-paid taxis to their destination or, preferably, have someone reliable receive them at the airport.

VISA EXTENSION

It is virtually impossible to get the 15-day or 3-month visa extended. Only the 6-month tourist visa can be extended. It can be quite a bother to extend it beyond a 15-day period. Avoid it unless there is an emergency.

A 15-day extension on the 6-month visa is issued by the **Foreigner's Regional Registration Office (FRRO)** Hans Bhawan,1st Floor, Bahadur Shah Zafar Marg (3319781 (**MAP 15** C4). It is open on weekdays, 9.30 am to1.30 pm and 2 pm to 4 pm. A I5-day extension is given only if confirmed air tickets are not available. No fee is charged.

The 6-month visa can be extended for a maximum period of one month, but any extension beyond 15 days is a complicated matter.

Here's trying to simplify it for you. Remember, it is a three-step procedure.

Step 1: Collect the long-term visa extension form from the Ministry of Home Affairs office located on the 1st floor of the **Lok Nayak Bhawan** (**MAP 21** C3) behind Khan Market (4697648 / 4697018.

Step 2: After filling up the form, take it, along with four passport-size photographs, to the FRRO for authorisation. A fee of Rs 775 is levied on a 1-month visa extension.

Step 3: After authorisation for visa extension is stamped on the form by the FRRO, take it back to the Ministry of Home Affairs, Lok Nayak Bhawan. Here you will receive the actual visa extension.

TRAVEL INSURANCE

Take a travel insurance policy, covering theft and loss, before coming to India. Also buy a medical insurance.

There are several kinds of insurance policies. Make the right choice after consulting a reliable travel agent in your country. Policies that cover adventure sports like trekking or river rafting are more expensive.

DRIVING LICENCE

A valid International Driving Licence is necessary if you wish to drive a car or a motorcycle in India and it is advisable to get one before coming. **Automobile Association of Upper India (AAUI)** 14F Connaught Place (3314071 (**MAP 2** E3), extends help to AA members from all countries. If you do not have an International Driving Licence and still wish to drive in India, you can get a Temporary Driving Licence, provided you are carrying a valid driving licence of your country. You may still be required to give a test to check your knowledge of road signs. The AAUI can arrange this.

INDIAN DIPLOMATIC
MISSIONS ABROAD

Switzerland
Effingerstrasse 45,
CH 3008, Berne.
((31) 3823111.
Fax (31) 3822687.

9 Rue de Valais,
CH 1202, Geneva.
((22) 7320859.
Fax (22) 7315471.

Thailand 46 Soi 23
(Prasarnmitr), Sukhumvit
Road, Bangkok 10110.
((2) 2580300.
Fax (2) 2584627.

Trinidad and Tobago
No.6, Victoria Avenue,
P.B. No.530, Port of
Spain.
((809) 6277480.
Fax (809) 6276985.

Uganda 1st Floor, Bank
of Baroda Building,
Kampala Road, P.O.Box
7040, Kampala.
((41) 244631.
Fax (41) 254943.

United Arab Emirates
Villa No.9, Street No. 5,
Sector 2/33, Khalidiya,
P.O.Box 4090, Abu
Dhabi. ((12) 664800.
Fax (12) 651518.

Al Hamaria Diplomatic
Enclave, P.O. Box 737
Dubai. ((4) 519666.
Fax (4) 524453.

United Kingdom India
House, Aldwych London,
WC2B 4NA.
((71) 8368484.
Fax (71) 8364331.

20 Augusta Street,
Jewellery Quarters,
Hockley, Birmingham,
B18 6JL.
((21) 2122782.
Fax (21) 2122786.

Fleming House, 6th
Floor, 134 Renfrew
Street, Glasgow G3 7ST.
((141) 3310777.
Fax (141) 3310666.

**United States of
America** 2107
Massachusetts Avenue,
NW, Washington DC
20008.
((202) 9397000.
Fax (202) 9397027.

455 North City, Front
Plaza Drive, Suite 850,
Chicago, Illinois 60601.
((312) 5950405.
Fax (312) 5950416.

3 Post Oak Central, Suite
No. 600, 1990 Post Oak
Blvd, Houston,
Texas 77056.
((713) 6262148.
Fax (713) 6262450.

3 East, 64th Street,
Manhattan, New York
10021-7097.
((212) 7740699.
Fax (212) 8613788.

540 Arguello Boulevard,
San Francisco, CA
94118.
((415) 6680662.
Fax (415) 6682073.

Vietnam 58-60 Tran
Hung Dao, Hanoi.
((4) 8253409.
Fax (4) 8265169.

Zimbabwe No.12, Natal
Road, Belgravia, Post
Box 4620, Harare.
((4) 795955.
Fax (4) 722324.

HEALTH

Your health during your travel in
India depends on three things:
precautions taken before arrival,
day-to-day health care, and
efficiency in tackling emergencies.

No particular vaccination is
required for coming to India.
However, visitors from designated
countries in Africa, South
America and Papua New Guinea,
even if they are on transit, are
required to bring valid yellow fever
vaccination certificates. In the absence of this certificate
they will be quarantined for six days.

Precautionary medication is the best bet against common
ailments like diarrhoea, dysentry and malaria. Malaria is a
problem in India during the rainy season. So, if you are
coming at that time of the year, do consult your doctor for
precautionary anti-malarial medication. While in India, use
mosquito repellent ointment.

If you are not already vaccinated
against hepatitis B, get it done
before travelling.

Those not accustomed to Indian
conditions are usually vulnerable
to stomach problems. It is
advisable to seek qualified
medical advice before travelling
and carry your own first-aid kit.

There are any number of good
doctors, private clinics, hospitals
nursing homes and well-
established government hospitals in Delhi.

NOTES

VISA EXTENSION
TRAVEL INSURANCE
DRIVING LICENCE
HEALTH

THIS PAGE

For travel health, it is best to use your common sense.
Take care what you eat or drink. This is the most
important health rule. Water is suspect, therefore, it is
best to carry your own mineral water. Bottled mineral
water and aerated drinks are easily avaliable and are a
good substitute for water. Hot tea and coffee are also
good alternatives.

Indian travellers do not worry too much about water,
because their constitution is tuned to local conditions.
Even so, contaminated drinking water remains the main
reason for most stomach-related diseases.

Diarrhoea (the English call it 'Delhi-belly') is the
most common stomach ailment. Take a three or
five-day course of anti-diarrhoea tablets duly prescribed
by a doctor.

Diarrhoea leads to dehydration. So, along with
medication, drink a lot of water with salt and sugar.
There are some restrictions on your diet, too. Alcohol,
milk, meat, fried and spicy foods should be avoided.
Porridge, stew and the local *khichri* are easy to digest
and, therefore, recommended.

If the bout of upset stomach persists, get a stool test
done because it might be amoebic dysentery.

The tropical sun is extremely strong during the summer months, so guard against sun stroke and dehydration. Wear a hat and dark glasses when you go out. Drink lots of non-alcoholic liquids, water and fruit juice. Allow sweat to evaporate, wear loose cotton clothes. Use sun screen lotions and talcum powder as a precaution against prickly heat rash.

THINGS YOU CAN BRING INTO INDIA

Visitors can bring in articles for personal use, including cameras with 5 rolls of film, a reasonable quantity of jewellery, a pair of binoculars, a portable musical instrument, a portable radio, a tape recorder, a portable typewriter, a laptop computer and professional equipment. On arrival, you will have to give an undertaking on a Tourist Baggage Re-Export (TBRE) form, available with Customs officials at the Airport, that you will take these items back when you leave. This form, along with the articles that are entered in it, have to be shown to the Customs officials at the time of departure.

Designated 'high-value articles' are also allowed in, but on a written undertaking that they will be taken back at the time of departure. Please obtain a Landing Certificate if you are expecting unaccompanied baggage and for mishandled baggage.

You can bring in 200 cigarettes (or 50 cigars or 250 gms of tobacco) and liquor and wines up to 32 oz (1 litre). You are allowed to bring in any amount of foreign currency in cash or travellers cheques. However, if you are carrying more than US $ 2500 (or equivalent), you have to declare it on arrival. Fill up the Currency Declaration Form (CDF) which is to be attested by the Customs Officer. Indian currency cannot be brought in nor taken out of the country.

Leaving India from Delhi
THINGS YOU CAN TAKE BACK
EXPORT REGULATIONS

A visitor can take back the following goods:

(A) Souvenirs (including Indian silk, wool, handicrafts, etc.) without any limit.

(B) Gold jewellery and silverware up to a value of Rs 100,000 (and in excess of that only after obtaining a permit from the RBI, the Indian central bank).

(C) Other jewellery and precious stones, but if of high value, these should be appraised by the Customs Appraiser at the airport before departure. As a general rule, get an RBI permit for goods of high value. There are restrictions on the export of antiques and art objects which are more than 100 years old. In case of doubt, consult the Director, Antiquities, **Archaeological Survey of India** Janpath (3017443 (**MAP 21** B1). It is advisable to get a certificate of proof.

Export of most wildlife products is either prohibited or strictly regulated. Do not buy articles made of ivory, reptile, tiger or deer skin, tortoise shell or *shahtoosh* shawls made by killing the Tibetan antelope.

TAX CLEARANCE CERTIFICATE

If you stay in India for more than 120 days (4 months), from the date of issue of the visa, regardless of your date of entry into India, you would be required to furnish a tax clearance certificate to leave the country. This is to prove that you did not earn money while in India and that your trip was financed with the money brought in. If you are planning to stay in India for more than four months, be careful with your documents relating to travel finance.

EMBASSIES / HIGH COMMISSIONS IN DELHI

Afghanistan 5/50F Shanti Path, Chanakyapuri. (6889155. Fax 6875439.

Argentina B8/9 Vasant Vihar. (6141345. Fax 6886501.

Australia 1/50G Shanti Path, Chanakyapuri. (6888223 / 6885556. Fax 6885199.

Austria EP13 Chandragupta Marg, Chanakyapuri. (6889050. Fax 6886929.

Bangladesh 56 Ring Road, Lajpat Nagar III. (6834668 / 6839209. Fax 6840596.

Belgium 50N Shanti Path, Chanakyapuri. (6875728. Fax 6885821.

Bhutan Chandragupta Marg, Chanakyapuri. (6889230. Fax 6876710.

Canada 7/8 Shanti Path, Chanakyapuri. (6876500. Fax 6876579.

China 50D Shanti Path, Chanakyapuri. (600328. Fax 6885486.

Denmark 11 Aurangzeb Road. (3010900. Fax 3010961.

Egypt 1/50M Niti Marg, Chanakyapuri. (6114096. Fax 6885355.

Finland E3 Nyaya Marg, Chanakyapuri. (6115258. Fax 6816713.

France 2/50E Shanti Path, Chanakyapuri. (6118790. Fax 6872305.

Germany 6/50G Shanti Path, Chanakyapuri. (6889144. Fax 6873117.

Ghana 50N Satya Marg, Chanakyapuri. (6883298. Fax 6883202.

Greece 16 Sunder Nagar. (4617800. Fax 4601363.

Iceland 41/2 M Speedbird House, Connaught Circus. (3321172. Fax 3321275.

Indonesia 50A Kautilya Marg, Chanakyapuri. (6118642. Fax 6874402.

Iran 5 Barakhamba Road. (43329600. Fax 3325493.

Ireland 13 Jor Bagh. (4626714. Fax 4697053.

Israel 3 Aurangzeb Road. (3013238. Fax 3014298.

Italy 50E Chandragupta Marg, Chanakyapuri. (6114355. Fax 6873889.

Japan 50G Shanti Path, Chanakyapuri. (6876581. Fax 6885587.

Kenya 66 Vasant Marg, Vasant Vihar. (6146538. Fax 6146550

Kuwait 5A Shanti Path, Chanakyapuri. (600791. Fax 6873516.

Malaysia 50M Satya Marg, Chanakyapuri. (601291. Fax 6881538.

If you are not an Indian passport holder and are planning to stay in India for more than four months, apply for the certificate at the **Income Tax Department, Central Revenue Building** (ITO), Vikas Marg. ℂ 3316161 / 3317828 (**MAP 16** D4).

FOREIGN TRAVEL TAX

Rs 500 has to be paid at the airport as Foreign Travel Tax when leaving the country. For travel to Pakistan, Nepal, Sri Lanka, Bhutan, Myanmar, the Maldives and Afghanistan, the tax is Rs 150.

Arriving in Delhi by Air

The Delhi airport is called the Indira Gandhi International Airport (IGI). It has two terminals: Terminal 1 (domestic flights) and Terminal 2 (international). Terminal 2 is new and modern, equipped with all expected facilities; Terminal 1 is the old airport, basic but efficient. The two terminals are 7 km away from each other.

NOTES

THINGS YOU CAN BRING INTO INDIA
THINGS YOU CAN TAKE BACK
TAX CLEARANCE
FOREIGN TRAVEL TAX
ARRIVING BY AIR
EMBASSIES / HIGH COMMISSIONS

THIS PAGE

Remember, if you are arriving by an international flight and have to take a domestic airline for an onward flight, you would have to go from Terminal 2 to Terminal 1.

The IGI is one of India's busiest tourist entry points. You would arrive at this airport also to go to the neighbouring regions of north and northwest India.

TERMINAL 2 (INTERNATIONAL)

Terminal 2 is located about 19 km from the city centre (Connaught Place). Like most airports Terminal 2 has restaurants, 24-hour snack bars, 24-hour currency exchange counters, one run by Thomas Cook, the other run by the State Bank of India. It has left-luggage facility, infant-care facility and first-aid. There are pay phones for international (ISD), domestic long distance (STD) and local calls.

Major travel agencies have counters in Terminal 2 which deal with inbound and outbound travel arrangements and offer travel packages.

Most accredited 5-star hotels also have their counters in Terminal 2 to provide information, accommodation and travel packages.

CUSTOMS

There are two channels for customs clearance: Green Channel and Red Channel.

GREEN CHANNEL

This is for unhindered exit from the airport. You can walk through the Green Channel if you are not carrying goods which attract customs duty, or electronic goods of high value. You cannot take the Green Channel if you have unaccompanied baggage or foreign exchange over US $ 2500.

RED CHANNEL

For those who have anything to declare, including money worth more than US $ 2500.

TERMINAL 1 (DOMESTIC)

This is located 12 km away from the city centre (Connaught Place). It has all basic facilities, a 24-hour snack bar, telephones for international, domestic and local calls, car rentals, among them.

Terminal 1 has separate areas for Arrival and Departure.

The Arrival area has an Indian Airlines counter. This state-run airline had a monopoly on flights within India until a few years ago. It provides the largest network of domestic flights. Private airlines do not have their counters within the terminal building, but have their booths just outside.

The Departure area, too, has an Indian Airlines counter, while the booths of private airlines which provide efficient and courteous service are outside.

TRANSFER FROM AIRPORT

TAXI

There are three kinds of taxis. Yellow-and-black taxis for city destinations, DLY taxis with all-India permits and the more expensive DLZ taxis. There is a pre-paid taxi counter for these taxis in the Arrival area. It is a good idea to hire a pre-paid taxi to avoid being over-charged.

DLY taxis, white cars of Indian make, have all-India permits. They are more expensive than yellow-and-black cabs and can be hired for both city and outside destinations.

DLZ taxis are cars of foreign make. Like DLY cabs, DLZ taxis have all-India permits, but are more expensive than DLY cabs.

International car rental companies like Hertz and Europcar, as well as Indian private companies run taxi services (*see : Car Rentals, p.335*).

INTERNATIONAL AIRLINES OFFICES

Major airlines that operate international flights from Delhi:

Air India 23 Himalaya House, Kasturba Gandhi Marg. ℂ 3311502. Fax 3324204. Airport: ℂ 5652041 / 5653132.

Aeroflot N1 BMC House, Ist Floor, Middle Circle, Connaught Place. ℂ 3723241 / 3312843. Fax 3723245. Airport: ℂ 5653510 / 5653730.

Air France 7 Atma Ram Mansion, Scindia House, Connaught Place. ℂ 3738004 / 3312853. Fax 3716259. Airport: ℂ 5652099 / 5652294.

Air Lanka Room No.1, Hotel Janpath, Janpath. ℂ 3368843 / 3368845. Fax 3368274. Airport: ℂ 5652957.

Air Mauritius c/o, Air India, Jeevan Bharati Bldg, 124 Connaught Circus. ℂ 3731225 (Extn. 4222).

Alitalia Airlines 2H DCM Bldg, Barakhamba Road. ℂ 3311019 / 3354666. Fax 3713699. Airport : ℂ 5652348.

Bangladesh Biman World Trade Centre, Barakhamba Road. ℂ 3354401 / 3354403. Fax 3314699. Airport: ℂ 5652943.

British Airways DLF Centre, 1 Sansad Marg. ℂ 3329906 / 3323099. Fax 3325545. Airport: ℂ 5652077 / 5652908.

Cathay Pacific G123 Tolstoy House, Tolstoy Marg. ℂ 3325789 / 3321286. Fax 3721550.

Druk Air Chandralok Bldg, 36 Janpath. ℂ 3310990 / 3310991. Fax 3320586. Airport: ℂ 5653207.

Emirates Kanchenjunga Bldg, 18 Barakhamba Road. ℂ 3324803 / 3324665. Fax 3324383. Airport: ℂ 5696851/ 5696861

Gulf Air G12 Connaught Circus. ℂ 3324293 / 3327814. Fax 3721756. Airport: ℂ 5652065.

Japan Airlines Chandralok Bldg, 36 Janpath. ℂ 3327104 / 3327108. Fax 3324244. Airport: ℂ 5653942 / 5653358.

Kenya Airways Prakash Deep Bldg, 7 Tolstoy Marg. ℂ 3357747 / 3324489. Fax 3721140.

KLM Prakash Deep Bldg, 7 Tolstoy Marg. ℂ 3357747 / 3324489. Fax 3721140. Airport: ℂ 5652715 / 5652420.

Korean Air Prakash Deep Bldg, 7 Tolstoy Marg. ℂ 3721913 .

Lufthansa 56 Janpath. ℂ 3323310 / 3327268. Fax 3324524. Airport: ℂ 5652064 / 5652843.

Pakistan International Airlines 102 Kailash Bldg, 26 Kasturba Gandhi Marg. ℂ 3737791 / 3737794. Fax 3737796. Airport: ℂ 5652841.

Royal Nepal Airlines 44
Janpath. ℂ 3321164 /
3323437. Fax 3327125.
Airport: ℂ 5696876

SAS Ambadeep Bldg,14
Kasturba Gandhi Marg.
ℂ 3352299 / 3350307.
Fax 3355959.
Airport: ℂ 5653708.

Singapore Airlines
International Business
Centre, M38/1 Middle
Circle, Connaught Place.
ℂ 3321624 / 3350131.
Fax 3722115.
Airport: ℂ 5653822 /
5653072.

Swissair: DLF Centre, 1
Sansad Marg. ℂ 3722993
/ 3722994. Fax 3326999.
Airport: ℂ 5652531 /
5652535.

Thai Airways The
American Plaza, Park
Royal Hotel, Nehru
Place. ℂ 6239988.
Fax 6239149.
Airport: ℂ 5652413 /
5652796.

United Airlines
Ambadeep Bldg, 14
Kasturba Gandhi Marg.
ℂ 3351265 / 3353377.
Fax 3719415.
Airport: ℂ 5653910 /
5653911.

US Airways 601 Ashoka
Estate, 24 Barakhamba
Road. ℂ 3714621 /
3311362. Fax 3722878.

Indian Airlines
Malhotra Bldg,F Block,
Connaught Place.
ℂ 3310517.
PTI Bldg, Sansad Marg.
ℂ 3719168.

Safdarjang Airport,
Aurobindo Marg.
ℂ 4622220 (24-hour
office).

Ashok Hotel,
Chanakyapuri. ℂ 6110101.
Airport: ℂ 5665121.

Alliance Air (a subsidiary
of Indian Airlines)
Sardarjang Airport,
Aurobindo Marg.
ℂ 4621267.
Airport: ℂ 5665313.

Archana Airways 41A
Friends Colony East.
ℂ 6842001.
Airport: ℂ 5665519 /
5665854.

Jet Airways BE
Hansalaya Bldg, 15
Barakhamba Road.
ℂ 3321317.
G12 Connaught Place.
ℂ 3320961 / 3320963.
Jet Air House, 13
Community Centre,
Yusuf Sarai (24-hour
office) ℂ 6853700.
Airport: ℂ 5665404 /
5665405.

Sahara India Airlines
Ambadeep Bldg,
14 Kasturba Gandhi
Marg. ℂ 3326851 /
3326853.
Airport: ℂ 5665234 /
5665875.

U P Airways
A2 Defence Colony.
ℂ 4638204.
Airport: ℂ 5665126.

Jagson Airlines
12E Vandana Bldg,
11 Tolstoy Marg.
ℂ 3721593 / 3328579.
Airport: ℂ 5665545.

COACH

There are coach services for transfer into the city which operate from both Terminals 1 and 2. These are run by Airports Authority of India (AAI), Delhi Transport Corporation (DTC) and Ex-Servicemen's Transport Service. The coaches leave every hour and go to the city centre (Connaught Place), New Delhi railway station, and the Inter-State Bus Terminal (ISBT) at Kashmere Gate. *En route*, they stop at major hotels.

There is no stand for auto rickshaws, which are cheaper than cabs, at either Terminal 2 or Terminal 1. But you may find one outside. The fare may have to be negotiated, although auto rickshaws are supposed to charge by the meter.

Travel Within India

AIR

There are several airlines that fly to domestic destinations. Among them, they cover the length and breadth of the country. All domestic airlines operate from IGI Terminal 2.

Hand Baggage: In all domestic flights, passengers are allowed one piece of hand baggage. All baggage is subject to security check whether carried by hand or booked in the hold.

Baggage Allowance: Domestic airlines allow 20 kgs check-in baggage for Economy Class and 30 kgs for Business Class. Excess baggage is charged as per the schedule available at the airline's counter.

The reporting time for all domestic flights is 60 minutes prior to departure, except for Srinagar, Jammu and Leh for which it is 75 minutes.

NOTES

CUSTOMS
TRANSFER FROM
AIRPORT
TRAVEL WITHIN INDIA
INTERNATIONAL &
DOMESTIC AIRLINES
OFFICES

THIS PAGE

Onward or return reservations must be reconfirmed whenever there is a break journey of over 72 hours. Failure to reconfirm may result in cancellation of reservation.

Tickets purchased in rupees for domestic travel are valid for one year. Tickets on the international sector, as well as those purchased with US dollars, are valid for a year from the date of journey or date of issue, as the case might be.

Indian Airlines and its subsidiary, Alliance Air, offer a 50% concession on the basic fare for senior citizens (above 65 years) and bonafide students, as does Jet Airways and Sahara India Airlines. Blind and cancer patients get a similar 50% concession from Indian Airlines. All the above concessions are available only to Indian passport holders. Indian Airlines offers a 25% concession on the basic fare to foreign students. Indian Airlines also offers two special travel packages (if paid for in US dollars):

Discover India Fare : US $ 500 for 15 days and US $ 750 for 21 days of unlimited travel with certain routing restrictions.

India Wonderfare : US $ 300 for 7 days of unlimited travel. Port Blair, however, is not included in this scheme.

RAIL

The Indian Railways run a gigantic, modern and organised network which connects Delhi to most major and minor destinations within India.

There are three important railway stations in Delhi : Delhi Main (in the old Delhi area of Shahjahanabad), New Delhi and Nizamuddin and a few smaller railway stations like Sarai Rohilla and Delhi Cantonment. Most long distance train services are from the three major railway stations.

New Delhi railway station is located in the heart of New Delhi, barely 2 km from Connaught Place. Delhi Main station is in the old city, close to Red Fort. Both are extremely busy and crowded stations. By contrast, the Nizamuddin station, which has limited train connections, is less crowded.

TICKET RESERVATION

Trains in India are very crowded and it is necessary to reserve a seat or a berth to travel in any degree of comfort.

Rail reservations start from 30 days before the date of travel. Reservations can be cancelled up to 24 hours before the train leaves, but a nominal cancellation fee has to be paid.

Train tickets must be bought before you enter the train. You will be penalised if you do not have one and intend to buy it on board.

There are several computerised reservation centres. New Delhi Reservation Centre, the largest, is next to the New Delhi railway station on Chelmsford Road in the Paharganj area It is open from 8 am to 8 pm.

Railway Reservation Centres

Azadpur
Kirti Nagar
Chanakyapuri
Karkar Duman
Delhi Cantt
Lajpat Nagar
Delhi Main RS
New Delhi RS
Delhi Univ
Sarojini Nagar
Okhla
Nizamuddin
Shahdara
Sarai Rohilla

Avoid offers of quick reservations from touts who hang around the stations. There are a number of travel agencies near New Delhi railway station which are not very reliable. It is best to buy tickets from the Railway Reservation Centres. The long queues are often daunting, but most of these Centres are computerised and it does not take very long to buy a ticket.

Delhi is a good place to buy onward and return journey tickets. **International Travel Bureau** on the first floor of New Delhi railway station has a special booking office for foreigners. It is open Monday through Saturday, 7.30 am to 5 pm. Tickets here are issued only to foreign nationals and non-resident Indians against payment in US dollars.

Such tickets get a priority on reservation under the Foreign Tourist Quota and are exempted from reservation fees.

There are tourist information counters at Delhi Main and New Delhi railway stations, although the service here is not necessarily courteous.

SOME IMPORTANT TRAINS

Rajdhani Express is a superfast long-distance train that connects Delhi with major Indian cities.

Destination	Train No	Days
Ahmedabad	2427	Sat
Calcutta (via Gaya)	2302	Tue, Wed, Thu, Sat, Sun
Calcutta (via Patna)	2306	Mon, Fri
Bangalore	2430	Wed, Sat
Bhubaneshwar	2422	Mon, Fri
Chennai	2634	Fri, Sun
Guwahati	2424	Tue, Wed, Sat
Patna (via Varanasi)	2310	Thu, Sun
JammuTawi	2425	Thu
Mumbai	2951	Tue, Wed, Thu, Fri, Sat, Sun
Mumbai	2953	Mon, Tue, Thu, Fri, Sat, Sun
Secunderabad	2438	Wed, Sat
Trivandrum	2432	Tue

Shatabdi Express is a superfast train which links Delhi to cities close to Delhi, including major tourist destinations. All Shatabdi departures are from New Delhi railway station.

Destination	Train No	Days
Bhopal (via Agra)	2002	Daily
Lucknow (via Kanpur)	2004	Daily
Kalka (via Chandigarh)	2005	Daily
Chandigarh	2011	Daily
Amritsar (via Ludhiana)	2013	Daily
Ajmer (via Jaipur)	2015	Mon, Tue, Wed, Thu, Fri, Sat
Dehra Dun (via Haridwar)	2017	Daily

ELECTRICITY

Electric supply is quite reliable in Delhi. The electric current in India is 220-240 volts AC, 50 cycles.

The sockets here are of the 3 round pin variety similar to the ones available in Europe or America, so 3-pin electric gadgets brought in from abroad can be used here.

INDRAIL PASS

Indrail Passes for travel in India by train can be booked in India or abroad. The fare has to be paid in foreign currency. The passes are valid for 7 to 90 days. You can buy Indrail passes at the International Travel Bureau in New Delhi Railway Station. Indrail passes are also available at the railway reservation offices at Chandigarh, Varanasi and Amritsar.

Indrail Pass Prices in US $

Days	Air-cond.	1st Class	2nd Class
7	300	150	80
15	370	185	90
21	440	220	100
30	550	275	125
60	800	400	185
90	1060	530	235

SPECIAL TRAINS

Palace on Wheels lets you luxuriate in royal comfort on a week-long rail journey covering Jaipur, Udaipur, Jaisalmer, Jodhpur, Bharatpur and Agra. Tariff (October to March) US $ 325 / 460 per day per person for double / single occupancy. Tariff (September & April) US $ 270 / 370 per day per person for double / single occupancy. For details, call Bikaner House.   3381884 / 3386069.

Royal Orient is a luxury train which takes you on an 8-day trip along the endless sand dunes of Rajasthan to the sun-warmed beaches of Gujarat. The Royal Orient has all the modern amenities of a first class hotel.

Tariff (October- March) US $ 200 / 350 per day per person for double / single occupancy. Tariff (April & September) US $ 150 / 263 per day per person for double / single occupancy. For details call Royal Orient Central Reservation Office, 12/4 First Floor, East Patel Nagar. Telefax 5783960.

(Palace on Wheels and Royal Orient do not operate between May and August.)

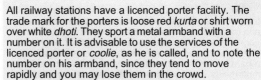

NOTES

RAIL
TICKET RESERVATION
INDRAIL PASS
IMPORTANT TRAINS
RAJDHANI & SHATABDI
SPECIAL TRAINS
TRANSPORT FROM
RAILWAY STATIONS

THIS PAGE

All railway stations have a licenced porter facility. The trade mark for the porters is loose red *kurta* or shirt worn over white *dhoti*. They sport a metal armband with a number on it. It is advisable to use the services of the licenced porter or *coolie*, as he is called, and to note the number on his armband, since they tend to move rapidly and you may lose them in the crowd.

If you are arriving by a late night train and happen to be in Delhi for the first time, railway stations are possibly the safest place to stay until morning. There are Upper Class Waiting Rooms in all stations and Retiring Rooms in New Delhi and Delhi Main railway stations.

The rooms at Rail Yatri Niwas in the New Delhi Railway Station complex have rudimentary facilities and are reasonably priced.

TRANSPORT FROM THE STATION

There are pre-paid service counters for taxis and auto rickshaws in all three stations. Buses are available but they are likely to be crowded. First timers to India are advised to avoid them especially if they have luggage.

BUS

Delhi is well connected by road to all major destinations in north India. The main bus station is the Inter-State Bus Terminus (ISBT) at Kashmere Gate, north of Delhi Main railway station. ISBT may jolt you with its chaos and pollution. However, like thousands of travellers everyday, you can find your way through the labyrinth if you keep your cool.

ISBT has all basic facilities including a tourist information office, a State Bank of India branch, a chemist, a post office, several phone booths and fast food stalls. Do not get influenced by touts, travel agents, auto rickshawalas and taxi drivers because there is a chance that you may be cheated.

There is a pre-paid service counter for auto rickshaws and taxis outside the main entrance. Connaught Place is half an hour from ISBT, as are New Delhi and Delhi Main railway stations.

Buses from ISBT go to destinations in Haryana, Punjab, Rajasthan, Uttar Pradesh and Himachal Pradesh.

There is a new ISBT at Sarai Kale Khan near Nizamuddin Railway Station. Buses from here go to Agra, Mathura and Brindavan, Gwalior and Bharatpur.

Getting Around in Delhi

Delhi is spread over an area of approximately 1483 sq km. According to a recent study, there are over 15 different modes of transportation by which people manoeuvre their way around the city, ranging from the latest model of the Mercedes Benz to the humble bullock cart. The level of noise in the streets of Delhi may unnerve the first time visitor.

In most areas there are restrictions on cycle rickshaws and *tongas* (horse-drawn carts), though a vegetable vendor pushing his cart is a common sight all over the city. This does not deter the Delhi driver, who has little regard for rules and speed. Teenagers zip about on fancy motorbikes, cars honk incessantly and overcrowded buses often screech to a halt in a haphazard manner in the middle of the road.

NATIONAL HIGHWAYS
leading out of Delhi

NH-1 Amritsar
NH-2 Agra-Kanpur-Calcutta
NH-10 Rohtak-Hissar
NH-8 Jaipur-Bombay
NH-24 Moradabad-Lucknow

ROADWAYS ENQUIRY

ISBT(General Enquiry)
(2961145
Delhi Transport Corporation (DTC)
(2968836
Haryana Roadways
(2961262
Himachal Roadways
(2966725
Punjab Roadways
(2967842
Rajasthan Roadways
(2961246
UP Roadways
(2968709

ISBT Sarai Kale Khan
(4638092

NEWS

Travellers to India remain connected with the rest of the world through all the major TV channels, BBC, CNN, NBC as well as the Asian channel, Star, and the state-run Doordarshan.

Major English dailies published from Delhi include The Times of India, The Hindustan Times, The Indian Express, Asian Age, The Pioneer, as well as The Economic Times and Business Standard.

24-HOUR CAR RENTALS

Apace Rent-a-Car
18 Community Centre, East of Kailash.
(6474835.
Fax 6460057.

Budget Rent-a-Car
78/3 Janpath. (3715657.
Fax 3739182.

Europcar Inter Rent
14 A & B Basant Lok Community Centre, Vasant Vihar. (6140373.
Fax 6145383.
112 First Floor, DLF Qutb Plaza, Phase I, Gurgaon.
(91352751.
F17 Sector 18, Savitri Mkt, NOIDA.
(91526446.

Hertz
GF29 Ansal Chamber Part I, Bldg 3, Bhikaji Cama Place. (6197188.
Fax 6197206.

TAXI

There are black-and-yellow taxis for travel within the city limits. However, you will rarely find a cruising taxi on Delhi roads. Each locality has its own taxi stand, as do all major hotels and commercial complexes. Usually you are required to call for a taxi from the stand. Delhi's taxis are mostly very old Ambassador cars, and although they rattle and shake they normally get you to your destination.

Taxi tariffs are to be paid by the meter reading, which could be checked against a tariff chart available with the taxi driver. The chart indicates how many rupees, over and above the meter reading, is to be paid to the driver.

CAR RENTALS

There are several international and local companies that operate car rental services. Most car rentals accept international credit cards. Foreign nationals are usually required to pay in foreign exchange, unless exempted by the Reserve Bank of India.

Hertz, Europcar and others have rates which are on a 4 hour and 40 km, or an 8 hour and 80 km basis, with and without chauffeurs. The rates vary according to the choice of car. As an example, the rates for 4 hours and 40 km range from Rs 495 for a Maruti 800 to Rs 2600 for a Mercedes 250.

For self-driven cars, the petrol cost is to be borne by the customer. Valid driving licence, passport (for foreigners) or proof of address is required along with a security deposit.

Another option is to engage the local white DLY taxi. These are available at all hotels and local taxi stands. The chauffeurs will always throw in a little extra insight while sightseeing and shopping, if you tip them well. It is a comfortable way to travel within the city and you can do things at your own pace.

THIS PAGE

AUTO RICKSHAW

No visit to Delhi can be complete without a ride on an auto rickshaw – a three-wheeled, black-and-yellow canopied contraption. These little vehicles are allowed to carry up to three passengers at a time. Auto rickshaws may be innovative in design, but they can turn into a commuters' nightmare. Auto rides are no joy rides, especially over bumpy roads with no discretion shown for speed. They are, however, a cheap way to travel from point to point.

In some parts of Connaught Place and Shahjahanabad there are *phatphattis* which operate on arterial roads. These are old Harley Davidson motorcycles converted into three-wheeled public transport vehicles with diesel engines, ferrying six to eight people at a time. Harley Davidson enthusiasts are unlikely to recognise the original.

CYCLE RICKSHAW

Delhi has an estimated three lakh cycle rickshaws which mainly ply in the Shahjanabad area. They are a convenient means of covering short distances. Not only do they precariously balance 2 to 3 people, but often carry merchandise as well.

There are some other localities where cycle rickshaws are available. For instance, at Nizamuddin Railway Station you may find it a useful vehicle to get out of the station and on to the main link road to catch buses, taxis or auto rickshaws.

There are still a few regular *tonga* stands in Delhi. The one in Paharganj is popular with young tourists. For an experience of a bygone era, ride on the horse-*tonga* through Daryaganj towards Lal Qila.

Beware of pickpockets in buses. It is not advisable for women to travel alone in buses after 9 pm. Women should not wear tight clothes or mini skirts or shorts, especially while travelling in buses as they may attract lewd comments and worse.

BUS

For a city as spread out as Delhi, buses are the cheapest and most popular means of public transport. Delhi has the Green Line service run by the state-owned Delhi Transport Corporation (DTC) functioning on all important and not-so-important routes.

In addition, there are the private Blue Line buses, which are notorious for speeding, but they are useful for the rushed traveller. The White Line buses are a little more comfortable than the Green or Blue Lines, though they travel only on limited routes.

Buses are a cheap mode of commuting and the prices range from Re 1 to Rs 5 for a single ticket.

There is a skeletal night service from point to point, mainly to and from railway stations.

Tips or *Baksheesh*

There is no rule which compels you to tip anyone for any service rendered. Courtesy demands that you tip a waiter in a restaurant or hotel. The general norm is to pay 10% of the billed amount. Taxi and auto rickshaw drivers, public transport staff, government officials or private service providers do not expected a tip. It is entirely up to you to tip someone for services rendered.

Sometimes the urge to tip can be misunderstood, as it may be considered an assault on personal dignity. In fact, it is a myth that nothing in India moves without baksheesh. People help and provide information, without expecting anything in return. Doing a good deed is a cultural trait, and is generally not measured in terms of money.

ENFIELD BULLET DEALERS IN DELHI

Amar Autos Shahdara.
(2452322 / 2212322.

Chowdhury Motor Agency 61 Gole Market.
(3735222 / 3734206.

ESS AAR Motors Jhandewalan Extn.
(7778836.

Lamba Enterprises Fateh Nagar, Jail Road.
(5144314 / 5419747.

Mahendru Motors Yusuf Sarai. (6963502 / 6852839.

Radhika Enterprises Ring Road, Naraina.
(5698906.

Ravinder Auto Centre Zamrudpur (service centre). (6479835.

BUS ROUTES

Chhatarpur - Safdarjang 519

Chhatarpur - New Delhi RS 590

Connaught Place (Super Bazar) - Malviya Nagar 520

Connaught Place (Jantar Mantar) - Kalkaji 440/490

Connaught Place (Plaza) - Hauz Khas 620

ISBT - Kendriya Terminal (via Kashmere Gate) 185

ISBT - Mehrauli 533

Kendriya Terminal-Nizammudin 4

Kendriya Terminal - Delhi University 185/220

Kendriya Terminal - Nehru Place 430

KendriyaTerminal - Mehrauli (via Hauz Khas) 530

New Delhi RS - Mehrauli (via Hauz Khas) 505

Nizamuddin RS - Mehrauli 413

Delhi Main RS- Chiragh Delhi (via Lal Qila) 419

Delhi Main RS - Nehru Place (via Lal Qila) 429

Delhi Main RS - Malviya Nagar (via Lal Qila) 524

There is a convenient bus service, **Mudrika**, that plies on the Ring Road. The express Mudrika service called **Teevra Mudrika** also operates on the Ring Road via Sarai Kale Khan.

GUIDED TOURS

There are full-day and half-day guided city tour options, on luxury coaches with qualified guides. The Delhi, New Delhi tours cover the city's major tourist spots : Lal Qila (Red Fort), Jama Masjid, Raj Ghat, Shanti Van, Qutb Minar, Jantar Mantar, Lotus Temple, India Gate, Rashtrapati Bhawan, Birla Mandir and Appu Ghar.

RING RAIL

The Ring Railway service is along a circular route within the city. The stops are not well connected by other modes of public transport. The route covers five important commercial areas - Chandni Chowk, Sadar Bazaar, Connaught Place, Pragati Maidan and ITO.

Money

INDIAN CURRENCY

Indian currency is called the Rupee. It is available in denominations of 500, 100, 50, 20, 10, 5, 2 , 1. One rupee equals 100 paise. Coins in common use are those of Rs 5, Rs 2 , Re 1 and 50 and 25 paise. The 20, 10 and 5 paise coins have become redundant in Delhi, but they still have value in smaller towns and rural India.

CREDIT CARDS

Credit cards are becoming increasingly popular, especially in urban areas. All major international credit cards are used, viz., Visa, Amex, Mastercard, Diners Club.

BANKS

State Bank of India IGI Airport (Terminal 2) ℂ5692807, is the only bank in Delhi with a 24 hour service.

Banks are open from 10 am to 2 pm Monday to Friday and 10 am to 12 pm Saturdays. Banks are closed on Sundays and national holidays. Most international banks have branches in Delhi.

Punjab National Bank
ECE House, 28 Kasturba
Gandhi Marg. (3310472
/ 3730565. Fax 3324788.

State Bank of India
11 Sansad Marg.
(3746265 / 3362635.
Fax 3732316.

FOREIGN BANKS

ABN Amro DLF Centre,
Sansad Marg. (3755130
/ 3755407. Fax 3755401.

**American Express
Bank** A Block, Hamilton
House, Connaught
Place. (3325221 /
3324765. Fax 3715352.

ANZ Grindlays
Mercantile House,
15 Kasturba Gandhi
Marg. (3320793 /
3361091. Fax 3324194.

Bank Of America
DCM Bldg,
16 Barakhamba Road.
(3715565.
Fax 3719821.

**Bank of Tokyo
Mitsubishi**
Jeevan Vihar Bldg, 3
Sansad Marg. (3733490
/ 3360248. Fax 3746329.

**Banque Nationale de
Paris** Hansalaya Bldg, 5
Barakhamba Road.
(3312836 / 3324211.
Fax 3731110.

Citibank Jeevan Bharati
Bldg, 124 Connaught
Place. (3712484 /
3714211. Fax 3329979.

Deutsche Bank
15-17 Tolstoy House,
Tolstoy Marg. (3724156 /
3721155. Fax 3316237.

Hongkong Bank ECE
House, 28 Kasturba
Gandhi Marg.
(3314355 / 3314359.
Fax 3719702.

**Standard Chartered
Bank** Allahabad Bank
Bldg, 17 Sansad Marg.
(3360321 / 3360151.
Fax 3342265.

ATM COUNTERS

Canara Bank
Jeevan Bharati Bldg,
Sansad Marg.
202 Padam Singh Road,
Karol Bagh.
E48 Hauz Khas Market.
DDA Bldg, Nehru Place.
Sector 12, Rao Tula
Ram Marg.

Indian Bank
C26 Community Centre,
Janakpuri.
DDA Market,
Shantiniketan.

Vijaya Bank
17 Barakhamba Road.
M53 Greater Kailash II.

State Bank of India
11 Sansad Marg.

ANZ Grindlays
B68 Greater Kailash I.
Malcha Marg,
Chanakyapuri.

Bank of America
M50 Greater Kailash I.
Hansalaya Bldg,
Barakhamba Road.
M1 South Extn I.

Citibank
Gurdwara Road, Karol
Bagh.
Jeevan Bharati Bldg,
Sansad Marg.
F42 South Extn I.
Archana Complex,
Greater Kailash I.

Hongkong Bank
ECE House, 28 Kasturba
Gandhi Marg.
302 Chandni Chowk.
Basant Lok, Vasant
Vihar.
Shankar Road Market,
New Rajendra Nagar.
Aditya Commercial
Complex, Preet Vihar.
Savitri Cinema Complex,
Greater Kailash II.

HDFC Bank
Archana Shopping
Complex, Greater
Kailash I.
Basant Lok, Vasant
Vihar.

**Standard Chartered
Bank**
17 Sansad Marg.
N Block Market, Greater
Kailash I.
Bhikaji Bhawan, Bhikaji
Cama Place.
Basant Lok, Vasant
Vihar.

**IMPORTANT
MONEY CHANGERS**

**American Express
Travel Related
Services**
Wenger House, A Block
Connaught Place.
(3324119 / 3712513.
Fax 3731420.

**LKP Merchant
Financing Ltd.**
M56 Connaught Place.
(3739797 / 3352468.
Fax 3350149.

Mercury Travels
Jeevantara Bldg, Sansad
Marg. (3362008 /
3362091.

**Money Exchange
Corp. International**
K19 Connaught Place
(3711400 / 3712800.
Fax 3711300.

**Okara Leasing &
Investment Ltd.**
RD Chambers,16/11
Arya Samaj Road, Karol
Bagh. (5766513 /
5766514. Fax 5784336.

Pheroze Pramroze
GF 9/11 Indra Prakash
Bldg, 21 Barakhamba
Road. (3352547 /
3352548. Fax 3357008.

R.R.Sen & Bros
49 & 66 World Trade
Centre, Babur Road.
(3353044 / 3719004.
Fax 3718032.

Sita World Travel
F12 Connaught Place.
(3734011 / 3353219.
Fax 3324652.

Thomas Cook
Imperial Hotel, Janpath.
(3342171 / 3340564.
Fax 3340563.

**Travel House
Exchanger**
M3 Middle Circle,
Connaught Place.
(3329609 / 3323171.
Fax 3324712.

**Transcorp
International**
G 4-5 Kanchanjunga
Bldg, Barakhamba Road.
(3323973.

Wall Street Finance
2E Caxton House, Rani
Jhansi Road.
(7525839 / 7536800.
Fax 7536799.

Communications

POST OFFICES

There are small but well-equipped post offices
in all parts of the city, and main post offices in
central locations. The latter have a wide range
of facilities, like telegraph, fax and a courier
service which operates under the brand name
EMS-Speed Post. Service for receiving mail is
also available in many post offices.

The postal system in India is relatively safe and
letters normally reach their destinations on time.
The ubiquitous local postman is still the friendly
visitor who comes every day pedalling his
bicycle. Here is one man who will occasionally
read out letters to the uneducated and perhaps
even write one for them. He deciphers the most
complicated of addresses and finds his way
through the bylanes with surprising ease.

If you need to dispatch an important letter or
document urgently it might be advisable to
send it by the government-run Speed Post
service available at most post offices, or
through one of the many private courier services.

For foreigners, receiving mail or *poste
restante* mail, is possible at the Foreign Post
Office at Kotla Road near ITO crossing. The
poste restante mail office is open on all working days,
from 9 am to 5 pm. The post office closes at noon on
Saturdays. The timings are the same in most post
offices. American Express has an exclusive clients'
mail service.

IMPORTANT POST OFFICES

Chanakyapuri PO Opp. Chanakya Cinema (4673645 / 4670138.

Eastern Court PO Janpath (24-hour service) (3321878.

GPO Gole Dak Khana (3364111.

GPO Kashmere Gate (2965118.

GPO New Delhi Ashoka Road (3364111.

Lodi Road PO (4692329.

Safdarjang Sorting Office Safdarjang Airport (24-hour service) (4611350.

Foreign PO Kotla Marg, Near ITO Crossing (3233304.

All Post Offices are open from 10 am to 6 pm Mondays to Saturdays.

MAJOR COURIER SERVICES

EMS-Speed Post Safdarjang Sorting Office (24-hour) (4611350.

Eastern Court PO (24-hour) (3321878.

GPO Gole Dak Khana (24-hour) (3364111.

Blue Dart Express Antriksh Bhawan, 22 Kasturba Gandhi Marg (24-hour). (3328874. Fax 3723145.

DHL Worldwide Express D1 Ashirwad Complex, Green Park (24-hour). (6854072.

Elbee Courier Service 1/18 Rani Jhansi Road (24-hour). (7778315. Fax 3550382.

Overnite Express 11098B East Park Road (24-hour). (3545311. Fax 3552411.

Skypak Couriers B6/4 Safdarjang Enclave (24-hour). (6194507. Fax 6194448.

TNT Express Worldwide E4 Defence Colony (24-hour). (4616969. Fax 4610980.

Mail receiving facilities are available at the Government of India Tourist Office, 88 Janpath (3320008 and the Student Travel Information Centre at Hotel Imperial, Janpath.

STD Rates

Full rate	8 am - 7 pm
Half rate	7 pm - 8.30 am and 7 am - 8 am
One-third rate	8.30 pm - 11 pm and 6 am - 7 am
One fourth rate	11 pm - 6 am

On Sundays and national holidays, half instead of full rate, is levied during the day

NOTES

FOREIGN BANKS
ATM COUNTERS
MONEY CHANGERS
POST OFFICES
COURIER SERVICES
TELEPHONES

THIS PAGE

Aerograms to anywhere in the world cost Rs 6.50. For communication within India, stamped envelopes cost Rs 2, inland letters Re1 and post cards, 25 paise.

Parcels by mail should not exceed 20 kgs. Books, documents, papers and printed material can be sent by book post which costs less.

COURIER SERVICES

There are several courier services available and most of them have at least one 24-hour service counter. It is advisable to insist on a receipt for payments made. For parcels over 20 kgs, a freight agent is required.

TELEPHONES

Within Delhi there are many ISD (international), STD (domestic long distance), and local call booths.

The rates for international calls are fixed, but calls within the country are charged on the basis of a pulse rate which varies for different cities, and for different times of the day.

Most booths remain open till midnight. Some of these booths have facilities for sending and receiving fax messages. Most of these are privately manned and the service is efficient and courteous.

Tourist Information Services

Government of India Tourist Office 88 Janpath (3320008. This is a reliable tourist information centre. The staff is helpful and the brochures and maps useful. These introduce the traveller to interesting places for excursions, not only in and around Delhi, but all over India.

Permits to visit Rashtrapati Bhawan (President's House) and the Mughal Garden are available here.

Delhi Tourism and Transportation Development Corporation (DTTDC) has a chain of offices all over Delhi. Their office at N Block, Middle Circle, Connaught Place (3313637 / 3315322, is open from 7 am to 9 pm.

It is advisable to go to an established travel agent to coordinate and organise your travel plans. The better known hotels have their own travel agents and tour operators.

STATE INFORMATION CENTRES

Andaman and Nicobar Andaman and Nicobar Bhawan, 12 Chanakyapuri. (6871443.

Andhra Pradesh Andhra Bhawan, Ashoka Road. (3382031.

Assam B1Baba Kharak Singh Marg. (3343961.

Bihar Bihar State Emporium, Baba Kharak Singh Marg. (3361087.

Goa 18 Amrita Shergil Marg. (4629967.

Gujarat A6 Baba Kharak Singh Marg. (3340305.

Haryana Chandralok Bldg, 36 Janpath. (3324911.

Himachal Pradesh Chandralok Bldg, 36 Janpath. (3325320.

Jammu & Kashmir Kanishka Shopping Plaza, Ashoka Road. (3345373.

Karnataka 3,4 State Emporia Bldg, Baba Kharak Singh Marg. (3363862.

Kerala Kanishka Hotel Shopping Plaza, Ashoka Road. (3368541.

Madhya Pradesh B8 State Emporia Bldg, Baba Kharak Singh Marg. (3341187 / 3366528.

Maharashtra A8 Baba Kharak Singh Marg. (3363773.

Meghalaya 9 Aurangzeb Road. (3014417.

Orissa B4 Baba Kharak Singh Marg. (3364580.

Rajasthan Bikaner House, Near India Gate. (3383837.

Sikkim New Sikkim House,14 Panchsheel Marg, Chanakyapuri. (6883026.

Uttar Pradesh Chandralok Bldg, 36 Janpath. (3322251.

West Bengal A2 Baba Kharak Singh Marg. (3732695.

TRAVEL AGENCIES

Aerotrek Travels Mercantile Bldg, E Block, Connaught Place. (3715966. Fax 3355468.

American Express Travel Related Services First Floor, Wenger House, A Block, Connaught Place. (3324119.

Ashok Tours &Travels Kanishka Shopping Plaza, Ashoka Rd. (3344422.

Balmer & Lawrie Core 8 Ground Floor, SCOPE Complex, Lodi Road. (4363425.

Cox & Kings H Block, Connaught Circus. (3738811.

Hans Travel Vishal Hotel, Main Bazaar, Paharganj. (527629.

International Travel House 14AB Community Centre, Basant Lok, Vasant Vihar. (6143400.

Mackinnon Mackenzie 16 Sansad Marg. (3323741.

Mercury Travels Ltd Jeevan Tara Bldg, Sansad Marg. (3732268.

Outbound Travel B2/50 Safdarjang Enclave. (6103902.

Royal Expeditions S43 Greater Kailash I. (6238545.

Sita World Travels (I) Ltd F12 Connaught Place. (3311122.

Thomas Cook (I) Ltd Imperial Hotel, Janpath. (3342171 / 3340564.

Trade Wings 60 Janpath. (3321822.

Travel Corporation of India C35 Connaught Circus. (3315181.

Emergency
HOSPITALS

Delhi has several goverment as well as many privately run hospitals and nursing homes. All government hospitals have modern medical facilities, but due to large patient turnout, medical assistance is slow. Service at the privately run hospitals and nursing homes is more efficient and assistance quicker.

IMPORTANT HOSPITALS / NURSING HOMES (AREA-WISE)

Civil Lines

Hindu Rao* (2513355
St.Stephen's (2511488 / 2511887
Tirath Ram (2522425 / 2522487

Connaught Place / Shahjahanabad

G. B. Pant * (3234242 / 3233001.
Kalawati Saran Children's* (3363609 / 3363728.
Kasturba* (3275024/ 3270390.
Loknayak Jaiprakash Narayan* (3232400 / 3230733.
Ram Manohar Lohia* (3365525 /3365960
Sanjeevan Medical Centre (3257145 / 3257143.
Sucheta Kripalani* (3363788 / 3363609.

Karol Bagh

Kolmet (5752055 / 5752056.
Sir Ganga Ram (5781837.

Saket / Sarita Vihar / Okhla

Batra (6982411 / 6983747.
GM Modi (6852112 / 6852113.
Holy Family (6845900 / 6845909.
Indraprastha Apollo (6925858 / 6925801.
Sitaram Bhartia Institute (6867279 / 6867933.

Safdarjang / Greater Kailash / Lajpat Nagar

All India Institute of Medical Sciences* (6864851 / 6861123.
Ashlok (6165902 / 6165903.
Mohinder (6852880 / 6852881.
Moolchand (6920218 / 6920217.
Mother and Child (6863110 / 664085.
Safdarjang* (6165060 / 6165032.
Sharma Nursing Home (6410333.
Spring Meadows (6432948 / 6430757.
Sukhda (6416440 / 6423073.

IMPORTANT HOSPITALS / NURSING HOMES (AREA-WISE)

Vasant Vihar

Holy Angels (6143411 / 6142842.
Vasant Lok (6149422 / 6149423.

Hari Nagar

Deen Dayal Upadhaya* (5145601.

Rohini

Jaipur Golden (7260935.

* Government hospitals

SPECIALISED HOSPITALS

Cancer Detection Centre (3716941.

Escorts Heart Institute and Research Centre (6844820 / 6833641.

Guru Nanak Eye Centre* (3233080 / 3236745.

Indian Spinal Injuries Centre (6894884 / 6896642.

National Chest Institute (6864012 /6964044.

National Heart Institute (6414156 / 6414157.

Orthonova (6987048 / 6989171.

Dr Shroff's Charity Eye (3251581 / 3251589.

Vimhans (Mental Health and Neuroscience) (6924300 / 6835042.

DAY AND NIGHT CHEMISTS

Batra Hospital Tughlaqabad Institutional Area Badarpur Road. (6983505 / 6983747.

Gulati Medical Store Shahdara. (2201540 / 2418275.

Hindu Rao Hospital Subzi Mandi. (2919706 / 2919625.

Holy Angels Hospital Community Centre, Basant Lok, Vasant Vihar. (6873411.

Kolmet Hospital Karol Bagh. (5754013.

Mohinder Hospital C5 Green Park Extn. (9852880

New Delhi Medicos R.K. Ashram Marg. (3347151 / 3732998.

Sucheta Kriplani Hospital Punchkuin Road. (3363609.

Springdales Chemists D4 Prashant Vihar, Madhuban Chowk. (7269450.

Spring Meadows Chemists East of Kailash. (6441782 / 6228713.

Super Bazar RML Hospital Connaught Place. (3364993.

POLICE

POLICE ASSISTANCE BOOTHS

Police assistance booths are located at the airport, railway stations and the ISBT at Kashmere Gate. There is a special booth in Connaught Place to help foreign travellers. There are police assistance booths at several important traffic junctions and other strategic points. In case of an emergency on the road, police patrol vehicles (white in colour), should be contacted.

NOTES

TOURIST INFORMATION CENTRES
HOSPITALS
POLICE STATIONS

THIS PAGE

LOST ARTICLES

In case of loss or theft, especially vital documents like passports, an FIR (First Information Report) must be filed at the Police Station nearest to the place where the loss has occured. In case of loss of documents the embassy concerned must be immediately informed.

POLICE STATIONS

Central District
Control Room (3270000
Daryaganj (3274683
Kamla Market (3230623
Karol Bagh (5726870
Paharganj (524746 / 520787

New Delhi District
Control Room (362229
Chanakyapuri (3011100
Connaught Place (3364139
Parliament Street (Sansad Marg) (3342700

North District
Control room (231552
Civil Lines (2522233
Kotwali (3276666
Sadar Bazaar (529792
Sabzi Mandi (2527354

North West District
Control Room (7234646
Ashok Vihar (7242917
Kingsway Camp (7231131

North East District
Control room (2295640
Shahdara (2285087

East District
Control Room (2209494
Gandhi Nagar (2212235
Preet Vihar (2210291
Vivek Vihar (2146040

South District
Control Room (6523967
Defence Colony (6253402
Greater Kailash (6429617
Hauz Khas (6867878
Kalkaji (6430607
Lajpat Nagar (6838945

South West District
Control Room (6182709
Delhi Cantt (5694444
Najafgarh (5566200
Vasant Vihar (6109299

West District
Control Room (5441909
Patel Nagar (5784034
Punjabi Bagh (533260
Rajouri Garden (5453990
Tilak Nagar (5407800

Further Reading

GUIDEBOOKS

Alexander, M., *Delhi and Agra: A Traveller's Companion* (London,1987).

Barton, G. & L. Malone, *Old Delhi: 10 Easy Walks* (Delhi,1988).

Bradnock,R.(ed.), *India Handbook* (London, 1997).

Conservation Society of Delhi, *Mehrauli Heritage Maps* (Delhi, 1993).

Eicher City Map, *Delhi* (Delhi, 1996).

Eicher City Map, *Central Delhi : Zonal Map 1* (Delhi,1997).

Everyman Guide, *Rajasthan* (London, 1996).

Insight Pocket Guide, *New Delhi* (Singapore, 1994).

Lonely Planet, *City Guide: Delhi* (Hawthorn, 1996).

Lonely Planet, *India & Bangladesh Travel Atlas* (Hawthorn, 1995).

Lonely Planet, *Travel Survival Kit: India* (Hawthorn, 1997).

Nicholson, L., *The Red Fort : Delhi* (London, 1989).

Nicholson, L., *Delhi, Agra and Jaipur India's Golden Triangle* (Hong Kong, 1996).

Nicholson, L., *India Companion* (London, 1996).

Sharma, Y.D., *Delhi and its Neighbourhood*, Archaeological Survey of India (Delhi, 1990).

HISTORY, ARCHITECTURE, LITERATURE

Ali, Ahmed, *Twilight in Delhi* (London, 1940).

Asher, Catherine B., *Architecture of Mughal India* (Cambridge,1992).

Bernier, Francois, *Travels in the Mughal Empire, 1656-68* (Reprint, Delhi,1972).

Blake, S.P., *Shahjahanabad: The Sovereign City in Mughal India 1639-1739* (Cambridge, 1991).

Brown, Percy, *Indian Architecture : Islamic Period* (Bombay, 1942).

Choudhary, Nirad C., *Thy Hand, Great Anarch! India: 1921-52* (London, 1987).

Cole, H.H., *Architecture of Ancient Delhi: Especially the Buildings around the Kutb Minar* (London, 1872).

Crowe, Sylvia & Shiela Haywood, *The Gardens of Mughal India* (London, 1972).

Dalrymple, William, *City of Djinns : A Year in Delhi* (London, 1994).

Dayal, Maheshwar, *Rediscovering Delhi: The Story of Shahjahanabad* (Delhi, 1975).

Fanshawe, F.C., *Delhi: Past and Present* (Reprint, Delhi,1979).

Festing, G., *When Kings Rode to Delhi* (Reprint, Delhi, 1997).

Frater, A., *Chasing the Monsoon* (Delhi, 1990).

Frykenburg, R.E.(ed.), *Delhi through the Ages* (Delhi, 1993).

A Gazetteer of Delhi, 1912 (Reprint, Delhi, 1992).

Gascoigne, Bamber, *The Great Moghuls* (London, 1971).

Gupta, Narayani, *Delhi Between Two Empires 1803-1931* (Delhi, 1981).

Gupta, Narayani, *Our City, Delhi* (New Delhi, 1987).

Hamilton, Walter, *East-India Gazetteer* (Reprint, Delhi, 1993).

Hankin, Nigel B., *Hanklin-Janklin, A Stranger's Rumble-Tumble Guide to some Words, Customs and Quiddities Indian and Indo-British* (New Delhi, 1992).

Hobson Jobson: A Glossary of Colloquial Anglo-Indian Words and Phrases (Reprint, Delhi, 1986).

Ibn Batuta, *Travels of Ibn Batuta, AD 1325-1354,* translated by H.A.R.Gibb (Reprint, Delhi, 1992).

Irving, R.G., *Indian Summer: Lutyens, Baker and the Making of Imperial Delhi* (Yale,1981).

Jhabvala, C.S.H., *Delhi: Stones and Streets* (Delhi 1990).

Karnad, Girish, *Tughlaq* (Delhi, 1972).

Kaul, H.K., *Historic Delhi, An Anthology* (Delhi, 1985).

Kaye, M.M., *The Golden Calm: An English Lady's Life in Moghul Delhi* (New York,1980).

Keene, H.G., *A Handbook for Visitors to Delhi* (Calcutta, 1882).

Khan, Sayyid Ahmed, *Asar-us-Sanadid,* translated by R. Nath as *Monuments of Delhi: A Historical Study* (New Delhi, 1979).

Koch, Ebba, *Mughal Architecture: An Outline* (Munich, 1991).

Lal, John, *Begum Samru* (New Delhi, 1997).

Lewis, Charles & K.Lewis, *Delhi's Historic Villages: A Photographic Evocation* (Delhi, 1997).

Important Business Addresses

Agricultural and Processed Food Products Export Development Authority 3rd Floor, Ansal Chambers II, 6 Bhikaji Cama Place. ℂ 6192141.

Associated Chamber of Commerce & Industry Allahabad Bank Bldg, 17 Sansad Marg. ℂ 3360704. Fax 3734917.

Association of Indian Automobile Mfrs Core 4B, Zone IV, 5th Floor, India Habitat Centre, Lodi Road. ℂ 4647810. Fax 4648222.

Automotive Components Mfrs Association 203-205 Kirti Deep Bldg, Nangal Raya Commercial Complex ℂ 5501669. Fax 5593189.

Confederation of Indian Industry 23,26 Institutional Area, Lodi Road. ℂ 4629994. Fax 4633168.

Engineering Export Promotion Council Vandana Bldg, 4th Floor, 11 Tolstoy Marg. ℂ 3314685.

Federation of Indian Chambers of Commerce and Industry Federation House, Tansen Marg. ℂ 3738760. Fax 3320704.

Federation of Indian Export Organisations PHD House, 3rd Floor, 4-2 Siri Institutional Area. ℂ 6851310. Fax 6863087.

Handloom Export Promotion Council XVI/ 784-85 Deshbandhu Gupta Road, Karol Bagh. ℂ 7770697. Fax 7776015.

Indian Chemical Mfrs Association 602 Vikram Tower, 16 Rajendra Place. ℂ 5733588.

Indian Machine Tool Mfrs Association IMTMA House, Plot No. 17 Nangal Raya Commercial Complex. ℂ 5599680.

Indian Medical Association IMA House, Indraprastha Marg. ℂ 3319009. Fax 3316270.

Indian Sugar Mills Association Sugar House, 39 Nehru Place. ℂ 6416711.

Indian Trade Promotion Organisation Pragati Maidan. ℂ 3371832. Fax 3318142.

Manufacturers Association for Information Technology 4th Floor, PHD House, Opp. Asian Games Village. ℂ 6866976. Fax 6851321.

Minerals and Metals Trading Corp. Ltd. Scope Complex, Core I, 7 Institutional Area, Lodhi Road. ℂ 4362200. Fax 4361912.

NRI Welfare Society of India D 253 Defence Colony. ℂ 4615055.

Organisation of Pharmaceutical Producers of India A 2/145 Safdarjang Enclave. ℂ 6192821.

PHD Chamber of Commerce & Industry PHD House, 4/2 Siri Institutional Area, Hauz Khas. ℂ 6863801. Fax 6863135.

State Trading Corporation of India Jawahar Vyapar Bhawan, Tolstoy Marg. ℂ 3313177. Fax 3320298.

Tractor Mfrs Association c/o Eicher Limited, 14 Commercial Complex, Greater Kailash II (Masjid Moth). ℂ 6445521. Fax 6431929.

NOTES

FURTHER READING
IMPORTANT BUSINESS
ADDRESSES

Further Reading

Mahajan, J., *The Grand Indian Tour: Travel and Sketches of Emily Eden* (Delhi, 1996).

Morris, Jan, *The Spectacle of Empire* (London, 1982).

Morris, Jan & S. Winchester, *Stones of Empire* (Oxford, 1983).

Seth, Vikram, *A Suitable Boy* (New Delhi, 1994).

Sharada Prasad, H.Y., *Rashtrapati Bhavan : The Story of the President's House* (Delhi, 1993).

Sharma, A.K., *Prehistoric Delhi and its Neighbourhood* (New Delhi, n.d.).

Singh, Khushwant, *Delhi: A Novel* (Delhi, 1989).

Singh, Khushwant, *Nature Watch* (Delhi, 1990).

Sinha, R., *Lalkot to Lodi and Gardens* (Delhi, 1996).

Spear, Percival, *Delhi: Its Monuments and History* (New Delhi, 1994).

Spear, Percival, *A History of Delhi under the later Mughuls* (Reprint, Delhi, 1995)

Tillotson, G.H.R., *Mughal India* (London, 1990).

Varma, Pavan & S. Shankar, *Mansions at Dusk: The Havelis of Old Delhi* (Delhi, 1992).

White, Stephen, *Building in the Garden : The Architecture of Joseph Allen Stein* (Delhi, 1993).

VHAI, *Delhi : A Tale of Two Cities* (Delhi, 1993).

Yamamoto, T. Matsuo Ara & T.Tsukinowa, *Delhi: Architectural Remains,* 3 vols. in Japanese (Tokyo, 1967-70).

THIS PAGE

Language in Delhi

What is the language of Delhi? For several hundred years it was *Zaban-e-Dilli*, the language known variously as Hindawi, Rekhta (the 'mixed') and finally Urdu. It was refined and polite. Today this refinement has been overwhelmed by the dynamism of a metropolis of nine million people - mostly outsiders - all bent on making their living, career and name. Lifestyle affects language, and the language of the street today is blunt and functional, laced with insults to sisters and mothers.

You could call this the lowest common denominator of language, either simple Hindi or Urdu - for they both share syntax, grammar and vocabulary. The difference is that Urdu uses the Persian script and takes higher vocabulary from Persian and Arabic, while Hindi uses words from Sanskrit and the Sanskrit-based Devanagari script. Urdu grew and flourished in urban centres, especially Delhi and Lucknow. During the independence movement the Urdu language became increasingly identified with the Muslim community alone. It was made the national language of Pakistan, while Hindi became the national language of India and the chief mother tongue of Delhi.

Punjabi, however, is not far behind in the race for the top Delhi language. Delhi has always existed on the edge of Punjab and tens of thousands of Punjabis from Pakistani Punjab settled in the city after Partition.

People from the south and east have brought their languages too, and any Delhi cable operator worth his salt shows channels in Bengali, Tamil and Malayalam - and, of course, English.

English was brought into the Indian education system by Macaulay in the nineteenth century to create a class of Indians, imbued with English culture, who would carry out the administration of the Raj. This is the class referred to by one of Delhi's most outstanding literary residents, Vikram Seth, in his poem *Divali*,

> *O happy breed of Babus,*
>
> *I march on with your purpose*
>
> *We will have railways, common*
>
> *law and a good postal service.*

But Delhi's army of central government servants does not have the monopoly of English. English has become identified with power, privilege and good education, in a way that no Indian language has. English is the first language of intellectuals, the upper ranks of businessmen, and the language targetted by the upwardly mobile middle classes who aspire to material wealth and prestige. In the process, Indian languages have been neglected. But English, like any invader which has settled in India, is being changed by its adopted land, expanding to include Indian words and concepts. Perhaps in time it will merge into a new *Zaban-e-Dilli*.

RANDOM WORDS FROM A NEW DELHI LEXICON

accha good; really?; well then, etc.

babu (derogatory) bureaucratic bureaucrat

chae tea

chamcha hanger-on; spoon

chatni chutney, as in 'I will make chatni of you'

gaali insult; swear word

gap shap gossip

garam hot, as in *chae* and *gap shap*

ghotala scam

ghazal now pronounced guzzle - background music in five-star restaurants

hangama uproar especially in parliament

havala illegal foreign exchange transactions

IMFL Indian Made Foreign Liquor, whisky, gin, etc.

is-teem upwardly mobile vehicle from Maruti Motors

izzat self-respect, honour

kabari wallah the dawn chorus of Delhi neighbourhoods – the man who recycles your newspapers and old bottles

kalab club, one of the five 'k's of the upwardly mobile Puppy (see below). Others being *kantract* (contract), *kuri* (girl), *kaar* (car) and *kaaktel* (cocktail)

laddoo round Indian sweets; what politicians say they have in each hand if they think they can't loose an election

maalish massage, nowadays often Kerala style

mirch-masala chilli and spice, what is used to flavour *gap shap*

mistri mechanic, creator of new terminology viz.

shaafat shaft

dolki silencer

broosh small rubber bits which wear out

denter a man who undents cars

naqli imitation

neta (giri) leader (ship)

pagri turban; the money you pay on the side for commercial property

PCO the life line of every citizen – the public phone booth

pranayam breath control to counteract urban tensions

presswallah the person on the corner with a charcoal filled iron who irons your clothes

puja worship, especially Durga Puja in Bengali neighbourhoods

puppy Punjabi yuppy with customised car

shadow/security man/men with sten guns

tarikh date; date of next hearing in a court case

thanda cold aerated drink

tamasha spectacle

VIP movement no movement for anyone else

yaar any sort of friend, up to the most intimate; generally like 'mate' in colloquial English or 'man' in colloquial American.

Phrase Book

IN EMERGENCIES

help! *bachao!*
stop *rukho*
medicines *davai*
Please call a doctor / ambulance
doctor / ambulance ko bulaiye
Where is the nearest hospital?
nazdeek hospital kahan hain?
I'm not feeling well
meri tabiyat theek nahin hai
Where is... ? *kahan hai...?*
When will... be back?
...vaapas kab ayenge?
Call the police *police ko bulaiye*

USEFUL WORDS

hot *garam*
cold *thanda*
good *achcha*
bad *bura*
open *khula*
close *bandh*
left *baayen*
right *daayen*
near *paas*
far *dur*
up *oopar*
down *neeche*
outside *bahar*
inside *andar*
fast *jaldi*
slow *dheere*
car *gadi*
bus *bus*
road *sarak*
way *raasta*
house *ghar, makaan*
fan *pankha*
electricity *bijlee*
train *train, rail gadi*
aeroplane
hawai jahaj

there *udhar, wahan*
food *khana*
water *paani*
girl *ladki*
boy *ladka*
woman *aurat*
man *aadmi*
who *kaun*
why *kyon*
what *kya*
where *kahan*
when *kab*
which *kaun*
how *kaise*
one, two *ek, do*

COMMUNICATION ESSENTIALS

greetings *namaste, namaskar*
yes *han*
no *nahin*
thank you *dhanyavad, shukriyan*
time *samay*
day *din*
night *raat*
morning *subah*
evening *shaam*
afternoon *dopeher*
today *aaj*
tomorrow *kal*
yesterday *kal*
here *idhar, yahan*

NOTES

LANGUAGE IN DELHI
PHRASE BOOK

THIS PAGE

USEFUL PHRASES

How are you?
aap kaise hain?
Very well, thank you
hum theek hain, dhanyavad.
What is your name?
aap ka naam kya hain?
My name is...
mera naam...hain
See you
phir milenge
What is the time?
kitna baja hai?
Where are you from?
aap kahan se aaye hain?
Do you speak English?
kya aap angreji bolte hain?
I don't understand
maine nahin samjha
Please speak slow
aap dheere-dheere boliye
How far is it?
kitna dur hai?

SHOPPING

money *paisa/rupaye*
What is this? *yeh kya hain?*
clothes *kapda*
shoes *joota*
big *bara*
small *chhota*
black *kala*
white *safed*
red *lal*
blue *neela*
yellow *peela*
green *hara*
Do you have change?
khule paise milenge?
Do you have...
aap ke paas...hain?
How much does this cost?
yeh kitne ka hai ?
Do you take credit cards?
aap credit card lete hain?
It is too expensive
bahut mehenga hai

Glossary

aarti the high point in traditional Hindu worship where the priest encircles the idol with lighted lamps to the accompaniment of the ringing of bells and the blowing of conch shells

achkan long coat for men, made of cotton, silk or wool

ashram hermitage

bagh garden

baoli step well

bazaar market

begum high-ranking Muslim lady

bhature deep-fried bread made of flour, popular in north India

bhawan mansion

Bismillah Muslim theological term meaning 'in the name of God'

Brahma one of the gods of the Hindu trinity, Brahma is attributed with the power of creating the cosmos. Hindu mythology tells us of a curse on Brahma owing to which very few temples are consecrated to him. The only Brahma temple in north India is in Pushkar

burqah long, loose garment worn by Muslim women covering the whole body from head to toe

chaat a tangy, savoury snack, popular in Delhi

chaddar large piece of fabric; a wrap

chapati a small, flat, round wheat-based bread usually rolled out and baked over a griddle; the staple food in north India

chhattri domed kiosk (also a Rajput cenotaph which commonly takes this form)

chandni moonlight (*chand* - moon)

choli short, fitting blouse usually worn with a *sari* or *ghagra*

chor thief

chowk open space where two or more roads meet; square

chhole chick peas cooked with spices and eaten with *bhature* or *kulche*

chowkidar watchman

churi bangle

dahi curd, yoghurt

dal pulses

dargah shrine of a Sufi saint

darshan an occasion on which one is permitted to see, for example, the image of a god; literally 'darshan' means sight

darwaza door, gate

darya river

desi local, pertaining to a particular region; euphemistically used to refer to country liquor

devi goddess; also used after the first name of a Hindu woman as a title of respect

dhaba a makeshift eatery originally located on highways catering to truck drivers

dharmashala public inns often found at Hindu pilgrimage centres where food and lodging are provided at nominal rates

dhrupad one of the nine forms of music in the Hindustani classical system. It is the oldest vocal style which can be traced to the ancient Hindu text, *Sama Veda*

dupatta a piece of cloth used to cover a woman's head, worn with *salwar-kameez* or *ghagra-choli*

durbar assembly of an Indian ruler where he met his subjects

dosa south Indian pancake made with rice flour and eaten with sambhar and coconut chutney

gali narrow lane

ganj market

gharana a particular style of Hindustani classical music which is passed on to the next generation of pupils by the teacher

ghat bathing place on the banks of rivers with steps leading down to it

ghazal form of poetry written in Urdu expressing the poet's love for a lady and which is set to music

ghee clarified butter

granthee person who reads from the sacred book of Sikhs, *Granth Sahib*

gumbad dome of a mosque or tomb

gurudwara Sikh place of worship

haat periodic bazaars held in villages

halim a rice preparation cooked with meat, popular among Muslims

hammam Turkish bath

haveli large impressive house

hookah pipe with a long flexible tube by which the tobacco smoke is drawn through a jar of water from a container

jaali net; intricate lattice work on marble or stone screen

jharokha small balcony with columns supporting a roof

jhula swing; hanging bridge as in Lakshmanjhula in Rishikesh

kabaddi game played by two teams of nine players each in which players take turns to hold their breath for a short time and catch members of the opposing team

kameez a long, loose shirt worn over a *salwar*

katha a tradition of telling stories usually myths and legends

kebab meat seasoned and broiled usually on a skewer

khayal one of the nine forms of music in the Hindustani classical style, said to have been evolved by Amir Khusro; a Persian word which literally means idea or imagination

khichri a cooked dish of rice, pulses and vegetables; has the dubious distinction of being both a sick man's diet as also a delicacy depending on the way in which it is cooked

Krishna one of the incarnations of Lord Vishnu; Hindu mythology is full of miracles wrought by him. It is Krishna who gives Arjuna the message of the *Gita* in the war immortalised in the Hindu epic, *Mahabharata*

kurta a long loose-fitting shirt worn over a *salwar* by women or over a pajama by men

lehnga ankle-length, flared skirt often in bright colours enriched by intricate embroidery

lok people

Lok Sabha lower house of the Indian parliament

loo a hot, dry wind that blows over north India during summer

madarsa traditional Muslim school

Mahabharata Sanskrit epic composed by sage Vyasa in which is depicted the battle between good and evil as personified by the Pandavas and the Kauravas. According to legend, one of the cities built by the Pandavas, Indraprastha, was located in the area that is today occupied by Purana Qila

mahal palace

maharaja emperor

mandir Hindu temple

marg road, street

masjid mosque

meenakari a technique of covering the surface of silver or gold jewellery with multi-coloured enamel work

qila fort

qutb axis or pillar of justice and Islam

rajya state, kingdom

Ramayana Sanskrit epic composed by sage Valmiki in which is represented the victory of Lord Rama over the demon king of Lanka, Ravana

puri deep fried bread made of flour but distinct from *bhature*, often served with a spicy dish of potatoes

Ram lila a popular form of theatre in north India, where events from the life of Ram are depicted ending with a ritual slaying of Ravana

Rashtrapati the head of a nation; the President of India

raja king

Ravan the ten-headed demon king of Lanka in sage Valmiki's epic *Ramayana*

Ritusamhara a literary work by the fifth century Sanskrit poet, Kalidasa; meaning the gathering of the seasons

riwaq cloister bordering the courtyard of a mosque

sabha assembly

salwar loose, pleated trousers, tight at the ankles, worn by women with *kameez*

sambhar a hot, liquid pulse preparation made with vegetables as a side dish along with rice, *dosa*, etc.

sansad parliament

sarai inn, rest house

NOTES

GLOSSARY

THIS PAGE

sarak road

sari traditional Indian garment for women

mihrab arched recess inside a mosque which denotes the direction of Mecca and hence of prayer

minar tower

muezzin the person who summons the faithful to prayer from mosque

munghphali groundnuts

nai new (when the first vowel is elongated, it means a barber)

Nataraj literally the 'king of dance', Shiva in cosmic pose

paneer cottage cheese

parantha wheat-based bread made without yeast usually fried on a griddle and often stuffed with fillings like potatoes, cauliflowers, eggs, etc.

Qawwali one of the nine forms of music in the Hindustani classical system. A gift of the Sufi movement, qawwali was evolved by Amir Khusro. *Qawwals* are persons who sing *qawwalis*

seth trader, usually belonging to the prosperous Marwari community; a title added to a name to indicate high social standing within the community

shatabdi century; Shatabdi Express is a superfast express train

sheesh glass

shikar hunt

Shiva together with Brahma and Vishnu, forms the Hindu trinity of gods

tandoori food cooked in an earthen oven with glowing coals placed at the bottom

tila mound

Vishnu the preserver of the universe and a part of the Hindu trinity of gods; his ten incarnations include Rama and Krishna

wala a suffix forming compound nouns to indicate a person residing in a particular area (e.g., Dilliwala) or selling something (e.g., fruitjuicewala, paanwala, etc.)

Shah Jahan's
SHAHJAHANABAD 1648 AD

DINPANAH Pur

Firuz Shah
Tughluq's
FIRUZABAD 1351 AD

Ashokan pillar

Sher Shah Sur's
DILLI 1542 AD

Yudhistra's
INDRAPRASTHA 14

Humāyūn's
DINPANAH 1530 AD

Mohd. Shah Lodi's tomb

nb

Humāyūn's tomb

Kos minar

Ala-ud-Din Khilji's
SIRI 1302 AD

Muhammad Tughluq's
JAHANPANAH 1334 AD

Prithviraj Chauhan's
QILA RAI PITHORA c 1170 AD

Tughluq

la 1530 AD

350 AD (c)

UGHLUQABAD
1320 AD

Maps

TIPS ON USING THE MAPS

The **Index** gives the map page and square number (in blue colour) in which the name falls.

For ease of reference some names are indexed under categories, e.g., Colonies, Roads, Hotels, Restaurants, etc.

The area adjoining any map page is indicated by the extension map page number given in the overlap. **9**

The top of all map pages are oriented towards the North.

Estimation of distances :

On map pages 1 & 2, the blue grid square is 200 metres x 200 metres.

On map pages 3 - 42, the blue grid square is 1/2 km x 1/2 km.

For better accuracy a scale has been given on the southeast corner of even numbered map pages.

Key to Map Pages, Legend and Abbreviations appear on the back end pages.

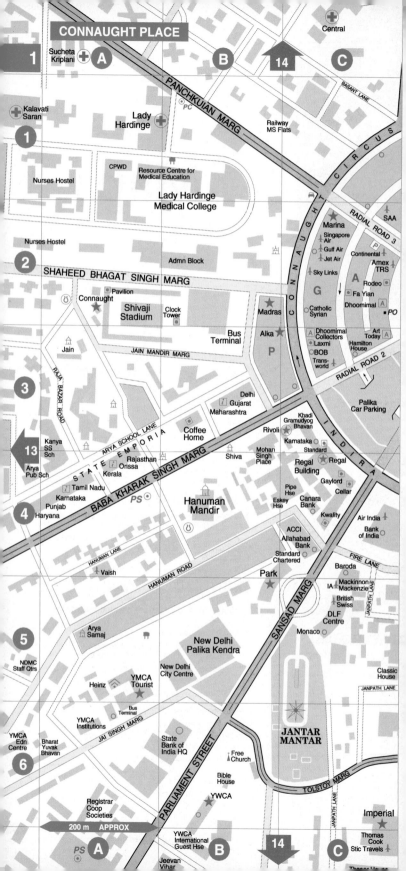

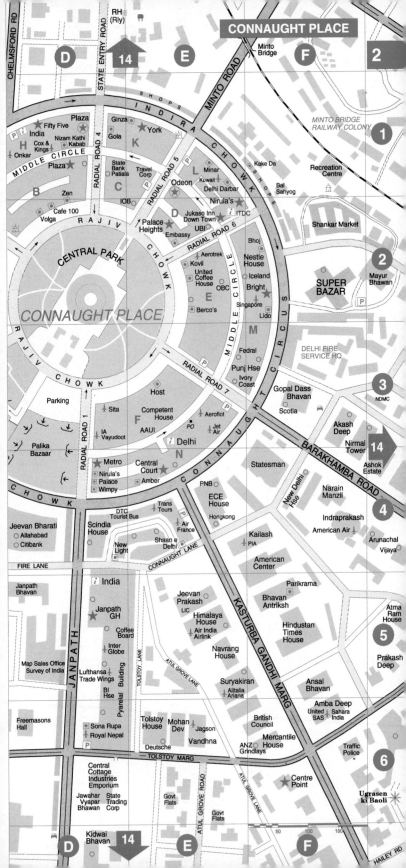

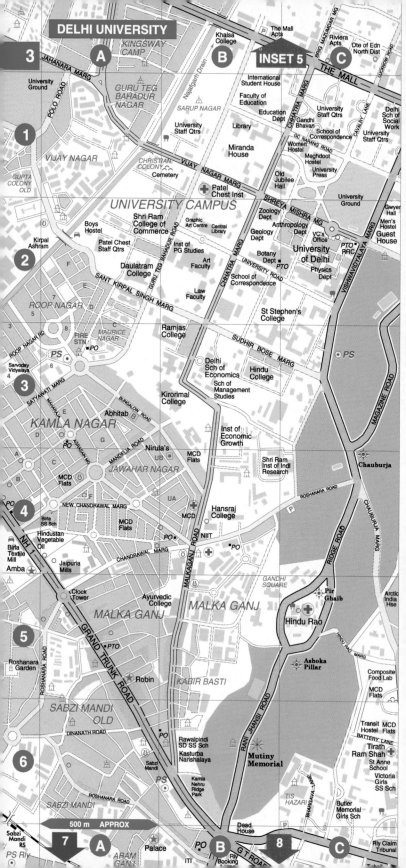

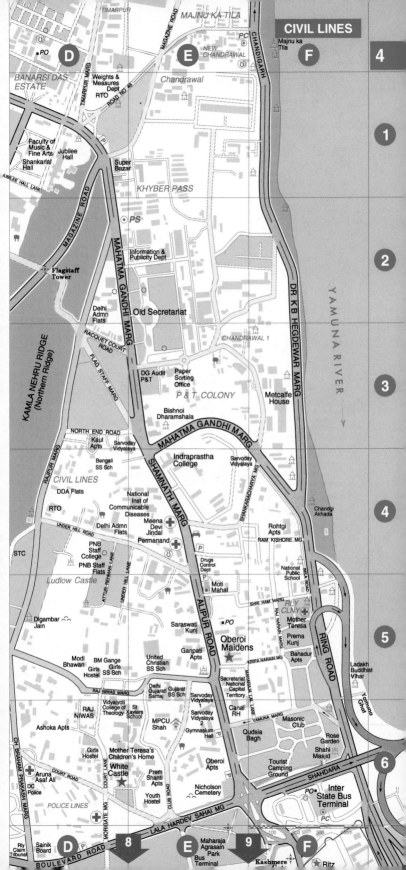

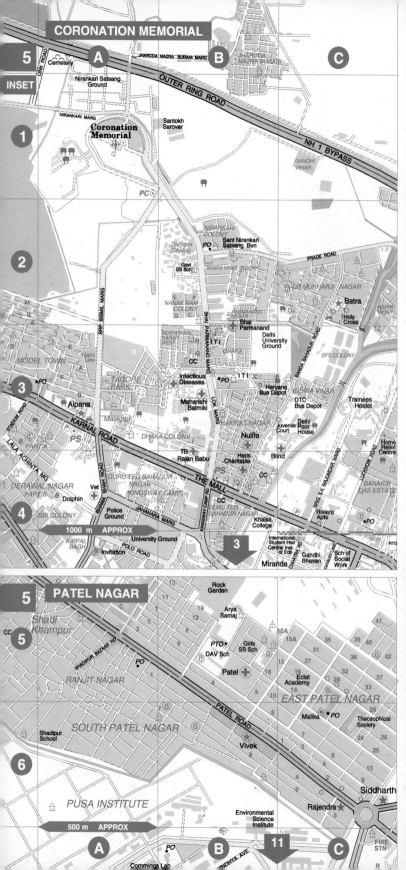

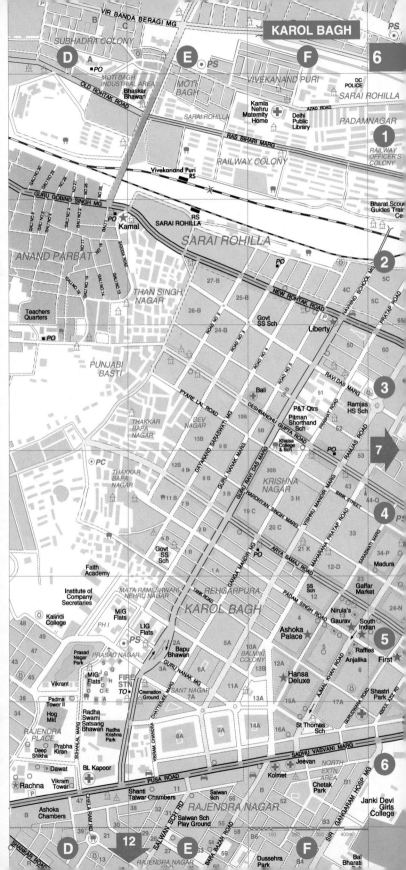

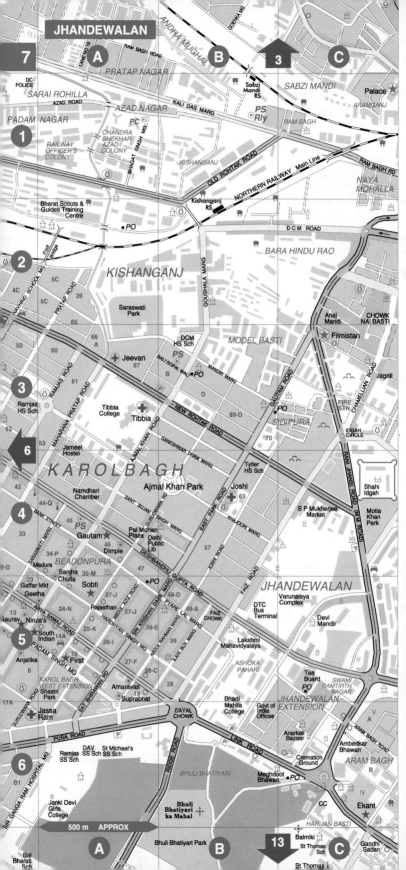

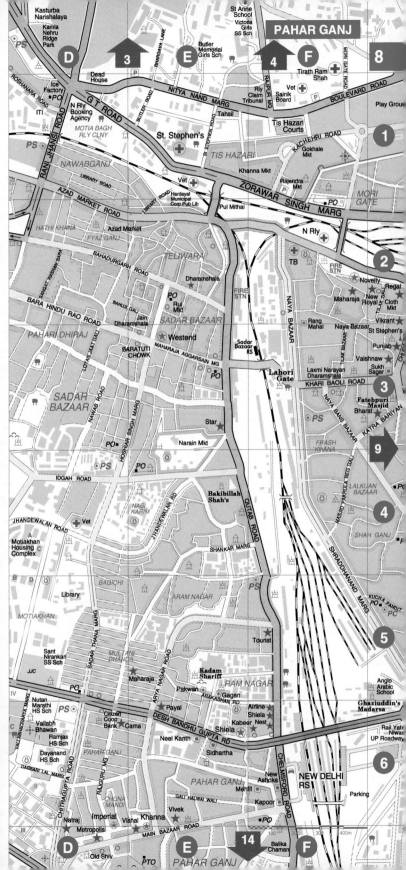

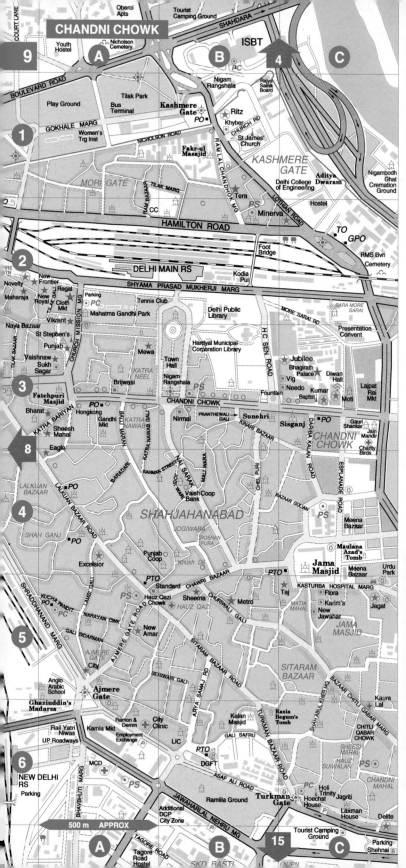

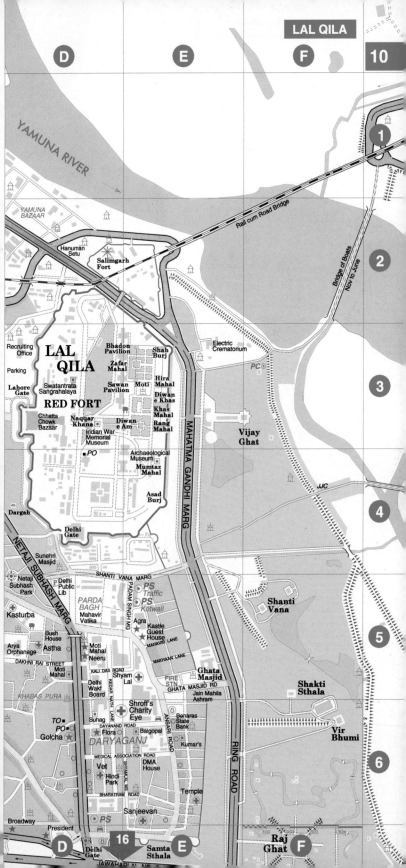

YAMUNA RIVER

YAMUNA
BAZAAR

Hanuman
Setu

Salimgarh
Fort

Rail cum Road Bridge

Bridge of Boats
Nov to June

Recruiting
Office

**LAL
QILA**

Parking

Lahore
Gate

Bhadon
Pavilion

Zafar
Mahal

Sawan
Pavilion

Moti

Shah
Burj

Hira
Mahal

Diwan
e Khas

Electric
Crematorium

PC

Swatantrata
Sangrahalaya

RED FORT

Chhatta
Chowk
Bazaar

Naqqar
Khana

Indian War
Memorial
Museum

PO

Diwan
e Am

Khas
Mahal

Rang
Mahal

Vijay
Ghat

Archaeological
Museum

Mumtaz
Mahal

JJC

Asad
Burj

Dargah

Delhi
Gate

Sunehri
Masjid

NETAJI SUBHASH MARG

SHANTI VANA MARG

Delhi
Public
Lib

PARDA
BAGH

Netaji
Subhash
Park

PADAM SINGH MG

PS
Traffic

PS
Kotwali

Mahavir
Vatika

Agra

Kastle
Guest
House

Shanti
Vana

Kasturba

Bush
House

Astha

Moti
Mahal
Neeru

MAHAVIR LANE

Arya
Orphanage

DAKHNI RAJ STREET

Moti
Mahal

KHABAS PURA

KALI DAS ROAD

Delhi
Wakf
Board

Shyam
Lal

KETNAL NATH LANE

MAKHAAN LANE

FIRE
STN

GHATA MASJID RD

**Ghata
Masjid**

Shakti
Sthala

Jain Mahila
Ashram

TO
PO

Golcha

Suhag

Shroff's
Charity
Eye

DAYANAND ROAD

Flora

Balgopal

Benaras
State
Bank

ANSARI ROAD

RING ROAD

Vir
Bhumi

DARYAGANJ

Kumar's

MEDICAL ASSOCIATION ROAD

Vet

Hindi
Park

BETHACHAL ROAD

DMA
House

BHARATRAM ROAD

Temple

Sanjeevan

Broadway

President

PS

16

Delhi
Gate

Samta
Sthala

Raj
Ghat

D   E   F

JAWAHAR

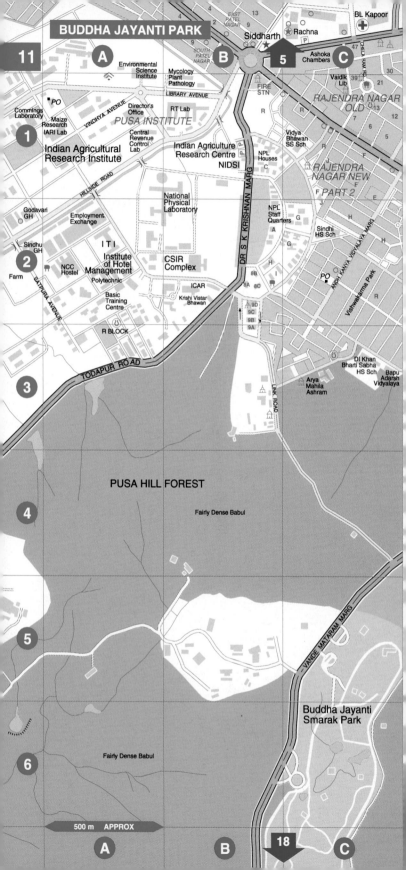

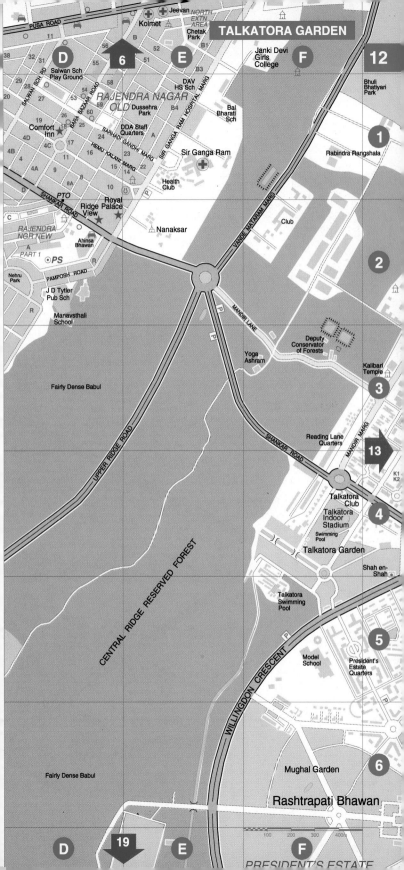

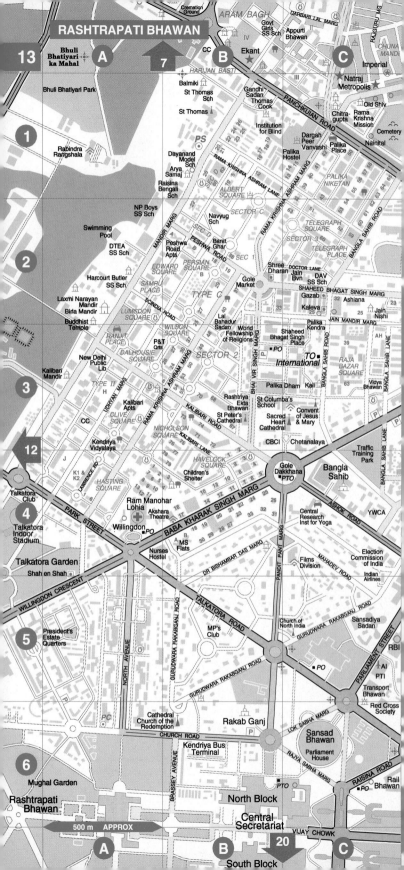

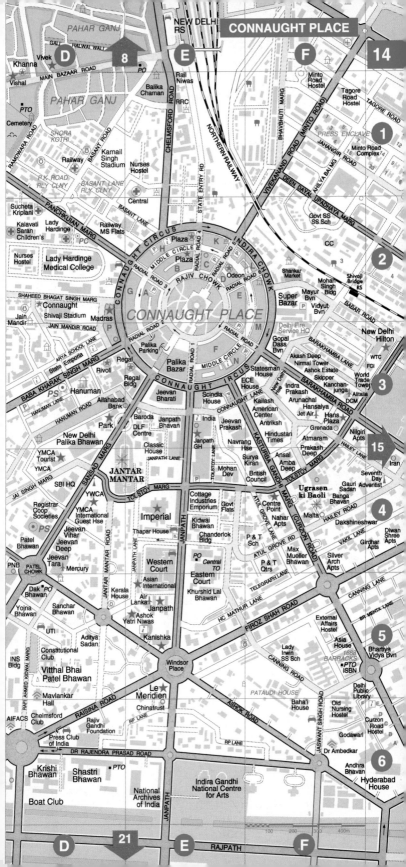

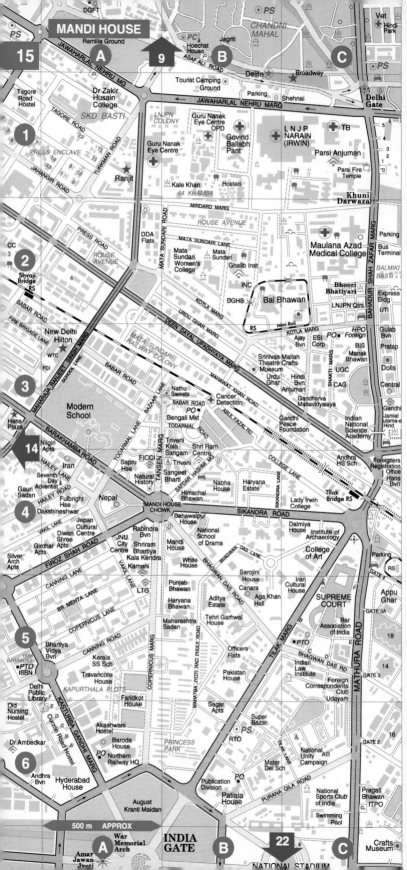

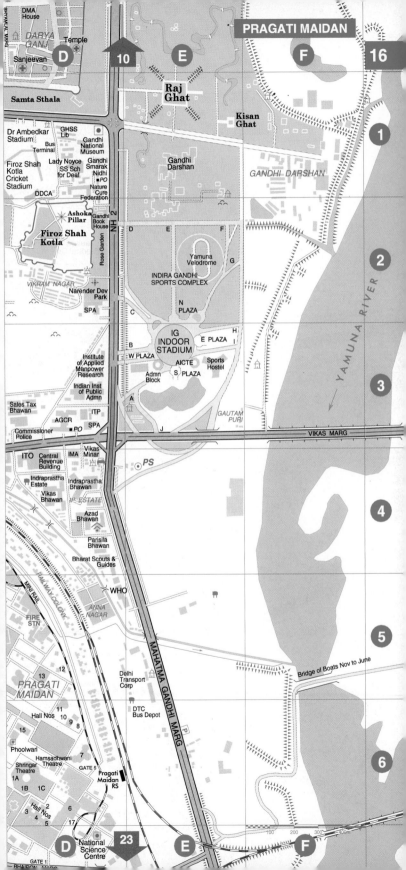

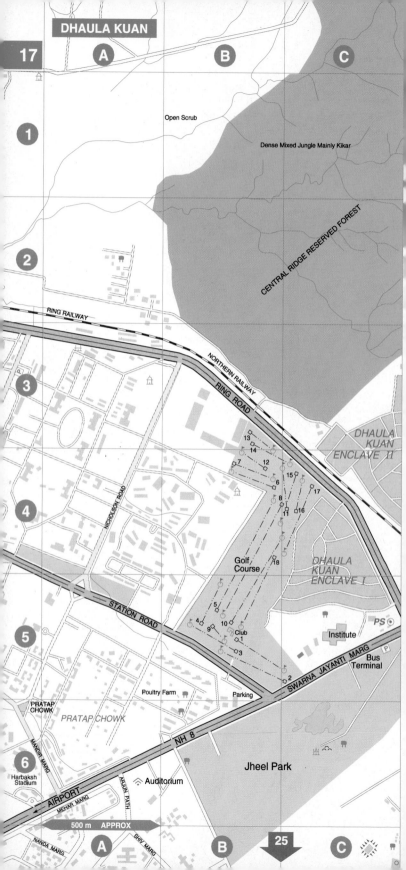

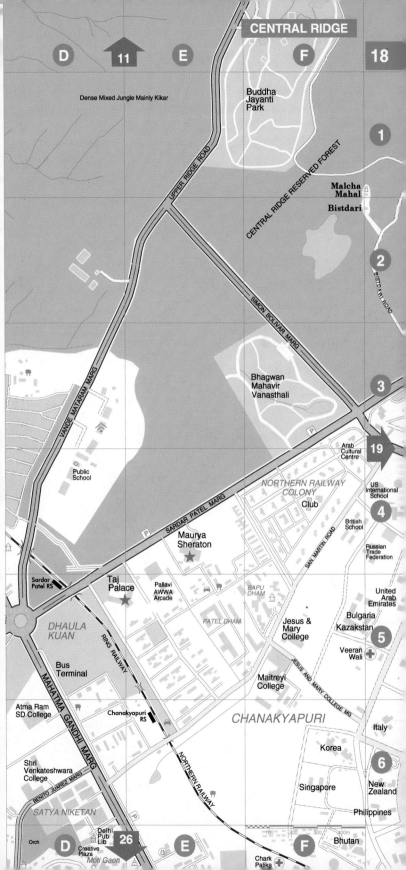

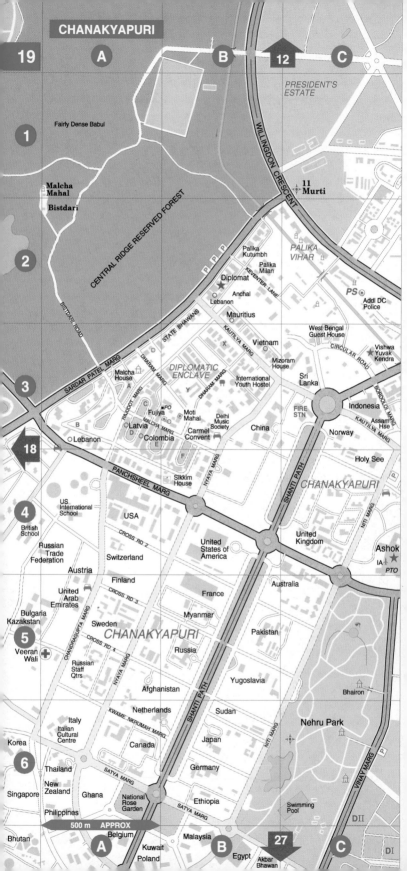

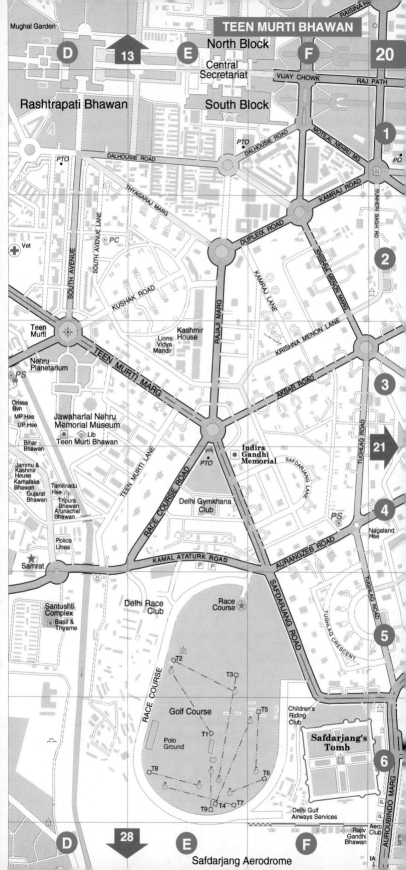

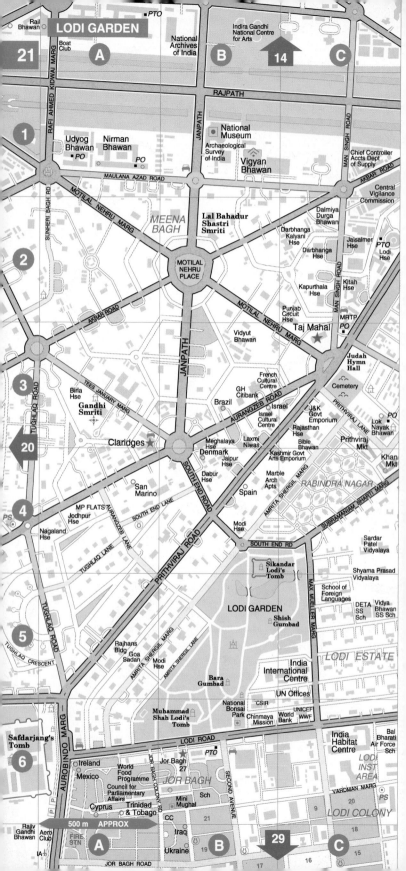

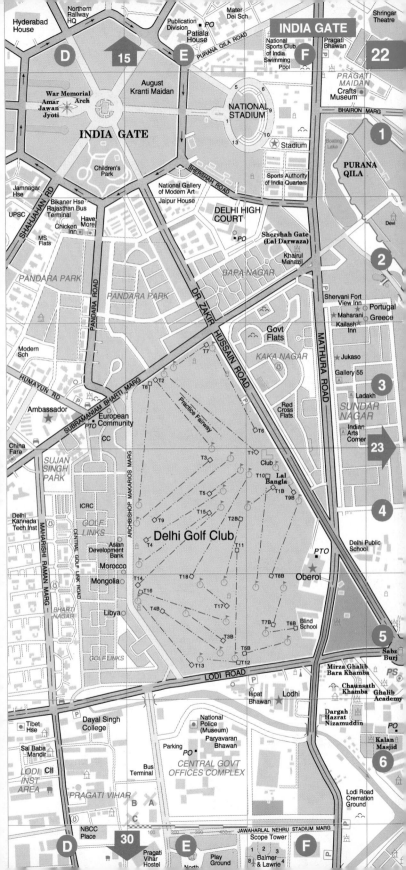

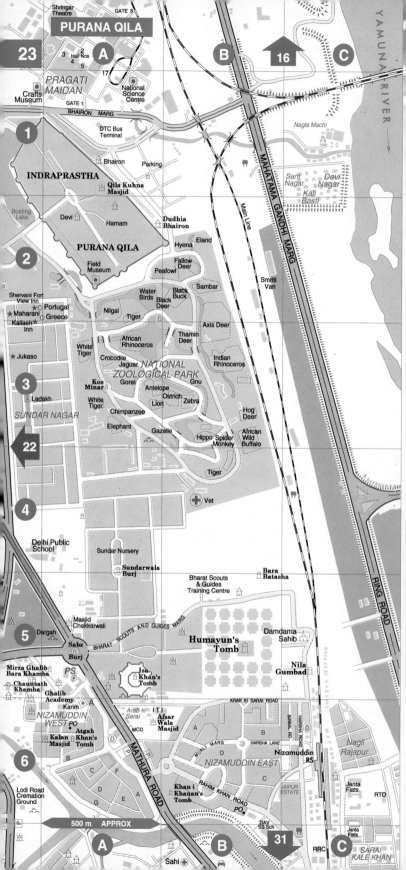

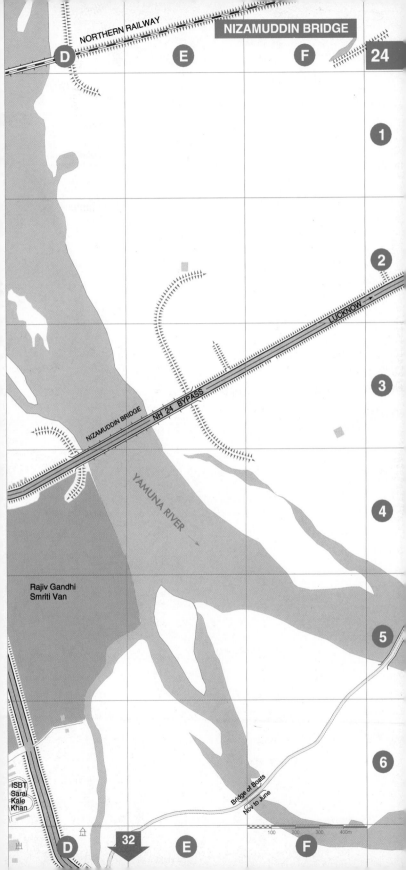

1

2

LUCKNOW →

3

NIZAMUDDIN BRIDGE   NH 24   BYPASS

YAMUNA RIVER

4

Rajiv Gandhi
Smriti Van

5

ISBT
Sarai
Kale
Khan

6

Bridge of Boats
Nov to June

100 200 300 400m

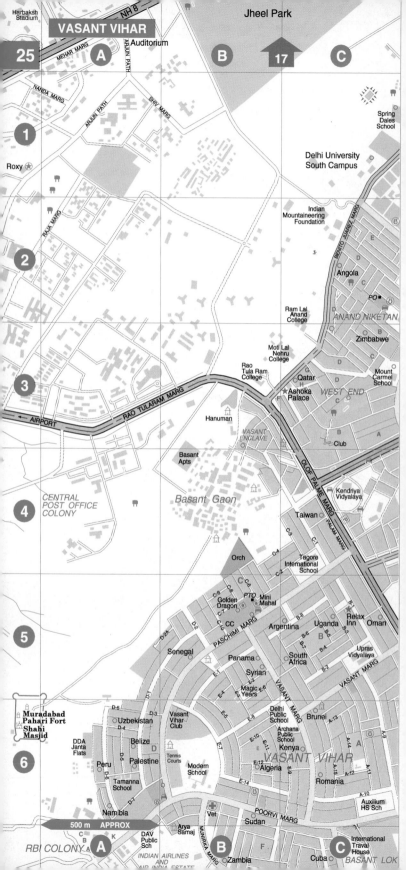

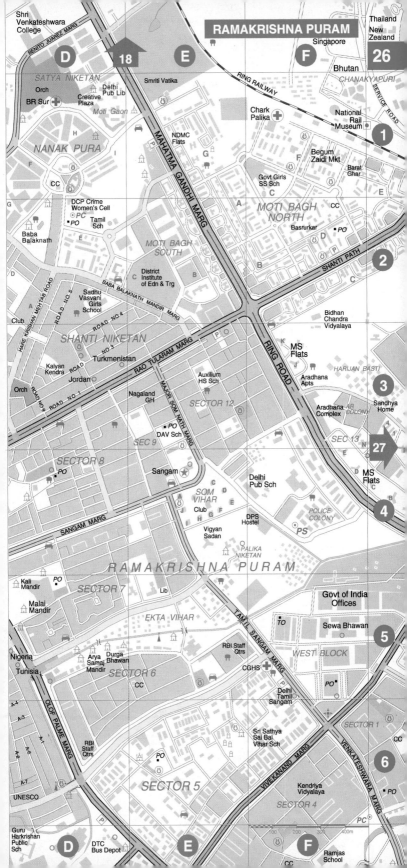

SAROJINI NAGAR

Thailand
Germany
Nehru Park
New Zealand
Ghana
A
National Rose Garden
Ethiopia
B
Swimming Pool
C
Philippines
SATYA MARG
NITI MARG
DII
Bhutan
Belgium
Kuwait
Malaysia
SATYA MARG
DI
CHANAKYAPURI
Poland
Egypt
Akbar Bhawan
SATYA MARG
1
National Rail Museum
Turkey
NITI MARG
Hungary
YASHWANT PLACE
CHANAKYAPURI
Naval Sch
Czech & Slovak
Nirula's
Chanakya
Chanakya Bhawan
Barat Ghar
Centre for Railway Information System
Naya Bihar Bhawan
PTO
STATE GUEST HSE COMPLEX
CC
RING RAILWAY
Safdarjang RS
Sarojini Nagar RS
PO
Vet
Railway Club
2
BRIG HOSHIAR SINGH MARG
CROSS ROAD 1
LANE J
CROSS ROAD 2
Arts & Commerce College
D
Delhi Pub Lib
SAROJINI NAGAR
HARIJAN BASTI
E
CROSS ROAD 3
LANE K
Nav Yug Sch
CROSS ROAD 4
3
F
CC
Sandhya Home
NETAJI NAGAR
DTC Bus Depot
AR COLONY
Women Technical Inst
P & T Staff Qtrs
AVENUE I
LANE H
LANE G
26
SEC 13
C
Scindia Potteries
MS Flats
A
4
B
IRCON
Palika Bhawan
Palika Mkt
Coffee Home
SHAHEED SUDHIR TYAGI MARG
LEKHA VIHAR
LANE G
RING ROAD
Hyatt Regency
FIRE STN
BHIKAJI CAMA PLACE
GAIL
Damania
Ansal
F
WEST BLOCK
Passport Office
NBCC Tower
EIL
NAUROJI NAGAR
Som Datt II
PNB Hse
Som Datt
PO
Sewa Bhawan
IG Police
Ansal II
A2
5
R K PURAM
EAST BLOCK
Organisation of Pharmaceutical Products
A2
Green Fields Sch
A1
PO
Govt of India Offices
NAUROJI NAGAR MARG
B1
B3
Govt Boys SS Sch
B4
Mohammadpur
SAFDARJANG ENCLAVE
KRISHNA NAGAR
B2
6
CC
Outbound
Humayunpur
SECTOR 1
Kendriya Vidyalaya
Ayyappa
RAMAKRISHNA PURAM
AFRICA AVENUE
PO
VIVEKANAND MARG
500 m APPROX
PC
Library
A
SECTOR 2
CC
B
33
C
B6
Delhi Lawn Tennis Association
CH HARSUKH MARG

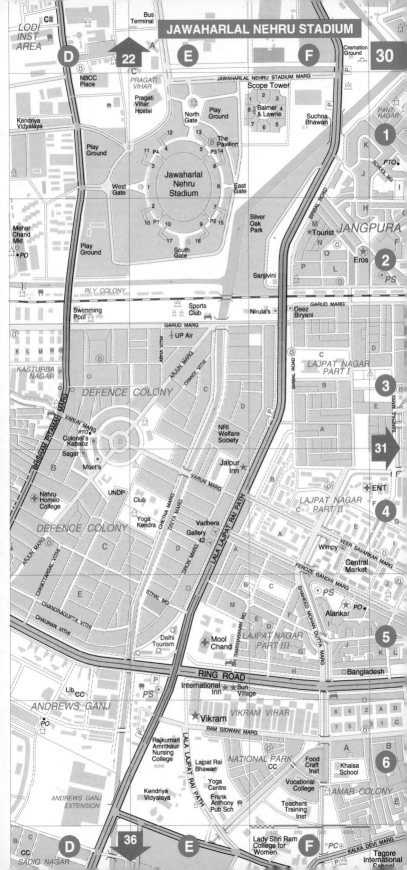

JAWAHARLAL NEHRU STADIUM

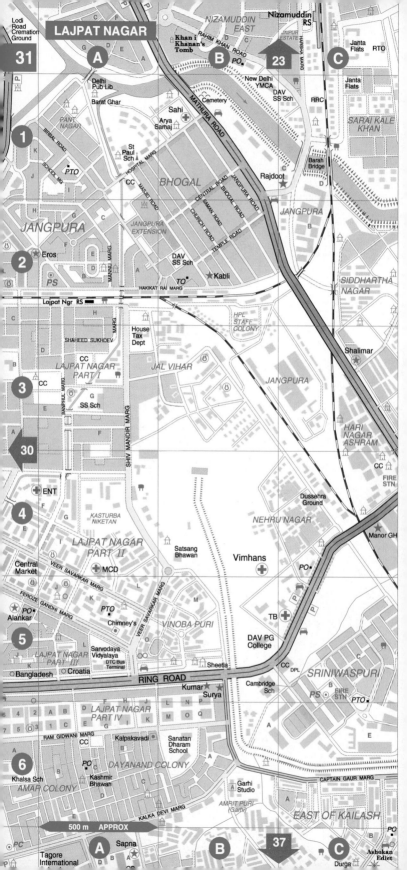

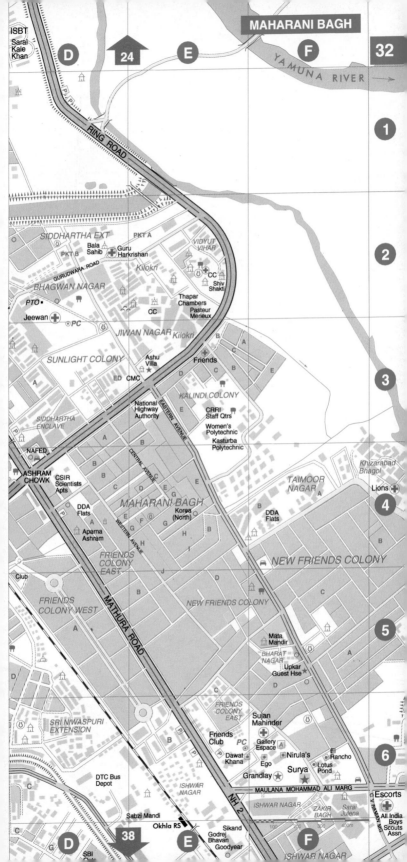

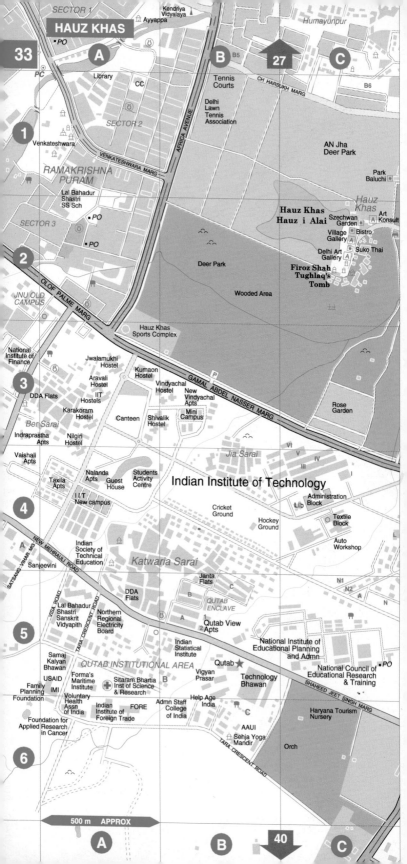

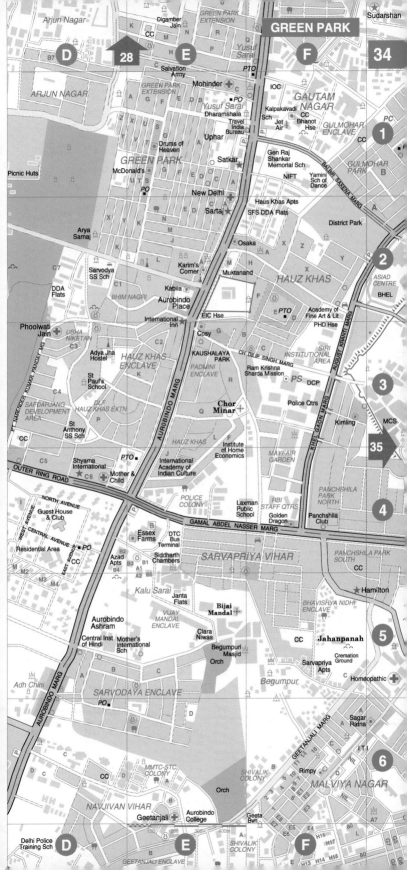

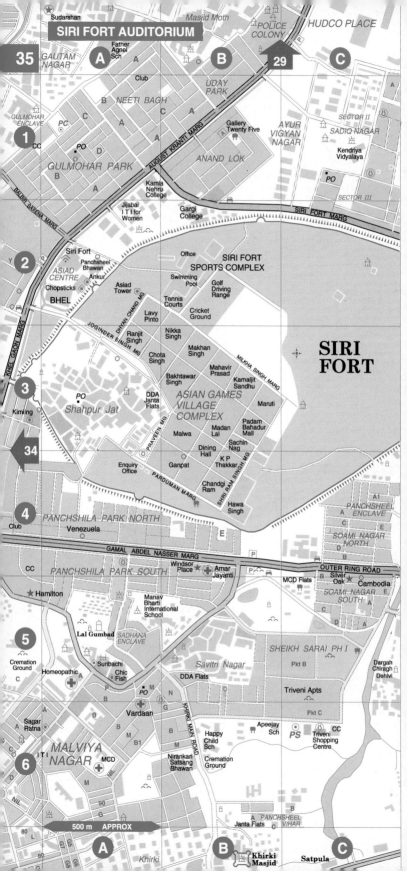

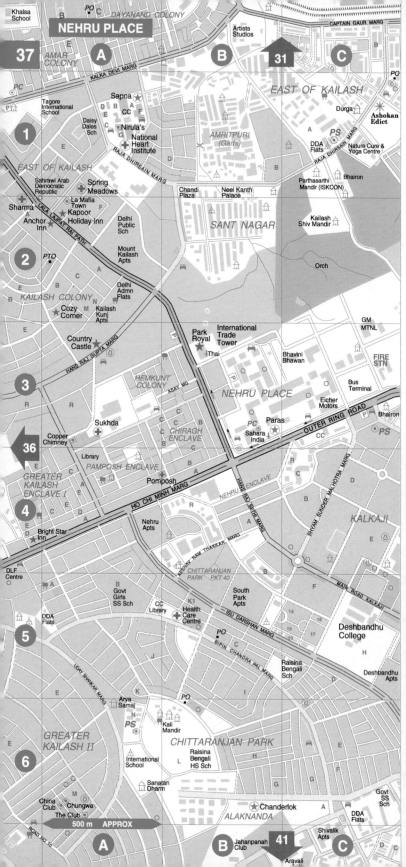

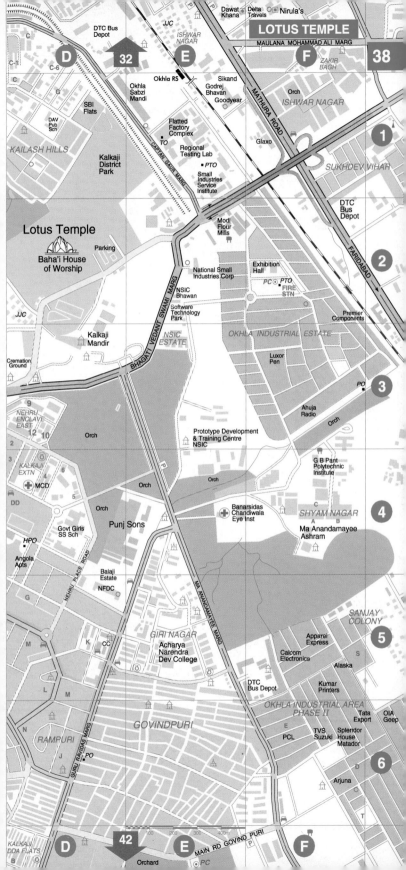

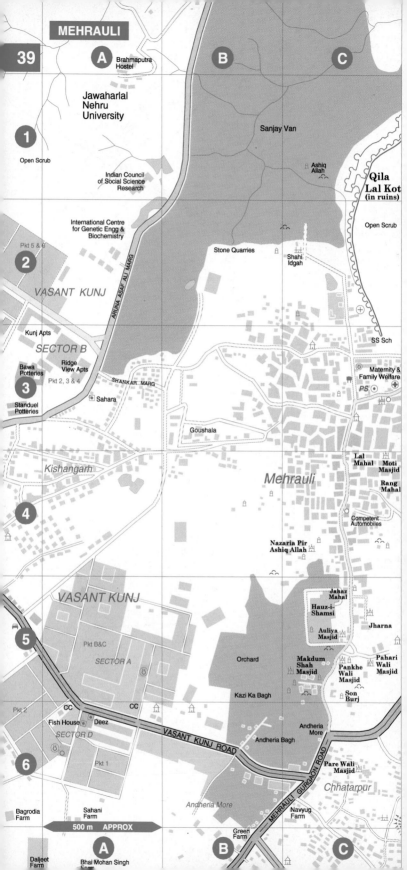

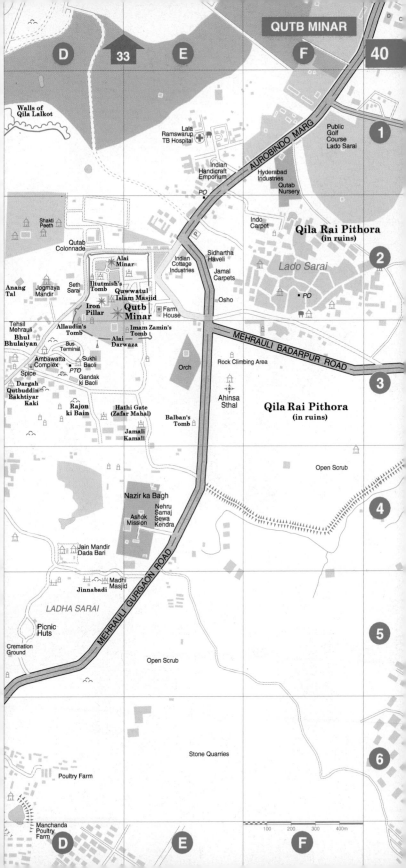

D 33 E F 40

Walls of
Qila Lalkot

AUROBINDO MARG

Public
Golf
Course
Lado Sarai

1

Lala
Ramswarup
TB Hospital

Indian
Handicraft
Emporium

PO

Hyderabad
Industries
Qutab
Nursery

Indo
Carpet

Qila Rai Pithora
(in ruins)

Shakti
Peeth

Qutab
Colonnade

Alai
Minar

Indian
Cottage
Industries

Sidhartha
Haveli

Lado Sarai

2

Jamal
Carpets

PO

Anang
Tal

Jogmaya
Mandir

Seth
Sarai

Iltutmish's
Tomb

Quwwatul
Islam Masjid

Osho

Iron
Pillar

Qutb
Minar

Farm
House

Tehsil
Mehrauli

Bhul
Bhulaiyan

Allaudin's
Tomb

Bus
Terminal

Imam Zamin's
Tomb

Alai
Darwaza

MEHRAULI BADARPUR ROAD

Ambawatta
Complex

Sukhi
Baoli

PTO

Rock Climbing Area

3

Spice

Gandak
ki Baoli

Orch

Ahinsa
Sthal

Qila Rai Pithora
(in ruins)

Dargah
Qutbuddin
Bakhtiyar
Kaki

Rajon
ki Bain

Hathi Gate
(Zafar Mahal)

Balban's
Tomb

Jamali
Kamali

Open Scrub

Nazir ka Bagh

Ashok
Mission

Nehru
Samaj
Sewa
Kendra

4

MEHRAULI GURGAON ROAD

Jain Mandir
Dada Bari

Madhi
Masjid

Jinnabadi

LADHA SARAI

Picnic
Huts

5

Cremation
Ground

Open Scrub

Stone Quarries

6

Poultry Farm

100 200 300 400m

Manchanda
Poultry
Farm

D E F

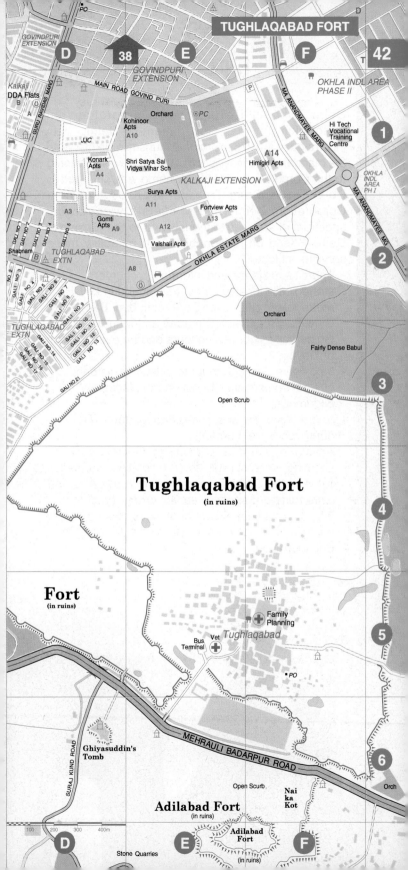

Delhi Tourism

Delhi Tourism Development Corporation, an undertaking of the Government of Delhi, was incorporated in 1975 to promote tourism in Delhi. When the mandate for construction of flyovers was entrusted to the Corporation in 1989, its name was enlarged to Delhi Tourism and Transportation Development Corporation. Delhi Tourism offers a wide-ranging spectrum of services to tourists and to the citizens of Delhi. Based on reasonability and reliability these services include :

- Tourist assistance and information counters strategically located all over Delhi and in key metropolitan cities such as Ahmedabad, Bangalore, Calcutta, Chennai, Hyderabad and Mumbai.
- Guided city sight seeing tours and an evening tour of Delhi.
- Innovative package tours to places of historic, cultural and scenic interest and to places of pilgrimage.
- Value based travel services through the IATA approved travel bureau.
- Adventure activities: parasailing, trekking, rock climbing, water sports, etc. (*For detailed information refer to the **Delhi Tourism pages in the Arts and Entertainment section,** earlier in this book.*)
- Transport: a fleet of cars and luxury coaches (air-conditioned and non air-conditioned) for smooth transportation.

- Festivals: these are held throughout the year. (*For detailed information see the* **Delhi Tourism pages in the Arts and Entertainment section,** *earlier in this book.*)
- Dilli Haat: a place for handicrafts, ethnic food and entertainment. (*For detailed information see the* **Delhi Tourism pages in the Arts and Entertainment section**.)
- Coffee Homes: wholesome meals at reasonable prices.
- Son et lumiere: a sound and light show at Purana Qila. (*For detailed information refer to the* **Delhi Tourism pages in the Arts and Entertainment section**.)
- Musical Fountain: at Ajmal Khan Park. (*For detailed information refer to the* **Delhi Tourism pages in the Arts and Entertainment section**.)
- Illumination of monuments.
- The Indian Institute of Travel and Tourism Management (IITTM -Delhi Chapter) : a centre of excellence for tourism education.
- Country liquor and IMFL retail outlets.
- Flyovers: to improve connectivity.

Delhi Tourism

Tourist assistance and information counters.
Delhi Tourism's information counters in Delhi and the regional information centres provide general information and other facilities such as accommodation reservation, tours and transport. These information counters are situated at the following locations:-

- N-36, Connaught Place, Middle Circle, New Delhi-110001.
  Tel.: 011-3315322, 3314229 Fax: 011-3313637
- Coffee Home Annexe, Baba Kharak Singh Marg, New Delhi-110001.
  Tel.: 011-3365358, 3363607 Fax: 011-3367322
- New Delhi Railway Station
  Tel.: 011-3732374
- Old Delhi Railway Station
  Tel.: 011-2511083
- Maharana Pratap Inter State Bus Terminus
  Tel.: 011-2962181
- Indira Gandhi Domestic Airport
  Tel.: 011-5665609, 5665126 Extn. 2297
- Indira Gandhi International Airport
  Tel.: 011-5691213,5652021 Extn. 2136
- NOIDA: DTTDC, C-117, Sector 18, Noida
- **DTTDC Offices outside Delhi :-**

Bangalore: C/o Govt. of India Tourist Office, K.F.C. Building No. 48, Church Street, Bangalore.
Tel: 080-5585417

Calcutta: C/o Govt. of India Tourist Office, 4, Shakespeare Sarani, Calcutta.
Tel: 033-2426215, 2421402, 2425813

Chennai: C/o Hotel Tamilnadu, No.3, EVR High Road, Chennai.
Tel: 044-589132, 560294

Delhi Tourism

Mumbai:	C/o M.T.D.C., Madame Cama Road, Mumbai.
	Tel: 022-2856736, 2026713, 2026784
Hyderabad:	C/o Andhra Pradesh Tourism, Yatri Niwas, Sardar Patel Road, Secunderabad, Andhra Pradesh.
	Tel: 040-816375
Ahmedabad:	C/o Tourism Corp. of Gujrat Ltd. H.K. House, Near Times of India, Ashram Road, Ahmedabad, Gujrat.
	Tel: 079-6589683, 6587217, 6589172

- **Currency exchange:** the facility of currency exchange is available at:-
- The DTTDC information counter, N-36, Connaught Place, Middle Circle, New Delhi-110001.
  Tel.: 011-3315322, 3314229 Fax: 011-3313637

Guided Tours of Delhi. Delhi Tourism offers guided tours of the city which give glimpses of its many facets. The 14th century description by Ibn Battuta of Delhi as, "the metropolis of India, a vast and magnificent city, uniting beauty with strength", still holds true of this city of cities, which abounds with the treasures of a splendid past and a pulsating present. Delhi is the confluence and repository of various cultures where the past and the present are infinitely linked to form a harmonious blend of majestic history and modern elegance.

Delhi Tourism

Sight-seeing tours, a full day and an evening tour, depart from the Central Reservation Office on all days. Complete details may be obtained from :-
DTTDC Central Reservation Office, Coffee Home1, Baba Kharak Singh Marg, New Delhi-110001.
Tel: 011-3365358, 3363607. Fax: 011-3367322.
Open 7 A.M. to 9 P.M. daily

Package Tours. For centuries Delhi has been the gateway to India, a land which is many things to many people. Some come to India to wonder at its magnificent past. Some seek the awesome beauty of its natural heritage, the majestic serenity of its mountains and the grace of its sacred rivers. Some wish to absorb the magic and mystery of this ancient land with its pot pourri of people and cultures.

To cater to all these different needs, Delhi Tourism has designed various itineraries which can turn one's travel experience into a personalised one. Good team work by a dedicated group of energetic and experienced personnel, along with a nationwide network of offices, provide comprehensive and reliable services with a professional touch.

Delhi Tourism has also evolved a series of LTC tour packages to different destinations which are immensely popular. Details on the tour packages can be obtained from any of the DTTDC information counters. All tours depart from :-
DTTDC Central Reservation Office, Coffee Home1, Baba Kharak Singh Marg, New Delhi-110001.
Tel: 011-3365358, 3363607. Fax: 011-3367322.

Delhi Tourism

Travel Bureau. IATA approved, Delhi Tourism's travel bureau has the advantage of easy accessibility due to its central location. It has computerised reservation systems, modern communication facilities and staff geared to cater to all travel needs. The travel bureau is situated at :-

N-36, Connaught Place, Middle Circle,
New Delhi-110001.
Tel.: 011-3315322, 3314229 Fax: 011-3313637

Country Liquor & IMFL Retail Outlets. Delhi Tourism has retail outlets for the sale of country liquor and Indian made foreign liquor. These outlets are strategically placed all over Delhi and remain open from 12 noon to 8 P.M. during winter and from 1 P.M. to 9 P.M. in summer.

The Indian Institute of Travel and Tourism Management (IITTM -Delhi Chapter). The IITTM was handed over to Delhi Tourism in 1993. Since then various courses and programmes pertaining to tourism and travel management have been successfully conducted by Delhi Tourism in order to strengthen the infrastructure required for tourism. The IITTM is situated at the following address :-

9, Nyaya Marg, Chanakya Puri, New Delhi.
Tel: 011-6118280

Flyovers. Diversifying its activities, Delhi Tourism has constructed a number of flyovers to improve connectivity in Delhi. In a city which is greatly spread out, this activity provides much needed relief from traffic congestion.

Illumination of Monuments. Delhi Tourism has contributed significantly towards dramatising and beautifying Delhi's skyline at night by illuminating the historic Qutub Minar.

Entries in blue colour indicate the map page and square number.

Entries in blue colour indicate the map page and square number.

402

Entries in blue colour indicate the map page and square number.

404

Entries in blue colour indicate the map page and square number.

Entries in blue colour indicate the map page and square number.

Entries in blue colour indicate the map page and square number.

PITAMPURA

WAZIRPUR INDL AREA

SHAKURPUR COLONY

SHASTRI NGR

ASHOK VIHAR

TRI NAGAR

KINGSWAY CAMP

KARNAL ROAD

INSET

5

CORONATION MEMORIAL

Majnu ka Tila

YAMUNA RIVER

MAGAZINE ROAD

THE MALL

Delhi University

KAMLA NAGAR

3

4

Hindu Rao

CIVIL LINES

DR. HEDGEWAR MARG

SHAMNATH MARG

NH 10

ROHTAK ROAD

MOTI NAGAR

SHIVAJI MARG

RAMA ROAD

KIRTI NAGAR

GURU RAVIDAS MARG

PATEL ROAD

NARAINA ROAD

TODAPUR ROAD

PUSA INSTITUTE

IARI

NARAINA

Todapur

Naraina

MAHARAJA NAHAR SINGH MARG

GRAND TRUNK ROAD

SWAMI NARAIN MARG

ANAND PARBAT

SARAI ROHILLA

RS

PATEL NAGAR

Siddharth

SHANKAR ROAD

RAJENDRA NAGAR

LINK ROAD

VANDE MATARAM MARG

11

12

D   E

Buddha Jayanti Park

SABZI MANDI

GULABI BAGH

BARA HINDU RAO

RANI JHANSI ROAD

KAROL BAGH

JHANDE WALAN

PUSA ROAD

SARDAR PATEL MARG

5

Siddharth

6

7

SADAR BAZAAR

RIDGE ROAD

ZORAWA SINGH MARG

ISBT

DELHI RS

CHANDNI CHOWK

Jama Masjid

8

9

QUTAB ROAD

NETAJI SUBH

MAHATMA

PAHAR GANJ

NEW DELHI RS

LAXMI NARAYAN

RML

MANDIR MG

JANTAR MG

CONNAUGHT PLACE

Delhi Gate

Delhi

13

14

15

Park

Meridien

SANSAD MARG

BABA KHARAK SINGH MG

JANPATH

H

Sansad Bhawan

Rashtrapati Bhawan

WILLINGDON CRESCENT

RAJPATH

INDIA GATE

NAT STA

Sup Cou

Taj Mahal

MOTI LAL NEHRU MG

Claridges

21

PRITHVIRAJ RD

Delhi Golf Club

22

RING RAILWAY

RING ROAD

STATION ROAD

17

DHAULA KUAN

18

Maurya

Taj Palace

19

Ashok

20

CHANAKYAPURI

SHANTI PATH

VINAY MARG

Race Course

Lodi Garden

LODI ROAD

CGO COMPLEX

Jawaharlal Nehru Stadium

SWARNA JAYANTI MARG

AIRPORT

NH 8

DU South Campus

RAO TULA RAM MG

WEST END

MOTI BAGH

NETAJI NAGAR

SAFDARJANG

SAROJINI NAGAR

LODI COLONY

BHISHAM PITAMAH MARG

30

DEFENCE COLONY

25

VASANT VIHAR

PASCHIMI MARG

OLOF PALME MARG

POORVI MG

Vasant Continental

26

RAMAKRISHNA PURAM

VIVEKANAND MARG

Hyatt

27

Safdarjang

MAHATMA GANDHI MARG

28

SOUTH EXTENSION

29

AIIMS

AUROBINDO MARG

AUGUST KRANTI MARG

LALA

Munirka

Mahipalpur

VASANT KUNJ

MEHRAULI ROAD

Masudpur

VASANT KUNJ

Farms

Jawaharlal Nehru University

NELSON MANDELA ROAD

AFRICA AVENUE

SAFDARJANG ENCLAVE

GREEN PARK

Hauz Khas

SDA

33

NCERT

Qutab

QUTAB INST AREA

GAMAL ABDEL NASSER MARG

34

HAUZ KHAS

Siri Fort

35

GREATE KAILASH

36

MALVIYA NAGAR

PANCHSHILA PARK

Chirag Delhi

DR AMBEDI NAGAR

SHAHEED JEET SINGH MARG

ARUNA ASAF ALI MARG

AUROBINDO MARG

Qutb Minar

39

40

MEHRAULI

VASANT KUNJ ROAD

MEHRAULI GURGAON ROAD

PRESS ENCLAVE ROAD

SAKET

PUSHPA VIHAR

Neb Sarai

SAINIK FARM

Khanpur

LAL BAHADUR SHASTRI MARG

MEHRAULI BADARPUR ROAD

OUTER RING ROAD

Madang

Bat